G is that YOU ME or the DEVIL

How to Confidently Know God's Voice

Kevin E. Winters

God, Is that You, Me, or the Devil?
How to Confidently Know God's Voice

By Kevin E. Winters
www.doinglifeonfire.org

Published by Kevin E. Winters, 12700 Denny Court, Upper Marlboro MD
doinglifeonfire@yahoo.com

International Standard Book Number:
978-0-9977334-3-3

Printed in the United States of America

Cover design and page layout by Artiest Design and Illustration

Dedication

I would like to dedicate this book to the most special people I have had the pleasure to know. First I would like to dedicate this to my mother Lynn Rose Winters. Thank you for your effortless and tireless approach to child rearing. Though you are not with us on earth I am very much a product of the wisdom that you spoke to us while you were here.

I would also like to dedicate this to my grandparents DeWayne and Queen E. Bush who have laid the foundation of a great legacy. This book is proof of that foundation. Thank you for being examples of godliness.

Then there are those in my life that are still on this side of Glory. I would like to dedicate this to my beautiful wife and friend, Tanya and our four children Autumn, Caleb, Aaron, and Noelle. Thank you for sharing me with the world. Thank you for putting up with daddy talking into the air. I am grateful that I have a family that allows me to be me. I love you all with every bit of my person.

Contents

Section 4: Hearing His Voice   145

Endorsement

God, Is that You, Me, or the Devil?, is a book that will help anyone seeking to hear God's voice. It is extremely practical, biblical and helpful. It is well organized and easy to read. It is a "how to" book, which makes it life-changing to those who desire to pursue spiritual intimacy. After reading this, you will have a new confidence and an enhanced understanding of how God speaks within you and how to determine that it is God speaking. You will become comfortable walking and living by the Spirit (Gal. 5:25).

Dr. Mark Virkler
Founder: Christian Leadership University

1

Introduction

How does one find himself in the place of writing a book about the topic of hearing voices? I know that admitting that I hear voices is not a popular admission to make, but the reality is that we all hear voices. Every time your Pastor speaks, or when friends and neighbors are attempting to give you counsel you are subject to a voice. These are all voices attempting to directly and/or indirectly make an impact on your life. Sometimes we give weight to these words and sometimes we do not. Then there is God, Satan, and even your own voice to consider. The real issue is not whether or not you hear voices, but can you distinguish which one belongs to God. That is what this book is all about. It is not about merely the hearing of voices. It is about discerning the voice of God among the myriad of voices.

For me, this all started in 1993 when a young charismatic healing evangelist was introduced to a young thriving church. He was being used by God mightily to expose both the church and its pastor to the reality of signs and wonders.

I remember that day so vividly. As He prayed for people they fell down under God's power. Sometimes it was just one individual and at other times whole sections fell at once under the power of God. I had neither seen nor heard of anything like this before. He also did such things as callout people's names and illnesses and they were healed. Even my girlfriend at the time was on the floor. But with all that was happening I have to admit that I was a bit skeptical even though I thought it was exciting to see. I had never been introduced to the concept of God as "personal". Even in this experience I thought to myself, 'Ooooh! God has come to visit with the lowly humans and when He's done He'll leave and go back to heaven.' I had always believed that He was in outer space somewhere ruling the universe and that He would come to retrieve us at some point in the future. It never crossed my mind that He was a person who wanted to be and could be known personally until later that night.

As the service concluded that evening the evangelist started expressing an interest in returning to our church to minister, but stated that his schedule was usually so busy that he had never been able to return to an area to minister a second time. However, in the middle of his statement he looked up and started talking to someone. The whole time I was asking myself, 'Who is he talking to?' The conversation went back and forth; it was not a one-way conversation. Finally, he said the Lord said, I will be returning! I thought, 'What? God spoke to him? God speaks to people?' I was in utter amazement and all else faded away in light of this information. I can't tell you much about what was said after that statement. I was completely captivated by the idea that God speaks to people. I wanted Him to speak to me too.

That led to an all-out search for how I could get God to speak to me. I so intensely desired this experience. With all of my being I craved this communion with God. My desires eventually led me to Benny Hinn's book *Good Morning Holy Spirit*, which started me down a road filled with rich experiences where my heart's desire was being satisfied.

I shall be forever grateful for what happened that day—the day when a young evangelist exposed me to a life changing reality. It was from that moment on that I had a life filled with rich experiences with the voice of God. Many of which I share in this book. This however is the good part of my story—the part that coincides with the first chapter about how God still speaks to people.

The rest of the chapters that follow are written from my second life changing experience. It is from this experience that I would begin a journey of learning how God speaks, what He talks about, and how to distinguish His voice from the other voices, and so many other topics.

At this point in the story I had been enjoying the most beautiful experiences and encounters with God, but I was enjoying them alone. The traditional Full Gospel Baptist church that I attended did not embrace the experiences with

4

the young evangelist quite like I did. The experience, for whatever reason, it didn't seem to have the same impact on them that it had on me. So God raised up for me charismatic co-workers from a work place Bible study. They were familiar with what was happening in my life. One of those individuals became a very close friend. He was a prophetic seer that God was using in the revelation gifts of word of wisdom, word of knowledge, and prophecy.

This guy could see with such clarity. It was very impressive. Everyone in the Bible study was absolutely astounded at how God was using him. As time went on I started to operate in the seer realm as well. God also began to pour into me supernatural wisdom and insight. After some time He began to move upon me to share these insights with the group. Exciting times right! I thought so but my friend was not as excited.

One day as we were in the midst of a discussion, I started to share with him a crazy lie that the enemy tried to plant in my mind. As I was sharing this lie with him he suddenly and sharply turned to me and said, "Kevin, you need to make sure that you're hearing God." His response stunned me. I had always known that the possibility of deception existed, but until that moment I had not considered the reality of that danger. In fact I had not considered the possibility that anyone else could have been teaching me and talking with me. It was from that moment onward that I began an incredible struggle with doubt. It tormented me to such a degree that any subtle communication from God became very hard to discern. When God spoke to me I went through the normal spill of, is that me? Is that God? Is that the devil? These questions tormented me. I only felt comfortable with the idea that I was hearing God's voice when He moved in a very obvious way. It was very hard for me to recognize Him otherwise.

It was such a problem, in fact, that it gave birth to the concepts outlined in this book. Every one of the concepts in this book was birthed out of those moments when the spirit of doubt was so strong that I felt paralyzed. I felt so hindered by this spirit that I sought out God's principles.

As you would expect, God was faithful to respond giving me more and more insight into the subject. With each principle He taught me I regained more of my confidence. This always resulted in a season of peace. However, after some time passed, I began to experience more attacks. Another attack always meant that God would give me another principle. This was a continuous cycle that lasted years. I hated it at the time but it yielded much fruit. Today I enjoy a very intimate and rich relationship with the Spirit of God and it is my desire to share with you what He has shared with me.

These principles have helped me so much. It was through the principles presented in this book that I was able to allow God to fix my life.

After high school I decided that I was going to be a rap star. From that moment on I did absolutely nothing in school. My grades were so horrible that the college I attended threatened to kick me out if I didn't leave. At the time I didn't care, because I didn't want to be there anyway. I had convinced myself that I was going to be a rap star and nothing else mattered. Then I gave my life to Jesus and I could not see how my dream was going to fit into my new lifestyle. This presented a problem because I had completely blown my educational opportunities and I had no marketable skills. I wondered what I was going to do for work.

At that time my father was a federal government employee. Having a likeable personality he pulled some strings and helped my twin brother and myself to get jobs with his agency. My first job was in the file room and this is where I would be for years. During this time however, I was learning how to hear God's voice. This eventually led to God rekindling a passion in my heart for creating art. Long story short, I am now a well-paid artist. Also, because of what God has taught me about hearing and discerning His voice, I have never had to seek another job. God always told me what to do along the way to get my life back on track. His guidance fixed my mess up, and his guidance can fix yours as well!

I can guarantee you this; the principles in this book work. They are biblical, will greatly enrich your relationship with God, better position you to operate in your destiny, and will save you from making life-changing mistakes.

One thing that I hope you will see in this book is the clear application to discerning the voice of God in many situations. You will notice as you read this book that I did not give much emphasis to God's voice speaking

6

through men and women, although we know that He does. Instead I wrote this book with the focus of equipping the saints to encounter God intimately. However, these ideas can also be applied to discerning God's voice in any given situation—Whether it is presented by your Pastor, a Prophet, a friend, a stranger, or even via God directly. No matter how the voice of God is presented to you, these principles will assist you in making the dividing line clear.

I would also like to invite you to consider this; God took me through a lot to learn the ideas presented in this book. I believe it was His goal to get it to me so that He could get it through me. He really, really wants to speak with you and He wants you to be confident in the reality that it is your Savior that is speaking to you. Many of you have heard God speaking to you and have encountered battles with those same nagging questions, Is this me? Is this God? Is this the devil? This book will illuminate His voice so that you can distinguish it from all others.

My suggestion to you before you start reading this book is that you pray and ask God to open your eyes that you might see, and that He would give you the spirit of wisdom and revelation in the knowledge of Him. Both of these are prayers in the scriptures that you will read many times as you read through this book. Second, I invite you to expect God to speak to you. Believe and know that this is His desire for your life. Expect your Savior Jesus Christ to take advantage of the opportunity to be reconciled to you. Of course we know that His completed work at the cross reconciles you to Himself, but will you take advantage of the opportunity to really know what that means.

Lastly, I want you to read this book with your Bible in hand ready to examine the scriptures mentioned throughout. I always encourage people to study, and to test the spirits. Make sure that the words are not twisted and scripture has not been manipulated to suit the idea. I am confident that this work is easily verifiable in the word. Why? Because God used His word to teach me how to commune with Him and as you read and research the contents presented, that will become evident to you as well.

If you are ready, let us get started on a journey to learn how to hear and discern the voice of God!

7

Section 1
The Speaker

Chapter One

The God Who Still Speaks

Yes God Is Still Speaking!

Is God still speaking today? A better question is why would God have stopped speaking? What scriptural reason would there be for God to stop communicating with His people? The most popular argument states that God only spoke to give us the cannon of scriptures we call the Bible. My challenge to those who hold fast to this line of thinking is simple. Find a passage of scripture that says He ever intended to stop speaking. Or find for me one passage that says which house to buy and when? Which used car to buy? Which job offer should you take? You won't find one.

I know more than a few well-meaning Christians who were victims of predatory lending. These Christians were trapped in homes in which they could not afford or sell. It was a very disheartening thing to watch. A lot of their pain could have been avoided if they were in a better position to hear God give them warning. I heard God clearly say 'no'. That "NO" allowed me to survive that difficult time in our American history. In fact, I was doing very well. I was still able to provide for my stay-at-home wife and four children because I was able to hear God say, "No, not now."

The Bible is the infallible written word of God and I put much emphasis on its value in learning God's voice in this book. In fact I have included a story that illustrates how obeying the practical principles of God's word along with obedience to His voice helped to position me for a supernatural promotion. However, the Bible doesn't show you that the housing market is going to crash. It doesn't show you that the used car you are purchasing is a lemon. These are things that only God can reveal to you. These are some of the practical things that God wants to show you to prevent you from being deceived. He wants you to know if a fraudulent preacher is taking your money. He wants you to acknowledge the Lord in all of your ways so that He can direct your paths.

Why is it important to develop the ability to hear God's voice? I would like to suggest to you that God never intended for us to live our life without Him. It has always been His intention for us to have a thriving, dynamic, and personal relationship with Him.

God Did Not Save You for Heaven

It may surprise most of you to know that your heavenly residence was not the driving motivation for Christ's suffering at the cross. Wait you say, 'He died for my sins so that where He is I may also be' (John 14:3).

He did die for your sins, and He does want you to be where He is, but that is not why He died for your sins. The Bible says, *"For God so loved the world that He gave His only begotten Son, that whosoever would believe in Him would not perish but have everlasting life" (John 3:16)*. We all know that verse very well. For most of us our focus has always been on what God saved us "from", but we give little to no consideration to what God saved us "for"? He loved us and saved us from destruction for what? Was it for a free trip to heaven? Did He take 39 lashes that ripped open His flesh, endure a crown of thorns' pressed into His skull, did he suffer the humiliation of mockery and nakedness, all for you to go to heaven? I think not!

The Bible says this, *"God was at work in Christ reconciling the world to Himself" (2 Corinthians 5:19)*. The word "reconciling" means to bring back or to restore. So God was in Jesus restoring what to Himself? He was restoring us to Himself. God was restoring what Adam forfeited in the Garden—a personal relationship with God.

12

Adam and Eve: Mouth-to-Mouth

If it was God's concern, through Jesus Christ to restore a broken relationship with mankind, it begs us to consider what the scriptures reveal about that relationship. Just think about the suffering at the cross. What was so valuable to God about this preexisting communion that He would allow His creation to treat Him with such disrespect and cruelty?

I believe we must answer that question by revisiting the story of Adam and Eve. Traditionally, this passage has only been considered in its revelation of man's failure. I, however, am going to use the fall of man as a reference for my point, because it is full of obvious truth that we have allowed go over our heads. We have become so overly consumed by what happened in the garden that we ignore what the passage shows us about what was happening in the garden. Careful consideration of the passage provides us with a glimpse of what was lost in the garden. It is really a love story gone astray.

There are several things in the story that show us how God intended and intends to interact with us as His beloved. The Bible says in Genesis. 3:8, *"And they heard the sound of the Lord God walking in the garden..."* This statement reveals to us two things. One, God visited Adam and Eve. This statement alone shows us that God initiated spending time with them. He enjoyed being in their company. In other words, there was fellowship. Second, they were able to fully recognize Him. They knew the sound of his footsteps. This really says something about their relationship. I have four children and I have learned that each one of them is distinctively different. They sound different, they move different, and they even walk differently. It is because we have a close relationship that I know the sound of their footsteps. I can distinguish who is coming into my presence based solely on what I have learned about them over time. This ability to know that it was God walking in the garden tells us that there was a real connection between God and His creation. We know that God was not the only figure in the Garden. There were animals of all kind, four legged creatures, the serpent, and more than likely the heavenly host were there. However, with all of the different sounds of footsteps they were able to distinguish the sound of their God walking. Folks, there was a real intimacy that had been established.

Further exploration shows us even more about the relationship in the garden. The Bible also shows us that the Lord spoke directly to them. In Genesis 2:15, "*And the Lord commanded them...*" and again in Genesis 1:28 He tells them to "*Be fruitful and multiply.*" Furthermore, we are allowed to see the dialogue that took place after they had eaten the forbidden fruit. *(See Gen. 3:9-20).* Even though this results in intense fellowship, it was interactive fellowship all the same.

Not only does this passage present a relationship in which man hears the voice of God, but we can also see that the relationship is interactive. God spoke to Adam and Eve and they heard His voice clearly. They were also able to respond to His questions. For it reads, "*And the Lord said to them what have you done? Have you eaten from the tree that I commanded you not to eat from? And the Man said (responded), the woman you gave me offered it to me and I ate.*" (Gen. 3:12)

Here is another indication of the relationship that existed before the fall of man. In Genesis 3:21 it reads, "*Also for Adam and His wife THE LORD MADE tunics of skins, and CLOTHED them.*" What does this show us in light of the subject of reconciliation of relationship? It reveals to us that God and mankind had an interactive relationship such as that of a Father fellowshipping with His children. He spoke directly to them: they heard His voice and spoke to Him. He also provided for them, even when they were in the wrong.

So God was in Christ restoring to Himself fellowship such as that seen in the garden experience. God wants to commune with you.

Cain and Abel: Relationship to Religion

You may be thinking to yourself, but that was Adam and Eve. What about everyone else? After Adam and Eve are exiled from the garden, we know that they produced two children. Those children show us that even after our failure in the garden, God continued to commune with man.

In Genesis the 4th chapter we are presented with the story of Cain and Abel and the first murder. As the relationship with God began to deteriorate, man started the religious practice of sacrificial offerings. They started a practice of giving to appease God. It is the same practice used by many religious cultures till this day. It is an attempt to bring about peace between God and man; another way to wash away the guilt.

How do I know that this is the situation in the story? I know this because a search of the scriptures between Gen 3 and 4 indicate no requirement from God to offer sacrifices—not one. We have assumed that this practice was handed down to them from God. However, there is no support for that theory anywhere in the scriptures, Old or New Testament. It also becomes clear in the story that the acceptance of Abel's gift brought him some sense of peace, while the denial of Cain's gift brought him into distress. So much so that God warns him that he is entering into the clutches of sin.

There was never a sacrifice in the garden. In fact there was never a sacrifice until man fell into the clutches of guilty conscience. This is what I consider the beginning of religion, and the death of the relationship between God and mankind. In religion we work to make God accept us, but in relationship we learn that He already does. We learn that He loves us with an agape— unconditional love.

Looking at the story again we can see that Able offers God a sacrifice of love and Cain offers God a sacrifice of guilt. For God says to Cain "*IF YOU DO WELL…*" *(Gen. 4:7)* if you behave yourself…if you live righteously…if you do what is right! It was not his sacrifice God had a problem with. It was His lifestyle. It was the condition of his heart as presented in the scriptures in Genesis 4:7, which reads, "*SIN LIES AT THE DOOR!*" (Gen. 4:7)

Please observe in Genesis chapter 4 that even in his sinful condition the Lord chose to speak to Cain. You will also notice that there is dialogue between God and Cain. The conversation is flowing both ways. Even the tone of the conversation seems to suggest the idea that there was a relationship. In other words, this was not their first conversation. Genesis 4:9 reads, *"Where is Abel your brother, and CAIN SPOKE TO GOD. I do not know. Am I my brother's keeper?"*

So far we have explored God's interaction with the first family, Adam, Eve, Cain and Abel. Now we are going to explore the relationship between God and their descendants.

Noah: The Silent Treatment

In the story of Noah, mankind is at their worst and God is absolutely frustrated by our behavior. This frustration leads Him to conclude that mankind is a decision that He regrets *(see Genesis 6:6)* and the Lord says, *"I regret that I have made man..."* Somewhere in His regret He decides that there is one human worth saving and He's going to use him to repopulate the earth. His name was Noah.

He was described as a righteous man amongst a wicked generation. At this point in history we can see that mankind is nowhere near having fellowship with the Lord. Someone once said that fellowship was two fellows in a boat. The Lord spoke to me one day and said, "If fellowship is two fellows in a boat and the fellows are going to different destinations, which way do they row the boat?" It is clear that God and mankind were headed in two different directions. God, however, was about to get off!

Even though there was no corporate fellowship, there was some fellowship between God and Noah. For Genesis 6:9-22, and Genesis 7:1-5 show us that God spoke to Noah and that Noah was able to hear His voice.

However, there was a difference in the fellowship when compared to the fellowship God had with the previous generations. This passage shows us that God spoke to Noah, but Noah never spoke to God. In fact there are no recorded conversations in the Bible between God and Noah—the man that God called righteous. Even when the rain ended Noah was at the mercy of a dove to determine when the waters had receded from the Earth. Finally God spoke to Noah and commanded him to leave the arc. God spoke to Noah on two other occasions after leaving the arc and we still do not see any dialogue between the two.

Abraham: Visions and the Call from Heaven

Everyone knows that Abraham heard the voice of God. He even had angelic visitations on more than one occasion. The Bible says that God called him "a friend" *(see James 2:23)*. His relationship with God was so intimate that he was allowed to negotiate with God. He actually challenged God's decision to destroy Sodom and Gomorrah and God considered his earthly counsel. wow, this is what I aspire to achieve in my relationship with God. I want Him to consider me a friend.

However, we must consider that we see God communicating with mankind in a way that He never did in the previous chapters. He began to communicate with man through dreams and visions. This is yet another sign of our falling away from God.

Am I implying that dreams and visions are bad? No, in fact I have a section of this book that speaks to the issue in detail. However, in light of this context, it is. It is a sign that mankind was no longer able to bear hearing the voice of God. In fact the Bible says this about dreams and visions. In Numbers chapter 12, God says to Aaron and Miriam, *"If there is a prophet among you I speak to him in a dream and visions and in dark sayings. Not so with my servant Moses, for I speak to Him face to face"*. So while in the New Testament church, dreams and visions prove to be a great resource for interacting with God, we must consider that in light of how we interacted with God in the garden in the Old Testament, it is not so good of a thing. Mankind clearly goes from having direct communication with God to a less intimate form of communication. In fact this less intimate fellowship was expressed in unclear communication, hence we see used the term "dark sayings!"

What about dreams? What does the Bible say about dreams? Job 33:14-18 says God speaks to man this way and that way and he (mankind) does not perceive it, so He waits until mankind sleeps and then He seals instructions in their hearts with dreams. As I said earlier it was a less intimate and indirect form of communication. This passage reveals to us God's passion to speak with us face to face. It further reveals His intentions are often hindered by the reality that we are never listening. So He waits until we go to sleep and then

He speaks to us. This is an obvious depiction of a broken relationship. This is the perfect description of two ships passing in the night.

Moses: Prophetic Text Messages

Moses introduces us to yet a new era. Like Abraham, everyone knows that Moses had the kind of relationship with God that just makes you jealous. God spoke to Him face to face. We don't have one recorded instance of God speaking to Moses in a dream or a vision. God spoke to him directly. In fact the Bible says that he saw the form of God, it also says that God once walked passed him allowing him to see His backside.

So what was new with Moses? Moses is our first look at a prophet. The Bible actually calls Abraham a prophet, but we never see God use him to speak on his behalf. Moses, however, is the first person we see speaking to mankind on God's behalf on a cooperate level. By cooperate I mean we see him speaking to crowds and generations. Are you seeing the digression? Are you seeing the "you shall surely die" that God was referring to in the garden?

Moses' life reveals to us that man's heart has gone so far from God that He has to send him text messages. He can no longer speak to him face to face. He tries but man doesn't recognize Him so He speaks to him at night. Now He has to use someone as His vehicle to speak to mankind.

Eventually we get to the place between the end of Malachi and the beginning of Matthew. The period referred to as the "silent period". But was God silent? I doubt it. We just were not in a position to hear from Him.

Jesus: God Visits Man

This all leads us to Jesus Christ. Who we understand as our God who came to Earth and manifested Himself in flesh? So what was the problem? At this point in time mankind is so far from God that He cannot perceive that God is visiting him. Mankind had no concept of the voice that was visiting with him because of the darkness in his heart.

Jesus Himself is amazed at just how bad the relationship had deteriorated. They had many prophecies that notified them that He was coming. Those prophecies were clear in revealing what He would be doing, and how they would be able to recognize Him. However, even though they had all of theses resources at their fingertips, they still didn't recognize the day of their salvation.

Jesus and His Sheep

We started this chapter out with the question, "Does God still speak today?" John 10:27 answers that question for us. Jesus says in this passage, that His sheep, "hear His voice!" Some may say that this passage is referring to Israel hearing His voice as He preached salvation to them. However, if you keep reading He says and He has sheep that are not of this fold. Who are these sheep that are not of His fold? Jesus is referring to the gentiles or those who are not of the Israeli culture. In other words, if you are not Jewish you are gentile.

Jesus is speaking of a latter time after His death when the gospel would be preached in all the other nations of the world. This denotes that even in the latter times that He would still be speaking to His people. What is the preaching of the gospel but God speaking to mankind? It is His invitation to come in and sup with God. It is His invitation to come into intimacy with God. Why would He invite you into His kingdom to say nothing else?

We also have as a testament to the idea of a God who still speaks, Joel 2:28 which reads, "*And it shall come to pass afterward, that I will pour out my spirit upon all flesh; and your sons and your daughters shall prophesy, your old men shall dream dreams, your young men shall see visions.*". This passage makes it absolutely clear that our God is one who is still speaking. Joel tells us that with the outpouring of the Holy Spirit will come "dreams", "visions", and "prophecy". This is contrary to any theological explanation that says God is not speaking today. And it clearly indicates that He still wants to speak. So now it is up to you to decide whether you believe men whose rational minds are darkened to this truth, or God whose word clearly says He is speaking in the last days!

Then there is your own testimony. All of us who are saved can attest to hearing God's voice. In fact every saved person has heard the Holy Spirit speaking to them. The day I gave my life to Christ I heard the tugging of my heart. It was so strong that I actually left church several Sundays prior to actually surrendering to His voice. It was so strong and loud and I was so uncomfortable that I literally could not wait to get out of church.

Many of you can attest to that same experience. You heard something saying to you "today is the day" or "give your life to Me" or even "repent and be saved." I want you to know that when you responded that was just the beginning. Hopefully, as you read this book you will be able to see where the great "something told me" has spoken to you at other times in your life.

Finally, I want you to consider 1 Corinthians 10:11, *"These things were written for our example…"* The context of this passage is a warning not to walk in the ways of Israel's wickedness, but the essence is simple. All of the things seen in the Bible are recorded for us to see an example of how we are to interact with God. That includes the interaction recorded between Him and every person mentioned in the scriptures.

For instance, Enoch walked with God and was not. You can too—that is our example in that passage. Abraham was called the friend of God. Moses was called the most humble man on Earth and God spoke to him face to face. Elijah leaves us an example of a man that walked with God in power. David's example was that God loved him because He was a man after God's heart. Peter, James, and John, teach us that there are different levels of closeness with God and those closest to Him see more revelation of Him. Paul teaches us that we can walk with God under the new covenant in revelation. I could go on and on with the examples that God inspired men to record that only have one goal. That goal is that you would have a relationship with God and that you would hear His voice. Every single one of these great men had this is common. They heard the voice of God!

I don't need to pull out thousands of passages of scripture to make my point. John 10:27, Joel 2:28, your own salvation testimony, and the great examples recorded for our example, are all I need to make this a valid argument. Of course God speaks today and He has plenty more to say.

Chapter Two
Ways God Speak

Jesus said, *"My sheep hear my voice" (John 10:27)*. If we are not hearing the voice God, this statement suggests to us that the problem is not a transmitter issue. It is a receiver issue. For this statement is an emphatic statement not a passive one. Jesus is not saying My sheep hear My voice. He's saying MY SHEEP HEAR ME! The stranger's voice they won't hear or give attention to, because they are not familiar with that voice.

I was teaching my children this concept and I was teaching it from the position of fear. If you are a parent you know what I mean. I was teaching them that they should to be careful because the devil can speak to them also. As I was teaching them my parental version of the word, the Lord interrupted the conversation and said rather forcefully, "MY sheep hear MY voice. But wanting to protect my children from deception, I continued to teach them my version but I adjusted my message slightly. Then again the Lord interrupted me and said, "MY SHEEP, HEAR MY VOICE!!!"

So I began to instruct them about how to study God in the scriptures and encouraged them to continue to seek the Lord. I left it in the in the hands of the Shepherd and made myself available to help them discern.

Why am I starting with this particular truth? I know that God's voice is not the only voice we literally hear. Satan and his cohorts speak to us as well. It is important, however, for us to know that Jesus' voice is so distinct and different. Also, real Christians do not need to worry themselves with Satan's voice because the reality is Jesus says that Satan's voice is one that "His sheep" won't follow! Therefore, you do not need to be overly concerned or consumed with the fear of being deceived. You will have seasons like Jesus in the wilderness when you will be tempted but you will know that is it is not God speaking because Satan's voice will always point you to YOU. Jesus leads us to Himself. One truth you will see presented often is that *"The spirit of prophecy is the testimony of Jesus Christ"* (Rev. 19:10). I am going to drill this truth into you because it is the safe guard against deception.

The understanding that Jesus points us to Himself will help us as we move forward in discussing how He speaks to us. It will also give us the peace we need to position ourselves to hear Him in ways that some consider controversial, even though they are biblical. The controversy is spawned by the fear of deception, and the many examples of those deceived in such ways. I have to point out though, that if we look as the David Koresh's, Daddy Graces, and many other self-proclaimed Christ's who claim that they came to such an idea through a voice, dream or vision, we will see that they violated a basic truth. That truth again is that God testifies and points us to Himself. "If we draw near to Him, He will draw near to us", and that can only be accomplished if you walk in the safety of this basic truth.

Now that we know that Jesus says that "His sheep hear His voice" and that He points us to Himself, we need to discuss how He speaks to His sheep. How does God communicate with us? That is the question we will answer in the pages to follow.

Audible Voice

One of the most incredible ways in which God may choose to speak to you is in an audible voice. This mode of communication is one of the most constant and visible attributes of how God communicated with mankind. As I pointed out in chapter 1, this is how He spoke to mankind until after the fall. After the fall we can see a progressive falling away and eventually, we see that God and man have a silent period.

So God speaks in an audible voice, and I believe that He desires to do so more often today. Some would describe it as a still small voice deep down inside. And usually to hear it you have to sit still and be quiet for hours waiting to hear a faint sound in your heart. This is not what God desires. I go into much more detail in my chapter on "Hindrances to Hearing". I also have a book that speaks to this subject in detail called *You Can Hear the Voice of God Clearly*. But God's voice is a voice, that can be heard clearly. It is not a still small voice. This is an important truth to accept because it will help you open up your faith to receive what He really wants to do.

The reason you hear a still small voice is because this is the teaching to which your faith has been applied. Therefore it's what you have come to expect to hear. However, if you open your faith to the reality that God speaks in an audible voice, you will find that it is much easier to hear.

God does not want you to strain to hear His voice. He desires fellowship with you and He has made it easy for that to happen. Also, this popular teaching violates the basics of biblical interpretation. One should never develop a doctrine around one passage of scripture. You will never see the term "still small voice" ever again in scripture when God is speaking. You will however see God speaking in a clear voice in hundreds of passages. And it is consistently seen in the Old Testament and the New Testament.

I can recall a particular time in my life when God spoke to me the first time in an audible voice. I had been working in the file room for years before I was detailed to another office as an office assistant. The detail was to be thirty days, but turned into three years. While in the job, I did a lot of small tasks and menial work, but I believed that the will of God was for me to always do my work as unto the Lord. And that's what I did.

One day as I sat in prayer before God, I heard a voice clearly say, "You are going to get a job offer tomorrow, do not turn it down". The moment I heard it I knew that it was the Lord, but I have to admit, it was a bit startling. I've had many experiences with the Lord but this one was new and different for me.

In the middle of the next day my boss approached me with a question about the job that God told me was coming. I quickly discovered why He said not to refuse the offer. I was at the time in a permanent employee status and the new job required me to go into temporary status. This meant that after a certain time my position would be terminated and I would be out of a job. Yes, I said, "out of a job!" This was not an easy instruction to follow.

I wish I could tell you that I was obedient, but I became afraid and the opportunity passed. The job was given to another co-worker and one month later it was converted into a permanent position. This could have been a perfect story, but the good thing is approximately 6 months later the offer was made again and I accepted.

I also want us to understand that in the Bible people heard the audible voice of God in different ways. It was obvious that Adam, Eve, Cain, and Moses heard an external audible voice. Phillip is one of our New Testament examples of God speaking in an audible external voice in Act 8:29. But there were some people who actually heard the voice of God internally in a dream or vision. Such was the case with Abraham when God gave him a dream that his descendants would be as innumerable as the sand on sea, (Genesis 40:23). Peter in Acts 10:13 is another example of God speaking to us in an internal audible voice. Peter says he saw a great sheet let down from heaven and he heard a voice say, "Rise Peter. Kill and eat".

So as you open up your faith to receive the audible voice of God, just understand that it may happen in one of the two ways.

Dreams and Visions

One of the other ways, in which, God may choose to speak to you is in a dream or a vision. Dreams and visions are mental images impressed into the mind during a conscious or unconscious state. The major difference between the two is that dreams are received during a sleeping state, while visions can be received while sleeping or awake.

Dreams and visions are fascinating to a lot of people and God uses them to speak to people for many different reasons. Some are used to provide direction as with Abraham when he left his family for the land that God would show him (Gen. 12:1). Or He may use them to challenge our perspectives and mindsets, such as He did when He helped Peter accept the gentiles (Acts 10:11-16) and Joseph when he was going to put away Mary for what he thought was an illegitimate conception (Matt. 1:20). Sometimes He will show us our future as he did with Joseph (Gen. 37:5-11), and to warn us as he did with King Abemelech who was going to sleep with Abraham's wife (Gen. 20:1-7). No matter how He chooses to deliver His message to you, just know that it is important.

Vision of Jesus

I have had many visions and dreams. One of my favorite occurred as I was writing this book. God initially told me that He wanted this book written within a certain time frame. Therefore, He impressed upon me often to write and I did. At some point in the process however, when I started writing a particular chapter, I could not figure out how to address the subject. Knowing what to do and explaining it to someone else are quite different. I had written maybe two paragraphs of that chapter when I finally said, "Lord this is not working."

In frustration I asked the Lord how He wanted me to approach this subject? I told Him that I really needed His help with this subject, because it was difficult to explain. Then I sat in my chair and waited. Then after 30 minutes or so, I got up and waited and waited. Later that night I returned to my chair and was waiting some more when all of a sudden, I saw a figure in an illuminated white gown fly into what I assume was the room I was in. He was at a distance and he had something in his hand. It was a rolled up piece of paper. As I was looking He unrolled it and there was writing on it. I could see the words but not clearly. The figure smiled at me and then flew away.

It did not dawn on me until the next day what was on that piece of paper. It was a vision from God giving me what I needed to write these chapters that I was struggling to complete. Once I accepted the vision the words for those chapters began to poor out me like rivers of living water.

This is an example of how God interacts with us in a vision to help us accomplish His will.

Vision of the Wolf Lamb

Sometimes God speaks to us in visions to get us to accept a truth. This was the case in this next story. I actually had this vision at a stoplight.

I was infatuated with a young lady at the time that I had only seen walking around on the job. This young lady was beautiful and friendly and she carried herself with such dignity and respect. She seemed meek and was always very polite. However, this was far from the truth.

I was so captivated by this woman that I had to talk to God about her. So one day as I sat at a stoplight I said, "Lord, what's up with the light skinned girl on the job". No sooner I said that, I saw in my mind a picture of a sheep and as I kept looking at it, the sheep began to turn into a wolf. This vision was completely contrary to what I had observed. I never saw or heard of anything that indicated that this woman was dangerous. So I asked the question again. And again I saw a clear picture of a sheep that turned into a wolf.

Having heard from the Lord I took the vision for what it was worth left this woman alone. Sometime later that year I was detailed to the position I spoke of earlier in the chapter, and guess who was there? Yep, this same woman! It was not even a day before I discovered that she was extremely promiscuous, a habitual liar, and a drunk. What happened to the nice young lady I had met? This was definitely a case of Dr. Jekyll and Mrs. Hyde!

This woman almost caused me to fall into sin, but God prepared me by giving me a simple image with a vital truth attached. You may be pondering how I received this vision. Some people think that being in a trance state is the only way to receive a vision from God. But what I experienced is something known as a mental vision. Mental visions happen to many of you more often than you may realize. After reading this book I pray that you will begin to recognize this more often. This becomes obvious in Daniel 2:29, which says, "Oh king as you lay on your bed ***thoughts entered into your mind...***" Later Daniel tells us that those thought came from God. What I want you to notice is that those thoughts were visual. So sometimes a vision will appear in your mind while you are awake and at other times while you are asleep. We call visions that happen at night dreams and those in the day visions or daydreams.

The Dream that Changed My Mind

Often times God will use a dream to challenge an idea or change our mind regarding an issue. He did this with the apostles Peter and Paul in the book of acts. I have discovered that some things are best shared and understood visually. This was the case with this particular dream. It would take years before it finally blossomed into understanding, but the reality it presented changed my life.

Years ago I dreamed that I received a phone call at work from a woman making an inquiry. As the conversation progressed I decided that I would minister prophetically to her. As I did, I tuned inward to hear the word of the Lord. As I did I initially heard the still small voice of God. It was an inner audible still small voice. As I continued ministering I started to notice that as I tuned in deeper that the voice of God became progressively louder. I remember so vividly in the dream thinking to myself, "How is this possible?"

This dream came at a time in my life when I was learning how to minister prophetically by choosing to exercise my faith. So when I awakened from the dream I was initially more focused on the reality that I could tune in to minister. It would be later that year that God would start teaching me about the audible voice. In fact He spoke to me about it while I was writing this book 20 years earlier. At the time I was writing about the still small voice as a way that God speaks, when God suddenly opened up the understanding of Elijah's still small voice experience. At first I struggled to break from this old tradition to embrace a new truth. I had heard and been trained to look for the still small voice and that idea prevailed over the voice of God. I just did not have the faith to embrace a new truth or to replace the one that I was comfortable with.

Then years later I came into other audible experiences. At which point I rediscovered this dream in my journal. And low and behold there was this truth. God had used this particular dream, years earlier to communicate to me that I could hear the voice of God and not just a still small voice.

He used this dream to not only challenge my mindset and understanding, but this dream also revealed to me how to hear the voice of God. This is something that I cover in detail in my book *You Can Hear the Voice of God Clearly.*

It is important that I note for you that it is God who determines which way or ways He will choose to speak to you. Since I began to teach this people have experienced the voice of God and have become fixated on only hearing His voice. This chapter is the spawn of the multiple ways that God continues to speak to me today. Sometimes He speaks in a voice and other times in dreams and visions. Yet at other times He uses simple gestures. So while you are embracing this reality I plead with you that you not box God into a corner. He will determine how to best communicate with you. As time goes on and your relationship with God blossoms you will come to fully understand that sometimes words are enough and sometimes only a picture or similitude will effectively communicate the idea He is presenting to you.

Vision for Warfare and Intercession

Sometimes God has a very specific reason for giving you a dream or vision. Spiritual warfare is one such occasion. God will sometimes show you how the enemy is operating against a church, organization, or individual.

We see this happening in 2 Kings 6:17-20 when Elisha is caught between a rock and a hard spot. He has been revealing the King of Assyria's plan to attack the King of Israel. Out of reasonable frustration the perplexed king assumes that he has a traitor in his camp. One of his servants tells him that the prophet in Israel is telling the kings secret. The king of Assyria then decides that he is going to capture Elisha and kill him. So he goes by night to the place where the prophet is lodging. When Elisha and his servant awaken they realize that they are completely surrounded by soldiers. Elisha's servant then became overwhelmed with fear and Elisha prays a simple prayer. *"Lord, open his eyes that he might see"* (verse 16). And God answered Elisha's prayer and opened the servant's eyes to the spirit realm. When his eyes opened he saw that there were angels all about protecting them. This allowed Elisha to divert the attack and deliver the enemy into the hands of the King of Israel.

I remember a few months ago as I was praying that I saw a vision of a church with a large dark, 200-foot principality over it with a sword. He drew the sword and struck the church and divided it in half. Soon after the hands of the Lord grabbed the side of the church and put it back together and it looked as if nothing had occurred.

This vision revealed that a principality of division was starting an attack against this particular church. This was God telling me how He needed me to intercede in prayer for this church.

On another occasion, God revealed the enemy's plan against a Bible study group that I attended. This was a mighty group of multi-denominational people who got together every week for prayer and to study the word. One day as we were in prayer I saw in a vision four evil spirits sitting on the counter behind us. They were canvassing the group looking for the weak person in the group. Once they found their victim they began to move in, but not all at once. One would create an opportunity of attack for the next. They were quite systematic and organized in executing their plan. After the last one moved into position the Bible study suffered chaos and soon the drama killed the group.

After the time of prayer I told the vision to the group, but they did not take it to heart. I think they were a little put off by the fact that I saw evil spirits. But anyway, it was not long after that one of the women started having romantic feelings, or should I say lustful feelings, for one of the teachers. This led to chaos, which led to gossip and all of a sudden this group that had 15-20 persons in attendance every week praying and interceding for everything possible, was down to 5-6 people every week. God gave them fair warning, but they did not hear. I will admit, that looking back, I should have presented the vision with more wisdom. I was young and inexperienced then, but now I can see how important wisdom is when administering such information.

The Most Beautiful Dream

God also uses dreams to provide us with direction. This is a dream that came at a time in my life before I received Christ as my Savior. The beauty of this dream is that God tried to communicate with me even though I didn't know Him. But the dream clearly shows that He watches over us, even the sinners.

My early years of years in high school were really boring and uneventful. I spent a great deal of time desiring to be recognized and not get lost in the vast sea of people. When I got to the eleventh grade I discovered something fascinating about myself. I discovered that I loved poetry and that I could rap. This began a new chapter in my life and changed my status as a student.

I loved my new talent and I worked very hard to be the best rapper the world would ever hear. This was to be my career path and I would pursue it until I got what I was after. That meant school did not matter, and so I did just enough to get by. Upon graduation I was going to move to New York to pursue my dream.

Then it happened. I dreamed that I was coming up from and underground metro system in New York City. When I got to the top of the staircase all I could see was the entire city of New York made of the most beautiful crystal. I mean it was absolutely fascinating. I still remember how real that dream felt. I could hardly believe it was a dream.

It would be a few years before I would receive the interpretation of that dream. The dream was an attempt by God to communicate a very important truth about the direction I was headed. In the dream the rising staircase was a depiction of my success in the rap industry. The crystal city communicated the beauty and fragile nature of the dream. One day God finally spoke to me about the dream and He said, that it would have only taken a stone to bring my fragile world to an end.

I'm so glad God saved me from going in that direction. He tried to warn me about me direction but I was not able to hear Him. Thank God for His mercy.

Revealing the Heart

Sometimes God uses dreams and visions to reveal our heart when we are stuck in certain patterns of life. For a long time I was timid about displaying anger. I had seen some things in my childhood that left me angry and even after I got saved I worked hard to avoid being in situations where I might get angry. Which meant I worked at avoiding confrontations.

So I started talking to the Lord about how to be free to be angry, but not sin. One day as I was walking to the mall I got another mental image. This time however, it was an image of the Incredible Hulk. God was showing me that I was afraid of the monster that I thought might manifest in time of stress. He then began to assure me that He had done the work to free me from my past and that anger was an emotion that I could now control. After this discussion I went on to have healthy confrontations with people that did not involve me becoming violent. I was free.

One thing that you may hear as you open yourself up to receive from God through dreams and visions is that the devil might speak to you. You will also hear that dreams can come from the busyness of the day or issues on your mind. These are both true. Ecclesiastics 5:3 says, *"For a dream comes through much activity"*.

While I understand their concerns, I tell people all dreams are important even though they are not all from God. If the devil has an issue inside of you and your flesh is struggling with something, then it will manifest in your dreams. Why should you care? These types of dreams assist you in knowing how you should pray and what issues are going on in your heart.

For example, for a couple of years I would have reoccurring dreams about a former girlfriend who made life a living hell. In the dreams I was always doing something violent to her, such as pushing her off the top bunk bed onto the floor. After sometime passed I started to realize that I never grieved the pain that she caused me during the relationship. I was still angry in my heart and it was manifesting in my dreams.

Not long after, I attended a youth retreat and the Spirit of God started moving and dealing with people, and I sensed that this was the perfect time to release this issue to God. So I walked up front with just a tear or two, but by time I hit the floor I was sobbing uncontrollably and I felt all that pain from five years prior that I had bottled up inside of me. I was completely surprised and I did not expect that to happen. After I gave the pain to the Lord I felt much better and I have never had a dream like that again.

I have also had demonic dreams as well. However, I need to tell you that the type of dream I am about to describe is not likely to happen to you. This happened in my life as the gift of discerning of spirits was just beginning to operate. If anyone has this gift you will know what I mean when I say it was not a pleasant introduction to the gift.

I had been having a great year and the Lord was moving in my life in a mighty way. I was witnessing to everyone even my bosses. I had a booming Bible study on the job and prophecy and revelation were flowing regularly. I was wreaking havoc on the kingdom of darkness.

This resulted in a dream in which I saw myself run up to a woman to cast the demon out of her. As I raised my hand to cast it out she turned around and I heard a creepy voice that was not in the dream say, "You don't know who you are dealing with". This stunned me into waking up. When I opened my eyes there was a large dark presence standing over top of me staring angrily down at me as I lay on my bed. So I got up on my bed, looked it in the eyes, (yes it was that large), and told it, "No, You don't know who you're dealing with". Then I rebuked it in the name of Jesus and it left.

This may scare some of you but this is not likely to happen. This was a training period of my life and while I did not enjoy these experiences, I did come to KNOW the reality of the POWER in the NAME of JESUS. They really do flee at that name.

So unless God gives you certain gifts you may never have this type of encounter. Even if you do have such an encounter, rebuke it and go back to sleep.

Sometimes demonic dreams are more subtle. In fact, at the conclusion of writing the first draft of this book I felt a presence fill the air of my bedroom as I was going to bed. It was fear and I could literally sense it in the air as an overwhelming fear. That night as I slept I had a dream about how traditional religious people, to include friends and family, would reject the book. It also attempted to torment me throughout the next day, but I exposed it, rebuked it and the presence left and so did the thoughts and dreams.

These are my personal stories, but the Bible is full of stories of God speaking in dreams and visions.

Impressions

This is probably the most common experience among Christians and occasionally non-Christians. It is usually characterized by the popular clichés "something told me" and " I had a feeling."

Impressions are intuitive feelings, senses, or an inner perceptions or a sudden awareness felt deep within the being of an individual. Impressions ,may come to us as light as a flash of thought or as strong as an urge. However they may come to us we can be certain that what we perceive, is spiritual in nature. This is the most popular form of communication with the spirit world. Even the psychics and the New Age materials refer to the intuitive feeling.

What does this mean to the believer? It means that we must learn how to recognize God, which is the purpose of this book.

I find this particular method of communication very re-assuring. It seems to provide the greatest sense of security. Just consider how many times you have sensed something and ignored it only to find out that it was true. For instance many of you have known that someone was lying to you. You can't explain it, you just knew deep inside that something wasn't right. I once heard a character on television make this statement. "I trust my intuition, and my intuition doesn't trust you!" This seems to sum up this idea.

Some of us refer to this as our knower or the leading of the Spirit. However you may refer to it, it is a good method for measuring the validity of the other three communication methods. If fact, when I am uncertain I weigh the voice against my knower. If I have an unmistakable "knowing" I know I'm good to go.

The hardest thing about this method is learning how to subject our rational minds so that we can trust our inner senses. Also, this method as do all the others, though not to the same extent, require us to make the distinction between what is the Spirit and what is our own imaginations and desires. Some people are prone to projecting what they want as what they sense God is saying. Such as the many prophets who prophesied that President Obama would not receive a second term. Some of them claim to have had dreams and visions, but really it was just what they wanted to see happen manifesting to their hearts. This is why checking the "knower" is valuable.

The Bible says that *"The word of God divides between soul and spirit"* (Heb. 4:12). It makes the distinction between what is us and what is God. The best examples of this concept that I have heard was a teaching on the voice of God by a prophet who said, that you could liken impressions to those things we experience in the conscience. In our conscience there is no sentence structure as with the audible voice. There are no words, just a sense of right and wrong.

There a lot of examples in the scriptures as well regarding impressions and the many ways we may experience God moving on our inner man.

Perception

One way we might experience an impression as seen in the scriptures is perception. When God is communicating with us we may perceive something. When faced with a storm Paul says, *"Men I PERCIEVE that this voyage will end in disaster..."* (Acts 27:10) We also, see perception at work in the ministry of Jesus. In Mark 2:8, it reads, *"When Jesus perceived within His spirit."* Perception can also manifest as a strong desire or an urge to some action. We can again take our example from Jesus in the Gospels.

Jesus was departing Judea and was on His way to Galilee when he needed to go to Samaria. While at Samaria He meets the woman we know today as the woman at the well (John 4:1-4) Notice how the scriptures read, *"He left Judea and departed again to Galilee. **But He needed** to go through Samaria."* We can see this principle clearly in this passage.

34

Sudden Motivation or Inspiration

The other way in which we might experience impressions from God takes the form of motivation and inspiration. We can see this in the scripture as well. The Bible refers to this experience as the stirring of the heart.

We see this idea in the life of Ezra in Ezra 1:5, when he sets out to assist Nehemiah with the rebuilding of the temple. This passage reads, *"...and all whose SPIRITS God had STIRRED..."* In this story we can see that God uses the stirring or motivation of our inner man to lead us in a direction to accomplish his will. I go into great detail about this in the chapter *"The Voice and The Unction."*

We can also see it in other passages such as Acts 17:16 which reads, *"Paul's spirit was provoked within him and he..."* And again in 2 Chronicles 36:22, *"God stirred up the spirit of Cyrus."* Also In Haggai 1:14, *"God inspired the spirits of the men in Haggai to work on the rebuilding of the temple."*

Burdens

The last way that I have found in the scriptures that indicates how God may choose to speak to us is found in Habakkuk 1:1. It reads, *"The BURDEN which the prophet Habakkuk saw"*.

Sometimes God uses our own senses to call our attention to a situation. Habakkuk is in such a situation. God is causing him to see and take notice of all of the debauchery that is happening around him. What he sees is bothering him and it is having such an affect on him that he seeks God about what is happening and God uses this to give him his first prophecy.

This is good information for some of you who are trying to find the purpose of God in your life. In a latter book I am writing on how God shows us our destiny, I use this principle to help people to understand why five people can see the same situation of need completely different. It all has to do with the way the Lord directs His burden of vision. Burdens actually combine two or more elements from this chapter. You will experience a perceptual vision and you may perceive what God wants to do through motivation and inspiration.

Or you may see a burden and have an experience such as Habakkuk, where Gods speaks to you in an audible voice.

Hopefully the lights are coming on and you are beginning to recognize other times when God was moving in your life by impressions.

Similitudes

The last method that I am going to address regarding this subject is similitudes. A similitude is an analogy or parable. It happens when God takes something natural and makes it relevant to a truth. God can use any number of objects to convey His message. This is probably very common to preachers, who rely on good illustrations to make their points clear.

As I address this subject you will see how perception works to create this experience. In my experience God has blatantly spoken to me in parables using an object to convey His message. At other times He has spoken to me in what I call "perceptual vision".

The Bible says, *"And without a parable He did not speak to them"* (Matt. 13:34, Mark 4:34). This passage refers to how Jesus addressed the many audiences that heard Him speak. Why did He speak in parables? You will find that sometimes the hardest thing to do is to explain a supernatural concept to a natural minded audience. Jesus is having this same problem. He is speaking in reference to the Kingdom of Heaven and the Kingdom of God, and such things as faith and what happen when a demon is cast out to a man. How else could He have explained such abstract concepts to an ordinary people? He used wisdom and decided to use physical elements, which were relevant to the audience. He does this as an attempt to help their understanding of the supernatural realm.

He still speaks this way today. You will see this in the dreams and visions that you will experience. Sometimes the dreams are literal but most of the time they are full of symbolism that the hearer is familiar with or understands.

Just consider my vision above of the sheep that turned to a wolf. He could have shown me the various sins of this woman. But it was much easier and more efficient to just show me an image, which I could relate to from the scriptures.

Later in the chapter on *"Signs of His Voice"* I tell how God spoke a word to me using HE-Man. Yes, He-Man. God used He-Man to teach me the importance of His word and how the Spirit of God empowers us through it. You can read the full account in that chapter, but God will use all sorts of objects to teach you wonderful truths about life and Him self. He knows how to make the complicated easy to understand.

Perceptual Vision

The paragraph above refers to parable similitudes, but what about perceptual vision. Sometimes God will cause you to see an object or situation and then He will inspire you with revelation. We can see this happening in Habakkuk, which we discussed in the last section. He saw something and it became the springboard for revelation. The same thing happened to Jeremiah when God asked him the question what do you see. Then he looked up and saw a boiling pot and it was facing north (Jer. 1:11,13). He saw something and then God used what he perceived with his eyes to speak to him a prophetic word.

One of the most evident depictions of this is found in Hosea 1:2-4. God tells Hosea to go find a harlot and have children with her. And in obedience Hosea finds a harlot named Gomer and their strained marriage, filled with multiple affairs, becomes a visible representation to communicate Israel's whoring ways. God also uses it to communicate to Israel that even though they break His heart, that He is committed to their union.

Again, Jeremiah 18 shows us a perfect example of this principle. In this chapter Jeremiah is instructed by God to go to the potter's house. While there Jeremiah observes the potter in the process of working with the clay. While observing the potter at work he notices that the clay was spoiled in the hands of the potter. It was so flawed that He made it into another vessel. (see Jer. 18:4)

This observation of the potter interacting with the clay is used as a form

37

of communication with Jeremiah. From the experience God gave birth to a word in Jeremiah. You will see a similar thing happen with a linen loincloth in the thirteenth chapter of Jeremiah.

Ezekiel is another example of this concept. God told him to make a hole in his wall and carry out his belonging through the hole (Ezek. 8:8). He also told him to lie on his side and eat filth (Ezek. 4:4). All this was a visual and dramatic production with one goal I mind. God wanted to communicate a truth.

My children have often been great tools for God to show me truth. I have four beautiful children and our custom at our house is that dessert is only served to those who eat all of their food. One night in particular they were not fond of what mommy had made for dinner. And they were slugging through eating their food. What they did not know was that I had bought something special for them to eat that night. However they would only be able to get it if they ate their food.

I could see that this was not going to end well for them. I so desperately wanted them to have what I had purchased. Suddenly I became aware of the fact that God was saying the same to thing to me. He had a blessing for me and He really wanted to give it to me but He really needed me to make the life adjustments that He required. This is what I call perceptual vision. It is the moment when God causes you to become suddenly aware of some idea He is trying to communicate to you.

All of the information I presented above outlines the ways that God has revealed to me that He speak to us. I know from the many conversations that I have had with people that they have experienced God speaking to them in one of the ways mentioned in this chapter.

Every once in a while, God allows me the privilege of pointing out to people when He is speaking to them. It's always heart warming for me, and eye opening to them to know that the creator has been trying to get their attention.

Hopefully, the information I presented in this chapter will have the same affect on you. I am also hopeful that it will allow you to come out from among those about whom God says, I speak this way and that way, but man doesn't recognize Me.

Section 2

Discerning the Voices

Chapter Three
Signs of His Voice

Pastor I had a feeling! Hey guess what, I heard a voice! I had a dream! I saw a vision today! All of these are prefaces to a lot of tragic stories, which range from light failure to the destruction of individuals.

How many serial killers have said, 'I heard a voice tell me to do it?' Or what about the heinous acts of September 11, 2011, when Osama Bin Laden said that God told him to perform the egregious acts of that unforgettable day. Or how about the many preachers, prophets, evangelists, and religious leaders, who rip people off in the name of the Lord? Or how about the many religions whose beginnings were inspired by a vision someone believed was from God.

Such experiences have made people very leery of the validity of such experiences. As a result, a lot of well-meaning Christians live with uncertainty when it comes discerning God's voice.

How can we be certain and walk in the confidence of knowing that God has spoken to us? How can we get to a place that allows us to freely pursue and develop intimate fellowship with Him?

Allowing for Mistakes

First let me begin by saying that you must be willing to fail if you are to learn. There is no great formula for discerning the voice of the Lord that will exclude you from missing the mark from time to time. Therefore, you need to accept the truth that sometimes you're going to get it wrong. The Bible tells us in Hebrews 5:14, that we "LEARN TO DISCERN between good an evil". How? We learn by the "EXCERSING of our SENSES by reason OF USE!"

Why Are We So Afraid?

Have you ever heard this popular saying before, "If it is not the will of God, God won't be in it. You'll be on your own!" Isn't that the scariest thing, to think that if you make a mistake and miss the voice of God, or if you choose your own way for whatever reason, that God is going to leave you to yourself? Or that He would watch you struggle and not offer His assistance.

I am so glad that God does not think like man. It pleases me to know that we can measure such statements against the Bible and the examples of God's character.

What makes this statement so unscriptural? It is unscriptural because one of the last things Jesus tells the disciples is that "He would be with us even UNTIL THE END OF THE AGE" (Matt. 28:20). Or how about the many examples where God proved to us that He "never" left Israel in spite of their propensity to go wayward.

The Permissive Will of God

Many people may have heard the terms *"permissive will"* and *"perfect will"* when referring to the will of God. But how many people actually know what they mean? Without a doubt, the perfect will of God is the ultimate place where God wants us to be. It is the center of His will. Most people understand that. It is, however, the idea of the permissive will that most of us struggle with because we think of it as the place beyond return. While I do agree that the perfect will of God is the best place to be, the permissive will is not exactly hell. If that were the case the majority of people are there now!

Why am I bringing attention to this issue? Because without a doubt if you miss God you are going to be in the permissive will of God. This is what causes fear in most people. This fear however, can be the start of an uncomfortable cycle when we don't understand what is happening.

44

Usually, after we miss God we panic and then it's, "Oh God, I missed the perfect will of God and now I am on my own!" The pressure of this reality sometimes causes us to make more rash decisions in an effort to return to the perfect will of God. This usually creates quite the mess and puts us further away from the perfect will of God.

The reality is that the idea of God abandoning us for our mistakes could not be further from the truth. The Bible says, "God is faithful even when we are faithless" (2 Tim. 2:13). God is the only infallible being and He understands that mistakes are inevitable. You are human and the perfect will of God involves faith and maturity.

The perfect will of God is not something that just happens to you by chance. It is something that you must discern and choose to embrace. Sometimes the perfect will of God is extremely difficult to walk in because it often calls us to walk where we cannot see, and to do what we cannot fathom. It requires a level of mature faith that some have not obtained. Therefore, turning down a high paying job when you don't have one at the request of a voice, intuitive feeling, or dream, is not always an easy decision to make.

This is one of my motives for writing this book. I desire for people to come to such an intimacy with God that they feel confident in what He instructs for their life. The relationship with God is just like any other relationship. It must be built and developed. Things like love, respect, and "trust" develop over time as you witness to one another that you can be trusted.

People find themselves in the permissive will of God for various reasons. Some people don't know God well enough to trust that His perfect will is what is best. While others assume that they know God better than they actually do and so they do what they think is the perfect will of God. Either way they miss God.

We can see examples of the permissive will of God in the scriptures. Adam and Eve are probably our best examples. The perfect will of God was for Adam and Eve to live in the Garden in His presence. However they made a decision that put them in a place where God allowed them to be. It was never His intention for us to live apart from Himself. Our condition of

45

separateness is what He permits us to do.

We also see it in the life of the Israelites. It was God's intention to take the first generation into the promise land. But they made a decision to focus on the giants instead of the GIANT-ism of God, and it resulted in Him placing them in His permissive will.

Again we can see this principle at work in Israel. In 1 Samuel 11:1-15 we read a story of Israel's request to Samuel to provide them a king like the rest of the nations surrounding them. Therefore, God gave them a king, but not before He and Samuel tried to talk them out of this idea. In fact, God says to Samuel *"Do not be dismayed, for they have not rejected you, but they have rejected Me as King over them"* (1 Sam. 8:7). The concept of kingship was never in the plan of God. It was not what He wanted as His perfect will. Saul was a part of the permissive will of God for Israel.

We can see it in the life of Moses as well. In Exodus God calls Moses to be a spokesman—a prophet. However He was not able to convince Moses of His greatness and ability to use him in spite of His speech impediment. Therefore God gave him his brother Aaron to speak to the people. Moses was the prophet to God, and Aaron was the prophet to Moses (Exod. 7:1). God's perfect will was to use Moses directly, but He settled for Aaron as the permissive will of God.

Abraham had a permissive will of God situation as well. He was told that his seed with Sarah would be the heir of promise. But Abraham created a child with Hagar the maidservant. While God did give him a child with His wife that was the heir of promise, Ishmael the son of the maidservant is a result of the permissive will of God. God never intended for Abraham to have child outside of His marriage.

King Hezekiah is another great example of this. In 2 Kings 20:1-6, God sends his prophet to tell the King he is going to die. Then when Hezekiah turns his face to the wall and prays, God sends the prophet back and extends his life by 15 years!

Finally, most of mankind is in the permissive will of God. 2 Timothy 2:4, says that "God desires ALL to be saved", but we know that all are not saved. The perfect will of God is for ALL to be saved.

So we can see from these many examples that there is a place where God allows us to be even though it is not what He desires as His best. And in all of these examples one fact remains true. God was still very involved in the lives of all to these people.

Adam and Eve still had some level of communion with God. He even made provisions for them. The Bible says that even though Israel was in the wilderness, that their clothes and shoes never wore out (Duet. 29:5). God took good care of them. God did not like the idea of providing Israel a king but He provided them the greatest king He could find in the person of Kind David. Moses was still used as a mighty prophet and performed many unimaginable signs and wonders. Abraham's illegitimate child was blessed and made into a great nation (Gen. 21:18). God even provided supernatural water for the child when He was dying in the desert (Gen. 21:19). As for mankind, even though we are wayward He still reaches out and has provided His greatest gift in the person of Jesus Christ.

Having said all of that, we can see that God still takes care of us even when we mess up. But I would not be providing the balance of truth if I told you that the permissive will is a great place. While God keeps us safe in this place it is not His desired best and it is reflected in the lives all of those mentioned above.

As you read the scriptures related to each of these stories you will see that the permissive will of God is a place of struggle. In the Garden, Adam and Eve did little to cause the ground to yield fruit to them. But in the permissive will, they worked harder to get what used to come to them easy. You will see this same idea with all of these stories.

The permissive will of God is a place where God is with you but the struggle to get what He wants you to easily receive gets harder. He gave Israel a king and they had a few good ones in all of biblical history. So make the choice to aim for the perfect will of God, but know that your "God is faithful even when we are not faithful" (1 Tim. 2:5).

Signs that God has spoken

Now that we understand the difference between the perfect will and permissive will of God, let's examine some concepts that will narrow the way. The concepts that follow are meant to provide you with information that will help to provide a basis by which you may know that you have heard from God.

1) Burning in the Heart

The voice of God is both exciting and captivating in the heart of the believer. When God speaks there is a sense of excitement and a captivation with the thought He has placed in the mind, or voice that is speaking to us. Please notice that His voice burns in our hearts, not tickles our ears.

This is an important distinction to make. Sometimes we hear voices that are interesting and their message may appear to be deep. Nonetheless, as we listen we often feel nothing inside that seems to connect us to the message. This happens for one reason. It is not the voice of God speaking. It may be truth. It may be a word from the Bible, but it is not God speaking.

This is where we must exercise caution and use discernment. It is moments like these when we hear ear tickling sermons, dreams, visions, and voices. When God speaks His voice may bring us a simple message. Or it may bring us a message that is contrary to what we want to hear. It may even be offensive to us. However, no matter what the message is, and how it is received, we can expect that it will capture our attention and burn in our heart with excitement.

This is why a preacher's message can seem so boring one Sunday and yet the next Sunday you can't take your eyes off of him. Another example of this can be seen in the experience of God seeming to lift the words off the pages of the Bible as you read. It is that "ah ha" moment when you see a truth you never seen before. This also explains why you can read a book one day and struggle to read with interest. Yet a year later that same book seems to almost come alive with excitement. This happens when God uses something to speak to us— He makes His voice burn in us.

We see this principle at work in Luke 24:31-32, when Jesus reveals Himself to two of His disciples on the road to Emmaus, they say, *"Did not our heart BURN WITHIN us AS HE SPOKE to us"*. Jeremiah describes the word in the same way when he says, *"His WORD was like FIRE shut up in my bones"* (Jer. 20:9).

2) A Sense of Authority

When God speaks He does not do so suggestively or passively. God speaks with assurance and absolutes. His voice is commanding. In fact God's voice creates a compelling sense that we should obey His instructions. It has an authoritative push behind it the same way we would feel when any real authority figure speaks.

In fact Jeremiah 20:7 says, *"You induced me, and **I was persuaded**: You are stronger than I, and have prevailed"*. In a nutshell, this simply means that God's voice is unlike another voice. It compels us. Ask yourself as you practice stillness if you are being compelled to action. One reason for this is the fact that He desires to be viewed as the Commander of the Lord's army. He is not going to ask you to do something; He's going to tell you to do something. This is very important because it is a stark contrast to how Satan speaks.

3) A Clear Conscience

The conscience of man is designed to give him a sense of direction regarding his decisions. While we can depend on this faculty most of the time, we must be careful for it is subject to defilement through the deceitfulness of sin. The conscience is man's inner awareness of fairness, right, and wrong.

When it is defiled we feel a sense of unshakable guilt. However, when it is functioning from a place of purity we may feel a simple sense of wrong. As for the Christian God uses it to bear witness to our decisions. When He speaks to us, His word responds to bring us into an inner peace that lacks a sense of guilt or wrong. We see this in Romans 9:1, when Paul says," *I tell the truth in Christ. I am not lying. THE HOLY SPIRIT BEARING ME WITNESS IN MY CONSCIENCE"*. This passage clues us into what and how the Holy Spirit convicts us of sin, righteousness, and decisions. He uses the conscience to either accuse us or excuse us. Romans 2:14,15 says, *"Their thoughts either excusing them or accusing them"*.

If you find yourself justifying your desires and decisions, then it is highly likely that you are missing God. Our attempt at justifying our actions is generally an acknowledgement of our awareness of wrongdoing. When we are doing what is right there will be no need to prove we are right. The same holds true with God's voice. The word of God is tested (proven) it stand as truth and needs nothing to pro it up.

For example, during the editing process of this book, I had an encounter with someone on social media. This person disagreed with the way I presented a truth in a passage of scripture and decided that she was going to make a judgment about my motives. She started her post with the words, "I probably shouldn't say this about you, but…" Then she proceeded to insult my character. This of course led to unpleasant fellowship between her and I, which we did later resolve.

This story is a classic example of how often times we ignore the promptings of the Holy Spirit in our conscience. If she had a sense of wrongdoing before she made the statement, then Holy Spirit was not excusing her to move forward with her decision. In fact her statement reveals that He was accusing her about the decision. He was tying to caution her not to move forward. She however, did what most of us do, and pressed beyond His warning. This is a great example of not having a clear conscience. How many time have we said, "I know I shouldn't but…" Please do not ignore the prompting of the Holy Spirit in your conscience. It could be the determining factor in you not making a life altering decision!

4) Sense of Peace
Jesus said of Himself, *"Me and My Father are one"* (John 17:21). What He was saying in this passage is that there is a lack of struggle between He and the Father. They were of one mind and of one accord.

This is really important and it really could have been lumped together with a clear conscience. A sense of peace means that I am not torn in my decisions. Often times the voice of God will conflict with what we want to do. However when we agree to God's idea our inner struggle will cease.

For example, we never see a separation between Jesus and the Father in the scriptures. We know that the trinity consist of three distinct personalities, but we only see one presented in Gospels. Not once is Jesus torn in His decision to do the will of God except in the Garden of Gethsemane. In the garden, Jesus and the Father are not one. We finally see the two distinct wills represented in the Gospels. There was the Father's will, which was for Jesus to go to the cross. Then there was Jesus' will in which He expressed that He did not want to go to the cross. He said, *"Father if you are willing take this cup from me; yet not "My will" but "Your will" be done (Luke 22:42).*

We also see this truth at work in the life of Jeremiah. He says I will not speak for you anymore (see Jer. 20:9). That was his desire. Then there was a separate part of him that burned to speak the word of God. He was not in a place of peace until He came into alignment with the will of God. The same was true with Jesus. His classic words, not My will but Your will be done brought Him back into the peace of God.

Ask yourself if there is a part of you that wants to do one thing and another part that wants to go in another direction. One of them is God. When you come into agreement with His voice there will be peace. Our agreement with God provides access to God grace in our life. It is a sense of peace with God and an awareness of His helping hand in whatever situation that we are faced with. For *"He leads me beside the STILL waters"* (Psalms 23:3)

5) Faith and Confidence
The voice of God produces a sense of expectation and hope. Not to say that we will not battle doubt from time to time, but His voices produces a sense of possibility in the midst of what may seem impossible. Romans 10:17, says, "Faith comes by hearing and hearing by the word or Voice of God".

Not only does it produce in us a hope for what is possible, but it also makes us confidently know something. Jesus said in John 8:32, "…you shall know the truth…" The main idea of this passage is "the truth" is something that we "know". The word know means that we are sure beyond a doubt. And our certainty is grounded in verse 31 which says, "If you abide in My word…" I want to note that Jesus is not referring to the Bible when He

51

speaks of His word. He is referring to what we hear or have heard from Him. It is in reference to His voice. It communicates to us the importance of being in the place of hearing from God consistently. It is consistency that gives us confidence. To be clear, that does include the written word. However as it relates to this passage it is not a reference to the scriptures. This means that we need to ask ourselves the question do I "know" that this it God.

As I am writing this I think of the many times that I have heard something from God and how I knew in that very moment that it was God. Then I think of the many times I have missed Him and again I can see the absence of that confidence. Every time I missed there was an absence of a sense of certainty.

There is a more practical example of this in our ever day life. Just think about how many time you heard a sermon and certain parts of it stood out to you as personal truth. You knew in that moment that it was that particular part of the sermon that was for you. You had a confident sense of absolute "knowing".

This goes back to #1, the burning in the heart. The truth is something that we know when we hear it. Remember this book is about the voice of God, not just the face-to-face voice, but also the voice that appears as dreams and visions, as preachers and prophets, as scriptures, or as similitudes. Regardless of how the voice of God comes to you be certain that you will know it when you hear it.

Finally, Jesus is very clear to say that His sheep "know" His voice. What are you hearing or reading or seeing that produces a knowing in you? If you have to force yourself to believe it then it's probably not God. That being said, the knowing leads to the next issue, the inner witness. And it is best felt when we learn about stillness, which I discuss later in the book.

6) An Inner Witness
"There is a spirit in man and the inspiration or Spirit of the Almighty gives him understanding" (Job 32:8). In each of us there is a spirit that recognizes spiritual things. Sometimes we can sense that things are wrong in our environment or surroundings. This is our spiritual man perceiving something

else spiritual. God uses it to respond favorably to people and situations in our environment. He also uses it regarding how we make decisions.

The Bible provides a really unique story that helps to illustrate this concept. The Bible says that *"The Spirit of God bears witness with our spirit... "* (Rom. 8:16) What this tells us is that God validates Himself in our hearts. He alone has a way of providing the assurance that we need to have a "knowing". One illustration of this is seen in Luke 1:41, when Elizabeth the expecting mother of John the Baptist goes to see Mary the expecting mother of Jesus Christ. The scripture says that when Elizabeth heard Mary's greeting the baby leaped in her womb and Elizabeth was filled with the Holy Spirit. This is a perfect example of this idea. The something in Elizabeth responded to the God in Mary. Likewise, when we encounter God's voice something in us responds to it.

For me, I experience this as an inner swelling (filling) that acknowledges a God idea and a feeling of emptiness when God is not involved. This also happens in the Book of Acts where we see several times a filling up before God moved. It was a form of validation. Look for that inner filling or swelling. Sometimes it will appear as a very light fill and at other times it may seem like a very obvious inner swelling. For the sake of clarity it appears as varying degrees of inspiration.

7) A Desire Towards What is Right in the Sight of God
The bible declares over and over again one simple truth... it is the will of God for you to walk in righteousness. If you are really hearing the voice of God, then you WILL have a desire to follow a path that is good in His sight. "For *He LEADS me in PATHS OF RIGHTEOUSNESS... "* (Psalms 23:3)

8) It Is Scriptural
Please note that I did not say, *is it in the Bible*? The appropriate question to ask is, is it scriptural? Scriptural means that the voice of God is consistent with what God has already revealed about Himself in the Bible.

It is very important to ask the right question. When we inquire as to whether or not something is in the bible, we set ourselves up for deception.

Satan used the scriptures in his attempt to lure Jesus off the path in Luke 4:1-13. You can find anything in the Bible to justify your point of view. However, what you cannot find is consistency in a lie.

God is consistent in how He speaks and what He has spoken. The Bible says, *"Let every word be established in the mouth of two or three witnesses"* (Duet. 19:5). This is something we can see clearly in any of the books of the prophets. They all testify to the same coming of the Messiah and the captivity of Israel.

Even when Elijah heard the voice of God as He hid in a cave, he heard a consistent message. God asked him the same question at the entrance of the cave that He asked him while he was sitting inside the cave.

Abraham is another great example. God spoke to him about the promised seed consistently. He was not changing His mind with every change in Abraham's circumstances. Even when he fell into error with Hagar, God kept His message consistent. This is really important because I have heard people say God told them to go in one direction, and then when the circumstances changed, they thought He was taking them in another direction, as if He was not sure of His direction. Please understand this point because God may change a circumstance to get you to the end goal, but His word to you will be consistent. Just learn how to be obedient and you will arrive at the place He has destined for you to reach.

This may be my most important point. There is a new version of Christianity called the Gospel of Inclusion. Created by a former mighty man of God who allowed a voice to dictate a theology that was not consistent with what the word of God teaches.

You should consider his example of folly to ensure safety from error. For by faith we understand that the times were framed by the Word of God. The word is a structure that provides the framework of safety.

These eight principles will help you to identify when God is speaking to you. While they may seem like a lot to remember, once incorporated into your life, they will become second nature to you. After a while you will just know that it is Him speaking and when you're not sure, you have these principles to review.

Lastly, I think you should know that these are not signs that occur outside of each other, but simultaneously. These are all things that we experience **"every time"** God speak to us.

Chapter Four
The Fruit of His Voice

Some time ago there was a well-known prophet who decided to declare the winner of a Super Bowl game nationally. He claimed that it was going to show the all-knowing aspect of God's power and win many to Christ. When all was said and done he proved to be way off. In fact this was one of those games where I thought only one team was playing because of how poorly the predicted winner played. Since this was prophesied via social media it went global. That being the case, when it proved to be in error the backlash was great. It was so great that all of social media was talking about how far off his word was. It gave the doubters fuel for the fire and that prophet suffered major embarrassment. What did he do wrong? How can I use this story to help you avoid such errors in judgment?

The writing of this chapter is inspired by a dream that I had in which God encouraged me that we can learn from the mistakes of others. In the dream one of my stubborn friends had gotten into an argument with someone and had come to speak to me about the situation. After sometime of listening to her rant I gently turned to her and said, "Maybe God is talking to you too!" This infuriated this woman and she accused me of being too spiritual. To which I began to show her how God can speak through the situations of others. Then I woke up with the passion and anointing to write this chapter in the wee hours of a Saturday morning.

Why am I sharing this dream with you? I'm sharing this because while some of you will instantly know the prophet to whom I am referring, some of you will not. I am not bringing this up to further the embarrassment of this prophet. But to the contrary, I am using it to set up the idea that God can speak to us in watching the failures of others.

This prophet is certainly not the only person who has failed in this regard. There have been many others including myself. In fact I can remember one such failure, though it was not publicized. Nonetheless I have made such mistakes as wells.

I work for a federal law enforcement agency. As such I am accustomed to having many different bosses. This is because federal agents come into the job understanding that relocations are always possible. So I had gotten accustomed to the constant rotation of one guy in, one guy out. And during this time of transition I wanted to strengthen my hearing skills by seeking a word of knowledge from God. On one particular morning I happened to look out of the window. As I did I saw my boss walking through the courtyard. I thought to myself, this is a perfect time to ask God where his next assignment would be. So I asked, "God, where is his next assignment?" I was hoping God would tell me so that I could use this as practice but the response I got back was far from what I was expecting.

Next, I heard a voice say, "God does not gossip." I thought to myself, what, gossip? But it was clear that what I was asking God to tell me was none of my business. It had nothing to do with me and there was no purpose in me having this information.

This all leads to my subject for this chapter. What is going to be the fruit of your experience in hearing the voice of God? It is true that you can have conversations with God, but what kinds of things does God converse about and how should you feel after the conversation?

These are all questions that are answered from the scriptures in this chapter. The word provides an iron clad way for us to know that God is speaking to us. It tells us exactly what He wants to speak to us about and how we should feel when He's done.

The Starting Point

The starting point for the answer to our question is 1Timothy 3:16, which reads, *"All scripture is given by inspiration of God and is profitable for doctrine, for reproof, for correction, and for instruction in righteousness"*.

First, Paul starts by telling us that "all scripture" is inspired. The scriptures are the recorded utterances of God. It was with these that He, the Holy Spirit, revealed the hidden mysteries concerning salvation (2 Tim 3:15, Acts 18:24-28). Many places in the New Testament writings refer to the Old Testament passages as reference material whereby, we receive sound doctrine. For it records that they are inspired, or in the Greek, "GOD BREATHED" (Pet. 1:21).

Some arguments have started over what the Bible means by the term inspired. To understand this concept we must gather a greater understanding of the words "spirit" and "inspired". It comes from the greek word *"pneuma"* which means "breath" or "wind". It is the innermost source of life, the motivating factor behind all that is visible. It can be defined as the animator of movement.

Inspired means: motivated; driven; compelled; or moved by. What Paul was saying here was that all scripture was written by men who were motivated, compelled, or driven by the actions or influence of God upon their hearts.

Leaves Inspired by the Wind

To help me understand what it is to be inspired God gave me the most incredible perceptual vision. It happened at work as I was going to the building next door to us. As I exited my building to go to lunch I happened to come upon a scene that I had seen many times before. Though I had seen it many times I never thought much of it until that day. It was fall and there was a pile of leaves on the ground. As I watched this pile of leaves, all of a sudden they were picked up by a passing wind. What I found unique about this very familiar scene was that the leaves actually revealed the pattern and direction of the wind.

"For the Spirit is like the wind, you don't see it coming and you don't see it when it is gone" (John 3:8). This passage likens the invisible property of the Spirit of God to the invisible property of the wind. This passage came alive for me that day. The leaves revealed the invisible nature of the wind. I

could clearly see the direction the wind was moving, the swirling pattern and tornado type shape, and how tall it was. It was an "ah ha" moment.

I quickly had a realization that I was looking at the very definition of inspiration. The great men and women of God did not see God coming (like the wind), but when He made contact with them as they yielded their vessel, He was allowed a moment to reveal His thoughts and intentions to mankind.

The Testimony of Jesus

Our reference passage in 1 Timothy 3:16 also says something that is very, very important for us to consider. It says that "All scripture is given by God, and that it is PROFITABLE". This is so important for us to consider as we seek to further our relationship with God.

You should know that when you have a conversation with God that it will profit you. Profit means that God is going to invest and/or deposit something in you that will benefit you and others. *"For all may prophesy that ALL may COMFORTED and ENCOURAGED!"* (I Cor. 14:31) You will benefit from the conversation.

Ultimately we must consider how we benefit. The Bible says that *"The spirit of prophecy is the testimony of Jesus Christ"* (Rev. 19:10). Also Ephesians 1:18 says that Paul prayed for the believers at Ephesus that they would receive the spirit of wisdom and revelation in the KNOWLEGDE OF HIM (Jesus). Any voice that you hear that points you to anyone other than Jesus Christ is not from God. The ultimate Goal of our interaction with God is to drive us toward Jesus and not away from Him.

Regardless of how supernatural the experience or circumstances are surrounding the receipt of any communication that is supposed to have to come from God, it must point and draw you closer to Jesus Christ. The Bible warns us about following voices that claim to come from God, with signs and wonders that comes to pass but lead us away from God. God warns us that if such a thing happens that it is a test from God regarding the sincerity of your heart (see Deut. 31:1).

This is always a concern to me when I see prophets who only seem interested in prophesying material blessings. God has a lot more to say to you about your life than He has a new house or car for you. Real prophetic ministry seeks to minister to the whole man, the body, soul, and spirit. It speaks to the issues of the secrets of men's heart to bring God glory.

You may have noticed that I did not list prophets, pastors, and people in general as one of the ways that God speaks to us. I omitted this form of communication from God intentionally. It is my goal to encourage the average believer that "if you draw near to God, God will draw near to you" (James 4:8). Then you will not need to rely on someone else to tell you how to live your life. There is a movement of prophets who are treating the prophetic ministry like a physic hotline. This disgusts me to no end, to see the gift of God that was received freely, being used to charge believers to tell them things like who they are to marry. Beware of these prophets. They have made themselves the gods to whom people look for their sustenance. This is not the spirit of prophecy. It points to a man and not to "The Man". It is for that reason that I encourage you to develop your own relationship with the Lord so that real prophets can confirm your word and establish your faith. You will find that having your words confirmed will sky rocket your confidence in the fact that you are hearing the voice of God. You should also consider that while God does want you to have the confidence to know that He hears you, He also, wants you to have the confidence to know that you have heard from Him!

What God Talks About

Doctrine: God the Teacher

Now that we understand that the ultimate goal of communication with Jesus is to draw closer to Jesus, we can look a little deeper into the types of things that we can expect from our interaction with God.

The first area I want us to consider is Doctrine. When we have conversations with God one fruit that might come from our interaction with the Father is Doctrine. Doctrine means: Teaching necessary for growth. One of God's primary concerns is your growth. The Bible says, *"That we may grow up into all things"* (Eph. 4:15).

For me this has been a primary blessing. In fact this book is the result of the many conversations that I have had with God regarding how to hear His voice. I am always amazed at the number of things that God has taught me that have allowed me to walk in joyful Christian living.

God led me into this understanding one day as I sat in Bible study. The pastor was teaching on how to study the Bible and had just introduced a new class dedicated to the subject. At this point I was really on fire for God and I wanted to take advantage of every available opportunity. So as I was purposing in my heart to take the class I heard God say, "I am going to teach you". This caught me off guard and I thought that maybe He meant that He was going to teach me through the class. Then again I heard, "I am going to teach you". Later that night as I was reading my Bible I had a vision of a flower that opened up and bloomed. When that happened, God began to open up the word to me in the most wonderful and adventurous way. It has been that way ever since.

One such example comes to mind. This was one of those surprise moments that occurred early in my Christian life. God used a very familiar similitude to teach and inspire me about Jesus. One day as I was walking around the house I heard the words "I have the Power". It was the familiar saying from He-Man, the popular 80's cartoon. Now I know you may be saying to yourself how in the world can God teach you anything from He-Man. But He did.

He showed me the spiritual similarities between He-Man and paralleled truths in the word. He showed me how a man named Adam would be transformed into a supernatural man when he raised his sword and claimed its power. He-man would raise his sword and say, "By the power of Greyskull! I have the power", then lightening would strike the sword and completely transformed his humanity.

Can you see it yet? Adam could only access the power of the word when he elevated it above his own thoughts. This parallels God telling us "His thoughts are *higher* than our thoughts" (Isa. 55:8) The lightening He referenced as the Holy Spirit working through the word (sword) to transform us into the new man whom God equips and empowers to fight against evil.

God actually spoke to me three and a half pages of spiritual truths with all the scripture to back it up. It was absolutely incredible and it encouraged me to establish His word as a priority in my life. What I am hoping that you will see is how God speaks to teach and impart to us something that we can teach to others.

You too will experience God teaching you all kinds of truths in various ways to assist you in growing into the person He has called you to be.

Reproof: The God Who Shines the Light

The second area that I want to discuss is reproof. Reproof means proof; test; convicting; and what exposes error. This one is precious to me as well because sometimes we are just wrong and that's where God helps to make our crooked places straight. Initially you may assume that reproving means that God is going to convict you in the sense that He is a judge handing down a sentence. While we know that God is a Judge and that He's going to judge the world, we must understand that this is not conviction in the condemning sense of the word. The Bible says that the Holy Spirit will convict us of sin, righteousness (what is right), and judgment (see John 16:8).

It is His job to alert us to these specific areas in our life. I use the word alert because it is an easier word to digest than convict and it is a more accurate depiction of what He does.

When you are engaging a relationship with God you will definitely discover that God will alert you to things that you might be doing that are either not pleasing or not safe. Yes, I said not safe. Sometimes what we want to do is not necessarily a sin, but it may not be beneficial to our well being. *"For all things are lawful for me but not all things are beneficial"* (I Cor. 6:12).

How might it look when God is reproving us? Some years ago I was babysitting my then three-year old godson while his mother was working late. It was a good night. However being a three year old and somewhat spoiled he decided to do something of which I did not approve. So I spanked him, put him on the couch by his self, and told him to stop crying. I was mimicking discipline the way it was modeled for me and I saw nothing wrong with what I did. God, however, did not agree. As I went on doing what I was doing God spoke to me and said, "That's not how I discipline you. I don't discipline you and leave you to console yourself. I let you know what you did wrong; I discipline you, and warn you not to repeat the action. Last, I comfort you".

The whole time God was speaking to me this little guy was crying his eyes out. He was so heartbroken. So I decided to do what God told me. I held him and spoke to him about what he did and explained to him that it was wrong. I warned him that if he repeated that behavior that he would be disciplined again. Last, I comforted him to reassure him that I still loved him. After all this he calmed right down and he and I felt so much better. And I use this same approach with all four of my kids. I discipline with love and it has led to a fruitful relationship between us.

Another story that comes to mind refers to how God used a dream to reprove me and show me my error. I felt the call to ministry years ago and as such I was invited out to speak at the church my father was attending. The first time I preached for this congregation it went so well that I was invited back a second time. The second time was more powerful than the first and this time. In fact I was invited to join their ministry staff. It was a great opportunity and I decided to meet with my pastor regarding my decision. The meeting did not go as I had planned and the pastor called my parents to let them know that he was really concerned about this move. He did not think I was ready for such a responsibility.

This angered me and I decided that this was an opportunity from God to do what He called me to do. That being the case I decided that I was going to go anyway. When I went to sleep that night I had a dream that I was outside the doors of this church waiting to get inside. Eventually the doors opened and when I went inside I turned into a black panther and some other animal and caused harm to the church. When I woke up I immediately understood the dream with one verse. *"The sin of rebellion is as the sin of witchcraft"* (1 Sam 15:23). After the dream I repented and followed some other advice my pastor gave me which helped me meet some really great people.

Jesus constantly reproved the Pharisees. On one such occasion Jesus was preaching in the synagogue and there was a man there with a withered hand. And the Bible says they were looking to see if He would heal him on the Sabbath. Jesus knowing their thoughts addresses their wrong. Notice that he does not condemn them. He merely points out the error in their heart and explains to them the simple balance of truth (Matt. 12:9-13).

When we converse with God we can expect God to do the same. He gently lets us know where we have gone in error and gives us the necessary wisdom to get it corrected.

Correction: The God Who Makes it Straight

The really great thing about God is the fact that He does not only expose the error in our lives, but He provides instructions to get us back on track. The word correction in our reference passage means, restoration; to return to a right state. Correction occurs when God tells us or teaches us what we need to make us right.

In our previous passage from reproof, we see examples of God exposing error and giving direction for correction. We can see God's correction in my story regarding my godson and we can see His correction in my dream. We can also see correction at work when Jesus corrected the Pharisees about their misunderstanding of the Sabbath.

We can also see Jesus operating in correction in Matthew 12:1-8, when He and His disciples were walking through the grain fields and the disciples were plucking and eating the grains on the Sabbath. This angered the Pharisees and they challenged Jesus on the issue. Then He reproved them and explained to them the purpose of the Sabbath. He didn't condemn them, but gently explained to them that they are wrong.

Instruction in Righteousness: God the Architect

Just looking at the life of Jesus in any of the gospels tells us that one of the most important aspects of His conversation is righteousness.

Instruction in righteousness means; to teach; to inform with information that structures a path for us to stay in right standing with God. Psalms 23:3 says, *"He leads us in the path of righteousness"*. In other words, when we are in communication with God, He will speak to us information that creates a path that leads us to what is pleasing to Him.

This is very, very important to understand. This is one reason why I was not given a word of knowledge about my boss' next duty location. God is not interested in idle conversation. He speaks with purpose. Remember I said I heard a voice say, "God does not gossip". It may not be evident, but this was a word of reproof, correction, and instruction in righteousness. God with one small phrase created a path for me to do what is right. What if He had said nothing and allowed me keep pursuing this type of behavior? It is possible that without His word of righteousness that I may have opened myself up to familiar and dark spirits to speak to me. And I have seen prophets operating under an anointing one minute, then pressing into the spiritual realm for more information after it has lifted and speaking by a familiar spirit. On one such occasion this happened and the rest of us sitting around had to stop the prophet and deliver him from the spirit.

Personally, I find these conversations with God are my favorite. I want to be right before God. I want the meditations of my heart and the words of my mouth to be pleasing before Him (Psa. 19:14). There is no better way to live than to have the creator Himself, teach you something that makes living an upright life easier.

As I consider this subject, I am reminded of an incident that occurred in my life regarding this subject. I was 25 years old at the time and still at home with my parents. I was sleeping in my childhood twin sized bed and my room was a mess.

One day upon awakening I heard God say, "Discipline, You need discipline." Discipline to me was a cuss word. Up until that point I had always been impulsive. I just enjoyed living life by the seat of my pants. But when I heard these words I looked around my room and for the first time I was convicted about my life status. However God did not stop there. He continued by bringing to my mind 1 Corinthians 13:11, *"When I was a child, I spoke as a child, I thought as a child, but when I became a man, I put away childish things"*.

All of a sudden I became fixated on the later half of the verse, *"...when I became a man I put away childish things"*. Then God began speaking to me that to become a man I would have to discipline myself to "put away" childish things. From that moment on I worked very hard on being disciplined. I researched strategies on the subject and completely transformed myself into a responsible man.

This is the benefit of conversing with God. Conversations with God can bring about change in your life, and create a path for you to be right before God. Most people who know me today think of me as one of the most responsible persons they know. Nonetheless, this was not the case before God spoke those life-changing words of instruction in righteousness into my life.

I have enjoyed all twenty plus years of my salvation. It has been an exciting ride filled with great things. Most of which, I attribute to the myriad of conversations that I have had with God that have been absolutely life changing. Not only has He spoken to me incredible life changing words of instruction, but He has also used His words to move me through difficult situations. He's lifted me up when I was low, and shown me the way out when I was trapped.

Doctrine, reproof, correction, and instruction in righteousness all help outline for us what we can expect God to speak to us about. Again I want to emphasize the importance of being open for God to speak, but I want you to know that He is not one of your homeboys or girlfriends. He is not interested in talking to you about random foolishness such as the Super Bowl. If God speaks to you regarding something such as a football game, you can be certain that He is using it as a teaching moment. He may emphasize the importance of teamwork, coaching, mentoring or any number of areas that He creatively extracts from these types to things.

How Should You Feel

Another really important concept to establish is how you will feel when God speaks. Why is this important? It is especially important if you are in a church that teaches that the motivational, manifestation, and or prophetic gifts are ministries that expose sin. One reason the Prophetic Movement suffers such resistance is the misunderstanding of what happens with the revelation gifts.

I have seen people who believed themselves to be prophets deliver harsh words that tore the recipient down. I have always wondered how someone could conclude that God is interested in destroying the person for whom He suffered and gave His life. They take this error in operation from I Corinthians 14:25 when it says that through prophesy the secrets of their heart are exposed and they will fall down and worship God. Please notice that it says "secrets" not "sins"!

Lately, there has been a lot of material correcting this error in teaching. Discerning of spirits was the most hated and misunderstood gift for a long time, but this too, has been reexamined and God has released fresh revelation that is making it a helpful gift instead of a hindrance.

So what should we expect to be the result of a conversation with God? How should we feel?

Edification: The God Who Builds

1 Corinthians 14:3, outlines for us what we should expect from an encounter with God. This principle applies to what we hear when God uses a human vessel, book, or when He speaks to us face to face. Regardless of how He speaks to us we can expect God to edify us, exhort us, and or comfort us.

The first area up for discussion is edification. Edification means: the act of building "the promotion of spiritual growth". Edification carries with it the idea that God builds us up higher. It would be seen visually as adding a second level to a one level house.

Often after a real encounter with the voice of God you will feel as though God has added something to you. Anytime we encounter a supposed voice that creates in us a feeling of being torn down, we can conclude that it did not come from God. God convicts us. He does not condemn us.

My example from the previous section serves as a great illustration of this concept. Earlier I told a story of how God spoke to me about discipline and growing up. This was a situation in which God edified me. He spoke reproof, correction, and instruction in righteousness that resulted in me going to the next level of life. Notice that He did not speak to me in way that pushed me away or created in me a feeling of failure. He spoke life. Jesus said, *"My words are spirit and they are life"* (John 6:63).

This was just one such example. On another occasion God spoke to me regarding time management after what I perceived to be a failed first date with my now wife.

My wife did not make for an easy catch. She believed deeply that it was the responsibility of the man to chase and catch, and she made me work for her hand. And I greatly admired that about her. She also did not believe in the idea dating. She believed that sufficient phone conversation was necessary to get to know someone and a date would only occur after she felt comfortable.

So we pursued a relationship on the phone for a while. We also went out on church group activities. After some time we did decide to go on a date alone. After all of the red tape I was a bit nervous but excited about our first date. When the day arrived I managed to get everything wrong. For starters, I did not know how to get to the restaurant (this was before GPS). And once we finally arrived at our destination I did not have any money on hand and the ATM machine was two blocks down from the restaurant. It was to me, a nightmare.

When I got home from the date I went straight to bed. When I arose in the morning the first thing I did was talk to God about how I messed up this date. During the course of our conversation He said, "Kevin, you failed because you failed to plan." Then He showed me how I could have prepared for the date and used Ephesians 6:16, regarding redeeming the time, to teach me the importance of time management and planning.

My life has never been the same. God took me up a level with an instruction in righteousness. My wife would now call me the king of planning and time management. This is how God edifies the believer. He speaks words that take you to the next level.

The parable of the sower and the seed serves as yet another great example to support the idea that God builds us up. He says in Matthew 13:1-23, that the word of God is like a seed that when planted in the fertile soil of our heart yields much fruit. Jesus shows us that one small seed is capable of producing growth in us so much so that we can be a fruitful place from which He may feed the lives of others.

Exhortation: The God Who Encourages

This brings me to the next concept. God exhorts us. Exhortation means: a calling to one's side; to empower with courage; to speak in such a way as to cause one to spring forth with a positive response.

Every Sunday morning at most churches in America you will see a person who stands in the pulpit and leads the worship service. Often that person is dynamic and charismatic. At my church there are few who are really good at empowering the audience to push past their life issues to give glory to a worthy God. They often speak and sing with such passion and creativity.

This is an example of exhortation. When God speaks to us one of His goals will be to empower us with the courage to push past our circumstances. Or He may empower us with the courage to trust Him. Regardless of what the issue is, God wants us to walk in courage and that is reflected in how He speaks to us.

The scriptures are full of such examples. In Jeremiah 29:11 God says to the captives of Israel, *"For I know the thoughts that I have toward you, thoughts of peace and not of evil to give you a future and a hope"*. He says to Joshua in Joshua 1:5, as *"I was with Moses so shall I be with you. I will not leave you or forsake you. Be strong and of good courage..."* He also says to Gideon in Judges 6:12, *"The Lord is with you. You mighty man of valor"*.

I could go on and on naming God's faithful servants and how He constantly exhorted them. There was Moses at the burning bush (Exod. 4:12). Hagar when she feared for the life of her son Ishmael (Gen. 21:17-18). Paul when God spared the life of him and all who were with him, when they were caught in a storm (Acts 27:23). There are many places in the scriptures that demonstrate this aspect of God's nature.

Comfort: The God Who Feels

The last area pertains to the comforting nature of God. Comfort means: soothing discomfort; to relieve pain or discomfort. Comfort is another almost self-explanatory concept that even the unbeliever naturally attributes to the nature of God.

Comfort, like exhortation, is something that we see about God defined in a multitude of scriptures. This characteristic of God shows us His caring nature and when you have heard from Him in a season of pain you should feel comforted. Even when He confronts you about your sin He does so in way that allows you to feel convicted about the issue and comforted regarding His love and acceptance of you. We see this is the story of Mary Magdalene (John 8:1-11).

When Mary is about to be stoned by her accusers Jesus came to her defense with a word of wisdom. After the crowd had dispersed He said to Mary, *"Woman where are your accusers? Has no one condemned you?" And She said, "No Lord". And He said to her, "Then neither do I, go and sin no more."*

In this passage we can see that even though Jesus did not approve of her sin He spoke to her in a way that expressed His dissatisfaction with her lifestyle, but also comforted her. This is one example of God speaking comforting words. His words provided so much comfort to Mary that she followed Him and served Him from that moment on. This story is a great example of how the spirit of prophecy leads to Jesus. His words comforted her so much that she was compelled to be closer to Him.

God demonstrates this in my life in the story of my first date. Not only did He instruct me in the way that was right but He also provided a great sense of comfort to me in a time when I felt really discouraged.

The following passages taken from Isaiah gives great testimony to our God who speaks comforting words. Keep in mind these are just a few passages from one book that clearly show God speaking a comforting word to His people, but there are hundreds more. Just look:

49:13 *says, "Though you were ruins and made desolate and your land laid waste, now you will be too small for your people, and those who devoured you will be far away"*

51:3 says, *"The Lord will surely comfort Zion and will look with compassion on all her ruins."*

51:12 says, *"I, even I, am he that comforts you. Who are you that fear mere mortals, human beings who are but grass?"*

Now that we've looked at what God wants to speak to you about. And how that information will impact your life. I think it is important to make a special note. While we know that God is good and He speaks to edify, exhort, and comfort us, we should also note that the scriptures provide a number of passages where God pronounces judgments. Please don't make the assumption that God is never going to have harsh words with you. He is a God of justice, but even in His justice there is mercy. His voice will always have a redemptive value and purpose, even when His word you may seem harsh. I have no personal examples of this (thank God), but the scriptures are full of such examples.

Chapter Five

Different Voices

One of the most heartbreaking things for me to hear comes from those who are tormented by the questions, is this me? Is this God? Or is this the devil? As I stated in the introduction, I too, have had to endure seasons of life when these questions tormented me. There were times when the struggle was so intense that I felt as though I had been through an interrogation with myself. So having been through this experience, I can completely identify with the frustration that it causes. This is in fact what motivates me to provide materials on this subject that are useful and practical.

Even though we hate this line of self-questioning, we must be honest and consider the reality that there are other voices. There is your voice, there is God's voice, and there is the devil's voice. While this may not be considered good news, you can find hope in the reality that each of these can be identified in scriptures as an individual identity. That's right! You can have assurance and know which is speaking because they are all different.

This chapter explores what the scriptures show us about two of the differences in two of these voices in particular. Those differences are what can be distinguished between you and Satan. We will not explore the personality of God in this chapter because the rest of this book is dedicated to that subject. So this chapter will only explore the two.

Your Voice

Learning to be Transparent

One of the things that I communicate to people often when they are torn between whether what they heard came from God or themselves is be honest with yourself. I cannot tell you the number of persons I have encountered in painful situations that could have been avoided, if they would have only been honest about their desires. For example, sometimes you have to admit that the person you want to marry is the person that "you" want to marry, regardless of whether or not you see red flags, and regardless of whether or not you have biblical grounds for the marriage.

A lot of people say that God told them things based on their own desires. Ephesians 2:3 says, "*...among whom also we all once conducted ourselves in the lusts of the flesh, fulfilling the DESIRES of our FLESH and of our MIND...*" and James 1:13-14, says, *"Let no one say when he is tempted, I am tempted by God," For God cannot be tempted by evil, nor does He Himself tempt anyone. But each one is tempted when he is drawn away by HIS OWN DESIRES and enticed"*.

These two verses make it absolutely clear that we are creatures filled with various desires, some good and some bad. Nonetheless, we have legitimate needs. When learning how to hear the voice of God you must be willing to be honest about what it is that you really want. I have met Christians who were more concerned about appearing holy and mature than being honest about their sinful heart. I have also seen these people wait around for years in hopes of marring people that God is clearly never going to give them, all because they are unwilling to consider the fact that the desire of their heart was not the will of God.

Therefore, following God requires us to be completely honest about who we are, what we struggle with, and what we are easily enticed by, "*Setting aside the sin which does so easily ensnare us*" (Heb. 12:1). Some people are materialistic. If this is you then you need to own this truth about yourself. There is a very strong chance that you are always going to be prone to believe

God is saying for you to have some materialistic item, when in fact, He may be telling you to give away the many things you have acquired.

If you are a person prone to fearfulness, you may find that you are also prone to believing God is calling you to riskless task, when He may be calling you to stretch your faith and get out of your comfort zone. The opposite may be true for the risk taker. The risk taker may find that God is calling him to stability.

One of the key ways that we can discern the voice of the Lord is by understanding that God often calls us to do things which are beyond us "... *For it is not by might nor by power, but by My Spirit says the Lord"* (Zech. 4:6). For example, He called Moses to be a prophet even though he had a speech impediment. He called Abraham to leave the security and familiarity of his family and homeland to go to a place He had not even shown to him. David was anointed to be king even though He was yet a child. And Gideon was called to be a deliverer and judge even though he was doubtful, timid, and insecure.

We can see in all of these examples that these people interacted with God out of their honesty about who they were and where they were. We can especially see this in the case of Moses and Gideon. Both stories show us how honesty and accepting the reality of our own weakness and limitations helps to create a distinction between what is of us and what is God. In these stories we clearly see man's weakness and God's greatness. As you become more honest about your own self and issues you will discover that the reality of God becomes visible in our weakness

One example from my own life comes to mind as I consider this subject. I saw this beautiful woman around the church that really caught my eye. I was at the time 6 or 7 years into my celibacy and I was on the hunt for a wife. She looked like a very nice woman, she was in church, and she appeared to really love the Lord. In my opinion she was a perfect prospect.

I felt drawn to this woman and so I sought the Lord about her and He gave me a dream. In the dream I saw this woman making a way to get close to me to start a conversation. As we were talking in the dream another guy came along and attempted to lure her away. Eventually in the dream he was successful. Later in the dream she returned to me and again he lured her away, but this time as she walked away with him her eyes were fixed on me. She never returned and I awoke from the dream.

Of course I interpreted this to mean that this woman was the person God had prepared for me. So I went full steam ahead. The first thing I did was join the ministry that she was involved in so that I would increase my chances of meeting her. After awhile we eventually met, and of course, we clicked immediately. So we exchanged phone numbers and proceeded to get to know each other. At this point there was nothing romantic we were just enjoying spending time getting to know each other—we also attended a lot of church functions together and spent a lot of time on the phone. All seemed to be going well. The dream was right on point. What I did not know, however, was that she was in an on-again off-again relationship with a guy at the church. In fact she told me that he was harassing her and she wanted him to stop calling her, so I thought nothing of the matter. A few months later I received a phone call at work from this young lady. She was near tears as she told me that she had just married this guy, of whom she had described as a nuisance. She then said to me that she should have married me. WHAT! She also stated that she wanted us to continue to be friends but I told her that was not possible. I said, it would not be fair to her husband and God would surely not approve.

I sure am glad this happened before we entered into a relationship and before I had a chance to develop any real feelings of affection. I could have avoided the whole scenario if I had just been honest with myself about the fact that I only wanted to be with her because she was so beautiful. She was so beautiful to me that I overlooked the fact that she was recently divorced and struggling with serious emotional issues. I also tainted the real interpretation of the dream because I was deceiving myself with my own desires. The dream showed me exactly what would happen. It was a forewarning from God that if I pursued that direction, that the results would not be favorable. But of course, that is not what I wanted to hear.

We can also find such examples in the scriptures. There is mention of one situation in particular, in which we can see what happens when we allow ourselves to be deceived by what we want to hear. It occurs in the book of 1 Kings 22 1:14. (read verses 5-8, 12-13, and 21-23)

In this story King Ahab and Jehospapt have agreed to go to war against the Amalekites. As they considered a strategy the prophets began to proclaim victory for the two kings. But somehow, King Jehosephat realized that these were not words from the Lord. Therefore he requested that they search out a prophet of God for counsel. One was found, but he was not a favorable choice in the eyes of King Ahab. This was primarily due to the fact that he prophesied evil against him continually.

When the prophet arrived he gave the king a word that was consistent with the other prophets. Nonetheless it was discerned to be a lying word. Then the prophet was forced to tell the king the true word of the Lord. When he did it was again contrary to the prophets. In fact he revealed that God had shown him that He had put a lying spirit in the mouths of the prophets. He also revealed that God did so because God wanted to lead Ahad to death. Eventually Ahad did die just as God had intended.

This story captures this idea is a very visible way. It is very evident that the king and the prophets were deceived by the desires of their own heart. The king wanted a word that would agree with what he wanted to hear and not what he needed to hear. Likewise the prophets just wanted to satisfy the king's heart. The result was that both the king and the prophets were easily deceived by their unwillingness to acknowledge their own desires.

This is one story but there are several scriptures that warn us of having "itching ears" (see 2 Tim. 4:3), "prophesying out of our own heart" (see Jer. 23:16), and so on and so forth. It all shows us that in our flesh we can sometimes be our own worst enemy.

Your Thoughts vs. God's Thoughts

One thing we must consider as we seek to distinguish our thoughts from God's is that His thoughts are not like ours. In the last section I lightly touched on this idea. I showed you that God called Moses to be a spokesman and David to be a king, even though their circumstances were contrary to their calling. Moses could not speak well and David was a teenager. As you look at these situations you may start questioning why God would make such decisions.

I always know that someone is headed in the wrong direction when God's ideas need to make sense to them. Isaiah 55:8-9 says, *"My thoughts are not your thoughts nor My Ways your ways, for as the heavens are higher than the earth so are My thoughts higher than your thoughts and My ways higher than your ways."* This simply means that God's way of thinking is beyond what we can fathom. Likewise, it is reflected in His voice. Many times His voice calls us to extend beyond our own reach. Our voice and thoughts however, generally conceives possibility by what we believe we can achieve in our own strength. It is our logic at work.

All of this means that there is little to no chance that you will by human logic come to an understanding of God's ways. For this reason God is revealed. Many times the Bible says that God revealed Himself to a person (see 1 Sam. 3:21). He is not a product of our logic. To most of us, making a teenager a king is illogical. We would never consider such a thing. It goes against our logic. This is also why we need faith! If God fit into our logic faith would be unnecessary.

For example, there is a story in 2 Samuel 6: 1-9 that helps to make my point. It is the story of a man that God killed simply because he tried to prevent the arc of God from falling. In his mind, and in ours, this was the logical thing to do. It was not only the logical thing to do, it was the ethical thing to do. However, God had established rules regarding how the arc was to be carried. Even though it was "our way" it was not "God's way". For that reason he paid a price. Many of us are paying a price right now for something that we did our way in an attempt to make God's way fit.

It is often our need for logic that prevents us from receiving God's voice. Many people ignore their dreams and other images and sounds passing through their mind simply because it does not fit into their logic. Our logic limits our perspective. *(I'll deal with perspective in a latter chapter)*

In the Bible Jesus tells on at least two occasions God the Father's location. He says, *"Our Father which is in heaven"* and to Peter, *"My Father is Heaven has revealed this to you."* What Jesus does in these passages is communicate to us that God has a different perspective. One that is not limited like ours. Therefore, God makes decisions based on His perspective. Consequently, so do we!

This is a clear depiction of Isaiah's quote *"My thoughts are Higher than your thoughts"*. From God's perspective He sees all of time. When He speaks to us, He speaks having knowledge of how what He tells us will impact us 20 years from now. He does so by His perspective. For this reason, your rational will never be able to think like God. You can only make decisions based on what you see today, in the very moment of time that you occupy. Your every move is a guess at how your decisions will impact your future. This is due to your limited perspective! For this reason we must apply our faith to God's understanding.

Today there are a lot of people attempting to explain things about God that they don't agree with: Things such as hell, divine judgement, how God loves, homosexuality, sex (God understands I'm a man…), and others things to say the least. They want God to make sense, or they want to make sense of God. My advice to you, as it relates to distinguishing His voice from yours, is that you embrace His revelation of Him self and stop trying to explain Him. His thoughts are not like yours!

This does not mean that logic bad. God gave us a brain for a reason. However logic does not equal understanding. So in your endeavor to learn how to discern you must come to the realization that your thoughts will not be like God's thoughts. Therefore, if you have all the answers, to who, what, when, where, and why, it is likely that you are operating in your own logic. God's thoughts will never sound like yours!

Learning to Walk Away

My other favorite piece of advice to persons caught in the dilemma of sorting God from self is to do nothing with what you hear. Waiting or walking away from what you hear will create a natural separation between soul and spirit. What you will notice is that the word or voice of God burns in the heart. This is because God is persistent with what He has to say. Jeremiah the prophet once decided that the hardship of ministry was more than he could bear. So he decided that he would not speak for God anymore and he went into an early retirement from prophesying. Even though this was his intent he soon discovered that the voice of God is not easily ignored. He eventually said, *"His word was like fire shut up in my bones"* (Jer. 20:9). Hebrews 4:12 likewise conveys to us that *"the word of God is active and alive"*. Jesus also said *"My words are spirit and they are life"* (John 6:63). The voice of God is active!

The voice of the Lord comes again and again until you either pass the time of obedience or yield and obey. Therefore, you should understand that God is very persistent. So if you think you have heard a voice, vision or dream, or an impression from God but you are not sure if it originated with you or with God, then walk away from it. If it originated with God it will come again. Sometimes it will just lay on your mind in a way that you cannot ignore. This is also true of dreams and visions as well. You will not forget the dream of the Lord. When a dream is from God you will find that you will possess an unusual sense of memory regarding the facts of the dream. In fact, you will remember it for years and years to come. He plants His word in you until it accomplishes His purposes and He gives us no room to say that we did not hear Him or know what He was saying.

Take Jonah for example. The word came to him and in disobedience to it He ran to the sea. Then God punished him and when He had granted Jonah forgiveness He gave him the same word again *(see the book of Johan)*. Or consider Samuel and how persistent God was in calling his name again and again until He got a response (see I Sam. 3). Balaam is our last example (see Numbers 22). This guy insisted on trying to get a word of cursing from God for one of Israel's enemies. However, though he tried very hard to persuade God to change His mind, God persistently and consistently spoke the same word. So remember God is persistent with His word because the voice of God reveals the character of God. This reveals to us that God is patient. Just because you get something now does not mean you need to act on it immediately. He says of the prophets in 1 Corinthians 14:32, *"the spirits of the prophets are subject to the prophets"*. In other words there is nothing that God has spoken to you that you cannot contain. If you are really hearing from God, you should expect that while He may be persistent, you do have control of how you handle what you hear. The point is this, God's voice is persistent.

In the next section I deal with Satan or demonic voices. It is important to address the idea that Satan is persistent as well. So if Satan is persistent and God is persistent, what then is the difference between the two? The major difference as stated earlier, is that God is patient this is why He lays on our heart until we obey. Satan on the other hand is impatient, and we will see this character trait during our exploration of the fourth chapter of Luke. He was very persistent with Jesus, but was not patient. Notice how quickly he changed his instructions to Jesus when he did not get an immediate or expected response. So separating your voice from God and Satan boils down to God's persistence and patience. The same can be said about separating God's voice from our voice. God is patient, but we as humans never are.

The Voice of Satan

This leads me to my next personality. If I had known then what I know now about how Satan works, I would have been able to avoid the situation with the young lady.

I want to start by acknowledging that there is a group of people who would rather not consider the reality of the devil. I am also aware that there is a group of persons who believe that any mention or study of the devil is somehow attributing to him some form of glory. However, I think that it should be noted that the scriptures are clear that he exist. It is also, equally clear in communicating that he has an agenda. Lastly, it warns us not to be ignorant regarding his devices (see 2 Cor. 2:11). Therefore, if we are to really know how to hear from God, we must consider this last point of uttermost value.

The beautiful thing about God is that He is not at all insecure. He is completely aware that Satan is no match for Him and so, while we may not think it godly to study him, we must consider the fact that God shows us who Satan is as a person in the scriptures. 1 John 3:8 sums up the creature's entire person. It reads, *"He that commits sin is of the devil; for the devil sinned from the beginning. For this purpose the Son of God was manifested, that he might destroy the works of the devil"*.

The Agenda

The first thing we need to understand is that he has an agenda. It is to steal, kill, and to destroy. This is his vision for your life and you can be sure that it will be reflected in whatever he tries to tell you. He also wants you to curse God and die. In other words, he wants you to say things such as God cannot do that, or God's does not love me. He ultimately wants you do die—to disconnect from God.

In Job 1:6-12 we see Satan going before God with the other angels and he challenges Job's loyalty to God. In his challenge to God he reveals that what he really desires is for Job to curse God. This is his vision. Then in Job 2:9 Job's wife says *"CURSE GOD AND DIE"*. This was the thought that originated in the heart of Satan. She was a conductor for his plan and we can clearly see the conversation that Satan had with Job's undiscerning wife. Satan is the voice of discouragement.

He is also a thief and murderer.

"The thief cometh not, but for to steal, and to kill, and to destroy" (John 10:10)

Second, the bible says that he is a liar and the father of them.

"Ye are of your father the devil, and the lusts of your father ye will do. He was a murderer from the beginning, and abode not in the truth, because there is no truth in him. When he speaks a lie, he speaks of his own: for he is a liar, and the father of it". (John 8:44)

"You are a child of the devil and an enemy of everything that is right! You are full of all kinds of deceit and trickery. Will you never stop perverting the right ways of the Lord?" (Acts 13:10)

He is also an accuser of the brethren.

"And the great dragon was cast out, that old serpent, called the Devil, and Satan, which deceives the whole world: he was cast out into the earth, and his angels were cast out with him. And I heard a loud voice saying in heaven, Now is come salvation, and strength, and the kingdom of our God, and the power of his Christ: for the accuser of our brethren is cast down, which accused them before our God day and night." (Revelations 12:10)

Lastly, he is our opposition.

"Then the he showed me Joshua the high priest standing before the Angel of the Lord, and Satan standing at his right hand to oppose him." (Zech. 3:1)

These are just a few key points to consider about the enemy. These passages all communicate to us very important indications of the types of conversations this being would be interested in having. These character traits provide us with a good reason why you do not have to worry about being deceived by the devil. Besides the fact that Jesus says, *"My sheep hear MY VOICE"*, the Bible shows us that Satan's plan is clearly different from God's. He is God's polar opposite. God speaks to us to lead us in paths of righteousness, and Satan speaks to lead us in paths of wickedness. Now, please, do not misunderstand my point. I am not suggesting that discerning the difference between God and Satan is as simple as one does good and the other does evil. We can see through the world around us that the devil does allow people to do good works, but what he does not allow, is good works that point to Jesus as the savior. Further into this discussion I will show you exactly how he operates to point you to your own self.

Therefore, you should ignore and/or rebuke any voice that encourages or inspires lying, gossip, and accusatory actions and words. Or any voice that steals the life out of, tears down, or causes destruction in the lives of others. This is not how God speaks to His children. We discussed this in a previous chapter "The Fruit of God's Voice". As you search the scriptures you will notice that God says very loving things to us in the scriptures. He called Israel the "apple of His eye" (see Zech 2:8). He also uses words like the beloved and the bride, royal priesthood, holy nation… (see 1 Peter 1:9) to express just how valuable we are to Him. You will not find this to be the case with your enemy. His voice condemns with words that produce guilt, shame, rejection, fear, discouragement, etc.

The Accuser is also an Abuser

Satan is an abuser. What do I mean by that statement? An abuser is someone who takes advantage of the weaknesses of others. This is what Satan does as well. The statement the Devil made me do is a half truth. The scriptures do not support the idea that Satan is capable of spiritually dominating the life of the believer. What it does teach us however, is that he will attempt to influence our behavior. This means that he will try to deceive the believer into partnering with him to accomplish evil. This also means that in order for his plans to have an affect in your life you must agree to follow him down the road of wickedness.

Please understand what I am about to say. Sometimes we see what appear to be conflicts in the scriptures. The Bible tells us to *"not to be ignorant of the devils devices"* (2 Cor. 2:11), and to *"Stay sober and vigilant because the devil walks about as a roaring lion…"*(1 Pet. 5:8) Then Jesus says, *"His sheep hear his voice and a stranger's voice they WILL NOT FOLLOW"* (John 10:27). So why do we need a warning about the enemy if we are not subject to following his voice?

What we must understand is that, when Jesus says that we will not "follow" a stranger, He is referring to the path of a stranger. God leads us in "paths". A path is a narrow road that leads to a particular destination. So when Jesus says we will follow Him, He is saying that we will follow his ways—We will imitate His life, His characteristics, and His righteous lifestyle.

What Satan seeks to do is to "distract" us or "hinder' us while we are on the path. His Goal is to get you off course so that you become discouraged in the journey. Also, the Bible shows us that he has a very systematic way to accomplish this task.

First you need to understand that he takes advantage of your weaknesses. This is why I started by saying how important is it for you to be honest about who you are. A long time ago a friend taught me that it is good to pray and ask the Lord to show you yourself. If you do you will find that the Lord does just that. I know that some people have a hard time with accepting their own nakedness. They do not want to see the issues in their lives. They seem willing to live in the deception that they are not that bad.

· These persons are perfect candidates for deception. The Bible tells us that *"Our righteousness is as a filthy rag"* (Isa. 64:6). This is something that you must first accept about what God has said about you. All this passage is saying is that your life on your best day looks raggedy like the clothes of a filthy homeless person. God's remedy for this is to clothe you in His beautiful righteousness. However if you are not willing to agree that you have areas of weakness, you will make it easier for Satan to tempt you. For you are like a man who sees himself in the mirror, but after he has gone away forgets that he is wretched (see James 1:23).

We see this type of self-delusion every year on American Idol. It never fails that someone comes into the audition delusional about his or her ability to sing. Have you ever wondered how a person could be so deceived? For the answer you need not look far. Usually the person is accompanied by parents and or friends, who are too afraid to tell him or her the truth. Therefore, every year millions of people watch the auditions to see those who deceived themselves. Sometimes, these people are devastated when they hear the truth for the first time on national television!

This is the point that I am trying to make. If you are unwilling to accept the loving truth of your own need, you will always be vulnerable to temptation. Also, Satan will take advantage of the opportunity to create pain and misery in your life. He is an abuser. He takes advantage of the weakness that lives in our flesh.

His Three-point Plan

Believe it or not, you are not dealing with an idiot. Please understand that Satan is not an idiot and you should respect the fact that even the Arch Angel Gabriel, recognized his power (see Jude 1:9).

The Bible says that he also has devices and schemes. A scheme is a systematic plan to accomplish a desired goal. Ephesians 6:12 also, tells us that his kingdom is highly organized and operates on the principles of order. He has a three-point plan and I am going to expose it in the next few pages.

His Primary Weapons

Satan has two primary weapons that he uses to try to deceive us. Those weapons are lust and pride. 1 John 2:16 says, *"For all that is in the world, the lust of the flesh, the lust of the eyes, and the pride of life is not from the Father, but is of the world"*.

I think that it is interesting that two-thirds of the battle is built on lust. It does not take much to know that the world we live in right now is fueled by lust. Our songs, have titles such as *More Money, More Power, I Kissed a Girl* and *Anti Up*, a rap song that glorifies robbery. Our movies and television programs are centered on characters and their quest for the things that they lust after, such as *Scandal*. Even our commercials are unnecessarily provocative.

The Bible says in James 4:1, *"From where do wars and fighting among you come? Don't they come from your lusts that war in your members?"*

Pride likewise has proven to be dangerous. In fact, there is a story in which King David decided to count his accomplishments. This seemly innocent act cost thousands of people their lives at the hands of an angel sent to punish David's actions. His moment of arrogance caused grief to many (see 2 Sam. 24:1-25). Also the Bible says that God hates pride (see Prov. 8:13). Pride comes before a fall (see Prov. 16:18). Last, it was because of King Nebuchadnezzar and his son's pride that they were removed from the throne of the known world (see DanIEL).

So we can see that these two weapons in the arsenal of the enemy pack quite the wallop. But how does he use these three against us? He uses these against us by perverting our desires. Lust is simply the perverting of natural desires. There is nothing wrong with sex…in the context of marriage! There is nothing wrong with money. The Bible says it answers all things (see Eccl. 10:19). It also says that *"The **love** of money leads to all evil"* (1 Tim. 6:10).

This is where we can see the value of boundaries. Lust does not respect boundaries—It is gluttonous. It is never satisfied. Therefore, Satan uses these weaknesses that exist in our flesh, to attempt to deceive and distract us from the path where God is leading us.

Lust of the Flesh and Eyes

In Romans 7:18 Paul says, *"For I know, that in me (that is, in my flesh) dwelleth no good thing. For to will is present with me: but how to perform that which is good, I find not."* There is something in us that wants to do wrong. This is called the lust of the flesh. It is that something that tells us to look at, to touch, to taste and to listen to something that God says don't look at, don't touch, don't taste, or listen to.

We can see in the scriptures how Satan uses this weakness in us to get us off course. We first see him using these two weapons against the first family. He was so successful in his initial attempt that it resulted in what we refer to as the fall of mankind.

Genesis chapter 3 gives us a full account of these events as Eve encounters the serpent in the garden. We can see the first part of Satan's attack in Genesis 3:6. For it reads, *"When she saw that the tree was good for food."* At first glance Eve appears to be having a completely rational thought process. The reality is that it was in fact a tree with fruit and it was good for food. There was nothing but truth in that statement. However, what Satan was able to do was get her to acknowledge her own lust. How did she know that it was good for food? What was she doing so close to what she knew was a restricted area? Maybe this was not the first time she was tempted. Satan simply got her to look beyond what God said was off limits. He tapped into her lust. He helped her to see something that would make her feel good. She was only deceived because she was able to relate the experience to the meeting of a legitimate need. It was food, it was off limits to her, but it was food all the same. As I stated before lust is nothing more than a legitimate desire perverted.

It is for this reason that we are so easily ensnared by various things. Sure we need sex. Sex is good, but God has provided boundaries around its proper use. Sure we need money, but having five jobs at the expense of your family is wrong. The same is true with all of our legitimate desires. Just because it feels good does not mean that it is good for you. If we are not careful, he will attempt to lure us off tract by giving us perverted ways to satisfy legitimate needs. This is what He was able to do with Eve and Adam.

Not only did he get her to lust with her flesh, he was able to sell her on the lust of her eyes. *"She SAW that it was good for food"* and Genesis 3:7 says, *"She saw that it was PLEASANT to the EYES"*.

The Bible says that, *"The eyes are never satisfied"* (Eccl. 1:8). How many times have we heard the phrase, "your eyes are bigger than your stomach". Most of us understand exactly what that means from experience. I can remember times when I would eat until I felt like I was going to vomit and most of you do too. This happens because we are prone chasing the things we see.

Our world today has created a society that is absolutely obsessed with our appearance. People are doing all kinds of things to their bodies attempting to make themselves *"look"* more appealing.

Likewise commercials are filled with the most beautiful people placed there to ensure that we watch the ad. Most people really do not have a clue as to the amount of strategic planning that goes into one ad. There is a reason why they cost millions of dollars to produce. Every color choice, texture, font, ethic demographic, etc. is considered in the making of a commercial, print products, and signage. It all has one goal and that is to appeal to your lust through your eyes. It is to give you something so visually strong that you would sacrifice and abandon all sense of responsibility to have the product in your possession. How do I know? I am a graphic designer and I have a first-hand knowledge of how important it is to ensure that the consumer has a great experience with the product through their eyes. The idea says that if I can get the consumer to look in the direction of the ad, then I can get him or her to see the message, which has also been strategically crafted. If the advertiser can get you to read the message, then they will increase the possibility of you making the purchase.

This is exactly what is happening to Adam and Eve. They SAW something and once they saw the ad, Satan ran his lines and they bought into his message. All of this took place because Eve lusted with her eyes.

She had seen that fruit many times, but this time she was tempted because Satan gave her a message that perverted her perception of the commandment that God had given to her and Adam. We must be careful if we are to really hear the Voice of God, not be lead by our natural eyes, but the eyes of our heart.

The Pride of Life

The last weapon in his arsenal is the pride of life. I call this EGO. It is our underlying drive to be someone important or to be engulfed in complete self-awareness. Eve was sold on truth. It has always been taught that Satan lied to her, but he really didn't. He said that they would be like God, knowing good and evil. He did not say that they would be like God! Likewise, during the Godhead council meeting God Himself says, *"The man **has become like one of US,** knowing good and evil"* (Gen. 3:22). But I'm willing to bet that she got caught up on the same thing most of us have read, You Will Be Like GOD.

Again, she saw something, but this time she saw it in her mind. She saw or imagined the possibilities of being wise like God. This is an example of knowledge exalting itself against God. It is our insistent desire to want to be in charge of ourselves. As you are learning the voice of God, you will quickly discover that Jesus is humble. The Bible says even though he was God, He took on the position of a servant (see Phil. 2:7). Jesus says, *"If you want to be first then be last"* (Matt. 20:16), *"For he who serves is greatest in the kingdom"* (Matt. 23:11).

This is in direct contrast to Satan's agenda. His voice wants you to exalt yourself. He wants you to imagine your greatness apart from humility. I always find it amusing, that people never have visions of themselves, on the mission field serving the needs of the poor. They always seem to have visions of grandeur and glory in which they are always the star. They always see themselves as preaching to thousands. I have met and heard several such stories, and seen prophesies go out over people's lives that were not from God. I look around now at all these great people and see that God has not done much of anything with their ministries. It is because they have not learned that God leads us in humility.

I have had these kinds of visions as well. I can remember times in church when I would have these great visions of myself standing on the platform at my church and doing all kinds of miracles. Next I would see people in awe of me and all that God was doing. I was hailed with greatness and all kinds of stuff. Then I would rebuke it and keep worshiping.

These were visions from the enemy that came at time in my life when God was using me to do great things. God had prepared me for this by cautioning me that if Satan could not stop me, then he would attempt to push me. This is what he did to Adam and Eve. He pushed them up in their own minds to want something they obviously did not need. That is what pride does—it makes us assume the responsibility of being god in our own lives!

Insecurity

Let me start by noting that insecurity is our worst enemy. Insecure Christians are those who do not understand their identity in Christ. It's the source of failure for Adam and Eve.

Insecurity is Satan's attempt to oppress us with feelings of inadequacy. He wants you to experience what I call thoughts of "not enough"—not good enough, not tall or short enough, not smart enough, not talented enough, etc. His voice led Adam and Even into feeling inadequate about their nakedness.

They were fine naked until Satan's voice convinced them they needed more than what God provided.

There is a story in the Book of Acts 8:9-25, regarding a sorcerer named Simon. The Bible says that Simon worked astonishing magic tricks and the people supposed him to be someone great. However after seeing the real Worker of Miracles, Simon repented and became a believer. Later he saw that the disciples were laying hands on people and that the Holy Spirit was given to all on whom they laid their hands. This ignited a lust for the power in Simon and Peter promptly rebuked him for his error.

Simon lusted for the power of God out of his own insecurity—his feelings of "not enough". Satan was able to move him because of the image of himself that he held close to his heart—the reminder of being someone great. We can see two of Satan's weapons in the story. When he SAW... he lusted for the POWER.

I have actually seen this happen. I tell more of this story elsewhere in the book. But I have seen people try to operate in the anointing after it has lifted and unintentionally find themselves operating by a familiar spirit. This happens because insecurity tells us it is more important to impress men than it is to obey God.

Selfishness

This leads me to the next area of concern. Adam and Eve allowed pride into the world. Their actions forever opened mankind up to idea of "ego". Cain killed Able when his ego was offended. Pride is something that we see all throughout the Bible and human history. Insecurity produces pride in our hearts. It happened to Simon, Adam and Eve, King David, Saul and a host of others throughout history.

All of this boils down to one simple word, selfishness! What Adam and Eve did was just selfish. Every word of her heart was aimed at how "she" would be satisfied. Even though she knew the consequences she still crossed the line of disobedience. She said this will satisfy *"my"* stomach. This really looks good to *"me"*. This will make *"me"* wise. To Hell, literally with everybody else!

This is Satan's plan for you as well. He wants you to exalt your throne above the throne of God. It is his ultimate goal to get you to make your decisions with the lust of your eyes, the lust of your flesh, and your pride.

Jesus in the Wilderness

If you are still not convinced that this is his standard mode of operation, the Bible provides a more clear depiction of this process when Jesus is tempted in the wilderness in the gospels. That's right, Jesus was tempted the same way—with the same ideas. The lust of the flesh, the lust of the eyes, and the pride of life are clearly visible in Luke 4:1-13.

Here is the set up. Jesus has just fasted 40 days and after He is finished fasting Satan appears to Him to tempt Him. His first attack is aimed at getting Jesus to change rocks into bread to satisfy His hunger. He wanted Him to use his power to serve His own needs. He wanted Him to use His power for selfish gain and he tempted Him using his own natural desires. He was speaking to the lust in His flesh.

Second, we see that he tries to tempt Jesus by taking Him up to the highest pinnacle and showing Him the world. Next he offers Him the whole world if He would bow down in worship. Again we can see that He is attempting to lure Jesus into his message through the lust of the eyes. Notice that he did not show him a cottage. He showed Him the world! Why is this a noteworthy point? It is noteworthy because it tells us that temptation is relative. Satan knew that he was talking to God, someone who already had abundance. He knew that Jesus would not be tempted by something meager. This is true for you as well. If you grew up with nothing then temptation to you may be a $300 handbag purchased with your rent money. However, for someone with abundance, a $300 handbag is not a temptation because they can afford it. So Satan tempts us with what we are prone to show weakness for.

Last, we see that he tells Jesus that if He is the Son of God that He should throw Himself off the temple and God would send angels to save Him. This is the pride of life at its finest. Satan attempts to appeal to Jesus sense of ego and reputation. He wants Jesus to assume arrogantly that He has no boundaries. He tempts him to believe that He was so special that all of heaven is at His mercy.

You will also see that Satan is attempting to push Jesus to die outside of the appointed time. He was attacking His sense of security, as to who He was and what He heard as God's ultimate the plan for His life. He could have said, Jesus, you are the Son of God do so and so, but he didn't. He said, *"IF you are the Son of God."* This is a ploy for Jesus to prove Himself, but Jesus demonstrates that the key to our victory in the season of temptation is humility and security.

Suggestive Thoughts

Finally, I think that we should note one very important element in all that you have read. One very distinct way that the voice of God differs from that of Satan can be summed up in the phrase "suggestive thought." Suggestive thoughts are indirect thoughts patterns that Satan gives us that are subtly tempting.

You will notice a subtle and suggestive tone in both the story of Adam and Eve and Jesus' ordeal in the wilderness. He says to Adam and Eve, *"DID GOD SAY…"* He Says to Jesus, *"IF YOU ARE* the Son of God…" These are both suggestions and they appear as subtle. One thing the Bible says about Jesus is that He spoke as one with authority. We can also read all throughout the Bible, wherever God is seen speaking, that He speaks with authority. His voice is commanding. In fact He gave Moses the 10 COMMANDMENTS not SUGGESTIONS. God does not speak in a questioning tone. He speaks with certainty because He knows what He wants to do. Only the insecure one speaks suggestively. I covered this in more detail in the chapter *"Signs of His Voice"*.

This is the voice of doubt. I deal with this is detail in the chapter *"Hindrance to Hearing"*. Doubt is a suggestive and passive voice. It IS THE ENEMY.

You will always hear the voice of doubt as the second voice. Its goal is to create two minds in you and to bring about confusion.

You will notice that Satan spoke "after" God gave Adam and Eve His commandment. We also see that He challenges Jesus' identity "after" he has been baptized by John and the Holy Spirit descending upon Him like a dove. It was "after" God had clearly spoken, *"YOU ARE MY BELOVED SON..."* Doubt is a questioning suggestive voice.

Here my personal example. In early 2015 the Lord told me to start preaching on social media. So the next day He immediately spoke a word to me to post online. The first video went over very well despite the fact that I was very nervous. I feared being ridiculed for being a social media preacher. With such a warm reception to the idea I continued to post videos. After approximately three videos I assumed that the novelty wore off because the "like clicks", comments, and encouragement drastically decreased. This led to an attack by the enemy. He started to whisper very faint indirect statements. One such statement said, "Are you sure God wants you to do this" and "If it was God, why are people not watching?" Knowing it was him I took this to God in prayer and He silenced this attack with a song from *"NEMO"*. He sang the Dory song *"Just Keep Swimming"*. He really encouraged, comforted, and edified me with that song. Later, I discovered that there were more views with each video. It turned out that a lot of people were watching but not liking or commenting. I discovered many were watching when they testified to me how the videos were impacting their lives. What I want you to notice is the difference in how God communicated versus how Satan communicated. God spoke to me directly as one in authority. He had no hidden meaning in His message. Satan however, attempted to deceive me by the use of tricky subtle speech patterns. He never communicates directly, he always speaks in a way that seeks to lead or influence you to draw a conclusion. It always leads to the "not enough"—feelings of insecurity.

If you hear his voice, you should immediately seek to nullify this attack the same way Jesus did. Jesus did not go into a lengthy dialog with Satan. He simply quoted the word of God. Even in my situation it was the word that God spoke to me, "Just keep swimming", that nullified his attack. Whether

God gives you a "Logos-Bible verse" or a "rhema-spoken word", just know that His word quickly and efficiently defends us against such attacks.

Whatever the situation, just remember that the voice of God is distinctly different from the voice of your enemy. I would also like you to remember that Satan is always going to attempt you to lure you away by the thing you lust for with your flesh and eyes. Lastly he will try to lure you away through your own over valued ego.

This means that his voice sounds more like yours than God's. If you've ever heard that Satan can imitate God's voice, be at peace. Again, God's thoughts are the ones that are least likey to sound like yours!

Chapter Six
Voices of Deception

Super Deceivers

In the last chapter we discussed a lot about the enemy and how he uses our weaknesses to deceive us. We also examined this type of deception from a natural and easily discernable standpoint. By natural, I mean that he uses everyday situations and things of the natural to which we can relate, such as things that tempt our eyes, flesh, and ego. Now I want to deal with what I call the super deceivers or "deceiving spirits". I call them super deceivers because these spirits confront us directly in supernatural ways. Often the supernatural gift of discerning of spirits is required to discern their presence. While some may not be aware of, or matured in this gift, there are some important "markers" that we can use to assist us in discerning such spirits naturally.

I want you to imagine how it would have been during the time when the first church was being established. Imagine the enormous task of putting into place sound doctrine from only direct revelations of Jesus Christ. Consider the reality that everything we know now through one consolidated writing, was at some point a bunch of scattered personal letters and writings to new Christians scattered throughout the known world. I don't know about you, but I am really glad I was not a member of the first church. While they had all kinds of incredible supernatural encounters and experiences that we today are still trying to create and surpass, they also had no foundation for which they could weigh and discern the revelations they received. They did not have a King James Version of the Bible from which to compare their supernaturally received insights. They were literally at a complete loss when it came to how to discern what they received and what to do with what they heard in the

Spirit. Their only hope was "learning to discern" the truth. While they did have all the revelation gifts available, there were no books on the "how to's" of ministry. And this lack of understanding is what led to other problems such as the Gnostic Gospels, and other false doctrines, and warnings about not believing every spirit but testing the spirits. It was the catalyst behind the verses of warning such as 1 Corinthians 12:3, *"Therefore I make known to you that no one speaking by the Spirit of God can call Jesus accursed and know one can say that Jesus is Lord except by the Holy Spirit."*

All of these passages arose out of a time period when people received the word and spoke fresh revelation from heaven. They are also the result of the many errors that the first church encountered because of the newness of the faith. These errors were the spawn of "deceiving spirits."

Deceiving spirits are not your everyday ordinary spirits. They are very powerful in the area of deception and to have the power to supernaturally encounter humans and to provide humans illegal access to the invisible world. Deceiving spirits feed on our insistence or fascination with things we really know nothing about. They are drawn to those who are always looking for an experience with the supernatural. Now as I have stated elsewhere in this writing, God is supernatural. All encounters with Him are supernatural and because He is supernatural you will have supernatural encounters. This chapter is not about discouraging you from experiencing supernatural encounters, but it is about discerning the source of such encounters. So it is not my intention to cause you to fear the supernatural, but that you would develop a healthy respect for a realm where the beings are absolutely real and the evil ones are ravenous towards the undiscerning and overly fascinated. The spiritual realm is not a playground. You need the Holy Spirit to guide you into such experiences. That is if He so chooses. It is for the mature saints who understand how to discern between good and evil.

The other really important thing to understand about these demons is that they are religious spirits. This is really amusing to me because most of those "high strung" on the supernatural, say that a 'religious spirit' binds those who are other-minded. And while there **"is"** such a spirit and it is a form of a deceiving spirit, it is not one who preys on those looking for experiences.

This particular spirit preys on those who are on the other end of the spectrum. I intend to deal with both in this section.

Don't be Deceived by the Power

As I was listening to my dramatized version of the Bible, God showed me something that I had never seen before in Luke 4:1-12. In the last chapter we dealt with this passage as a backdrop to explain how the Devil uses the lust of the flesh, the eyes, and pride to deceive us into cooperating with him to obtain his promises. As we delve deeper into these passages of scripture, we will see an even deeper level of deception was at work in the passage. A level of deception that I am sure is still very much at work today.

This is the most fascinating time period in which to be alive. People are hungrier for the supernatural more than I ever remember seeing in my lifetime. There are more horror movies, more false religions, more angel sightings, and more focus on things such as supernatural travel and the spirit world, positive focus and all sorts of things. With all that is happening, you have to conclude that some of it is of God and some of it is of Satan. So what are we as Christians to do with all this hyper spiritualism in the atmosphere? Should we shy away from the supernatural or should we embrace it? I believe that we should embrace what is happening and **learn to discern**. When we look at this ordeal in the wilderness again we see that Jesus not only learned how to resist temptation, but He also learned how to discern what was of God and what was of Satan.

When we look at Luke 4:5, we see an interesting thing happen, it says, *"Then the devil, TAKING HIM (Jesus) up on a high mountain, SHOWED HIM the kingdoms of the world in a MOMENT OF TIME."* How did Jesus get up the mountain? Why was He following Satan? I would like to suggest that He got there by supernatural means. The passage does not say that He "walked" up a mountain, but that He was "taken" to that location. He was supernaturally transported, *whether in the body or out of the body, I don't know!* Either way, we can see that the wilderness was a very important time in the development of the ministry of Jesus. He was having supernatural encounters with a *"deceiving spirit"*. And it moved supernaturally with the intent to influence His behavior and gain His loyalty.

This tells us a very important thing. Everyone who wants to encounter the supernatural needs to and will have a season like that of Jesus. It also tells us that there is a need to be discerning and watchful.

Some of you will obviously be repulsed by me saying that Jesus had a moment of being led by the wrong voice. So let me be clear. I am not saying that He was deceived, but that He was tempted with deception. Also we know that on two of those occasions He was supernaturally transported to the location. Luke 4:8 likewise says, *"Then he BROUGHT HIM to Jerusalem, and SET HIM ON THE PINNACLE of the temple*. Again, Jesus was supernaturally transported to another location.

Now that we can see this clearly in the scriptures, we must ask the question regarding how Jesus was taken to the point of temptation. What I mean is that it seems as though Jesus would have recognized Satan before He got to the top of a mountain, or before He got to the top of the pinnacle ready to take His own life. How did the devil get Him that far? I believe the answer lies in Mark 1:13. It reads, *"And He was there in the wilderness forty days, tempted by Satan, and was with the wild beast; and the ANGELS ministered to Him."* Another version says that the angels ministered to Him at the end of the season of temptation, but their presence is a key factor in how Satan appeared to Jesus.

How did Satan come to Jesus in the wilderness? I believe he came to Jesus the way he always came before God. He came with the sons of God; the angels. The Bible says in Job 1:6, *"Now there was a day when the sons of God came to present themselves before the Lord and Satan also come among them."* The Bible also says of this creature in 2 Corinthians 11:14, *"and no marvel; for even Satan disguises or transforms himself into an ANGEL OF LIGHT."* I believe that Satan came as an angel among the angels. Or that he came with the appearance of an angel before the real move of God came.

History has been full of religions started by visitations from angels. Mohammed started Islam because of an angelic visitation. The Jehovah Witnesses and Mormons both have their roots in angelic visitations. The

New Age Movement as well and many others have been started because of one person's supernatural encounter with a deceiving spirit appearing as an angel.

How to Recognize Deceiving Spirits

As I have stated before in other places in this book, the purpose of this book in not to focus on the "how to" of hearing the voice of God. There are many other good books on this subject. However my focus and my assignment from God is to give you what He has shared with me regarding "discerning" God and His voice. There are a lot of supernatural things happening right now and I believe that the Body of Christ is in an awakening stage. Also with this awakening to the world of the supernatural we are also learning how to operate in the beginnings of an outpouring of the Spirit of God on all flesh. Many assume that we are there now, but in reality we are just in a preparatory place where God is teaching us how to move in the supernatural. We should however, expect that with this move we will see counterfeits appearing as having come from God. We must also be taught how to discern in the supernatural. Right now a lot of spiritual realm pioneers have shallow standards such as "if it's peaceful" and "how do you feel in the experience". If you had asked Joseph Smith, the creator of the Mormons, about his encounter with the angels that turned him away from the faith, he would have described for you the most incredible feeling of peace and love. In fact, he does in his testimony of the experience. We cannot depend on how an experience feels, alone.

As I was pondering this I asked the Lord, how He knew that it was Satan if he was disguised as an angel, and His response was simple. He said, *"The testimony of Jesus Christ is the spirit of prophecy."* I have said this many times before in this book and I will say it a thousand times more, it is imperative that you make this a foundational truth of *"all"* that you hear. This is the essence of the voice of God. The angels of the Old and New Testament testify of Jesus. The Old Testament angles testify of His coming, and the New Testament angels testify of Him now. The Bible also tells us *"That no one speaking by the Spirit of God can call Jesus accursed and that one can only say Jesus is Lord by the Holy Spirit."* (1 Cor. 12:2)

I also want to reiterate the fact that the deceiving spirit is a "religious" spirit. By religious I do not mean restrictive, but that it is a spirit that is focused on ideas that have to do with religion and deity worship. The Devil reveals the purpose of the deceiving spirit in Luke 4:7. It reads, *"Therefore, IF YOU WILL WORSHIP before me…"* This is an aspect of religion and it is what a deceiving spirit is ultimately after, your worship!

Please do not be deceived, the Bible also lays out for us what this looks like in Colossians 2:18, false humility and the worship of angels. I want you to see that there are two aspects of this deception—one is traditional, ceremonial, and restrictive, the other is supernatural. I love the angles and while they are fascinating and a wonder to see and experience, they are not suppose to be the most important subject of our conversations and books. I understand that there is a need to understand their role in our lives and ministries since the Bible says in Hebrews 1:14, that *"They are all ministering spirits sent forth to minister to the heirs of salvation."* However we should not be so overwhelmed with focusing on inspiring angelic visitations. Angels have jobs, hence the term "ministering spirits". When they appear, it is for a reason, and they have in mind the same goal that you should have in mind— the glorification of Jesus the Christ.

We can see what a deceiving spirit looks like in 1 Kings 22:19-23, when a spirit is put into the mouths (plural) of the prophets. It was one spirit creating an atmosphere of inspiration. This is important to note, because sometimes we are deceived by the peer factor. We as humans are overwhelmingly peer-oriented. If we see two or more people having an experience we sometimes struggle to be right, even though we may know that something is wrong. That is what is happening here in the passage. These prophets were so easily deceived by this spirit because there was an atmosphere of deception. They all had the same dream, vision, and heard the same voice. Yet it was a deceiving spirit. Then one man with eyes to see and ears to hear, and a heart turned toward the worship of God gave a contrary, but accurate word. Again we can see that this is the work of a religious spirit operating in a religious environment.

As I have said before, these are not spirits that are always easy to discern naturally, but one thing remains true about these deceivers. They do not testify of Jesus. They may testify of your leader. They may testify of the greatness of some other deity. They may even testify of your own greatness, as was the case with David Koresh—But they will not testify of Jesus.

There is a really good story in Acts 16:16-19, which helps to drive this point home. It reads:

> *"And it came to pass, as we went to prayer, a certain damsel possessed with a spirit of divination met us, which brought her masters much gain by soothsaying: The same followed Paul and us, and cried, saying, These men are the servants of the most high God, which show unto us the way of salvation. And this did she many days. But Paul, being grieved, turned and said to the spirit, I command thee in the name of Jesus Christ to come out of her. And he came out the same hour. And when her masters saw that the hope of their gains was gone, they caught Paul and Silas, and drew them into the marketplace unto the rulers."*

This passage is another great example of this type of spirit at work. We can see from the passage that it was a spirit of divination. We can also see it at work preaching among the people. It was a religious spirit. It was hiding in the religious community, and what it was saying from just a simple observation really does not appear to be wrong. Paul and Silas were servants of the Most High God and they did in fact, come to show them the way of salvation. So where is the problem in this story? The spirit of prophecy is the *"TESTIMONY OF JESUS CHRIST"* not the testimony of "Paul" and "Silas"!

The Other Fella

There is another kind of deceiving spirit called a "religious spirit". Colossians 2:18 is the scripture of choice for this subject in Charismatic circles. They somehow overlook the worship of angels and jump right into the "touch not" and "taste not" portions of the verse. However when you look at this passage it is clear that these are not people opposed to the supernatural, but people that embraced it without discretion. They believed that their holiness was how they would obtain such encounters with the supernatural. This is what sets the stage for the Evangelicals and Protestants that are at the other extreme. They are deceived into believing that their self-imposed restrictions accomplished in their own strength are what God wants. They are partly turned off to the supernatural because of the fanatical behavior, inconsistent theologies, and blatant disregard for scripture as the final word of those who pursue the supernatural.

The religious spirit is a deceiving spirit as well. This next story I tell hesitantly. Time, wisdom, bad experiences, and maturity have all taught me that it is not always wise or beneficial for me to share my encounters and experiences, but I believe this will help make a great point. I had been in conversations with God about all the new things happening in the kingdom, some of it good and some of it bad. In fact as I read one guy's book or looked at a video of him teaching, I started to notice that demons were always present and that I would find myself in a position where I was forced to move into doing spiritual warfare. I naturally assumed that I was being attacked as an attempt to keep me from what he was teaching. I must admit that I did have some problems with some of the things he was saying but for the most part a lot of it was solid. Therefore, I pressed upon myself, to at least make an effort to hear the entire teaching, before I drew a conclusion. After a couple of attempts at trying to read this book and encountering unwanted guest, I decided to leave it alone and ask God what was going on with this book. He simply said, "doctrine of demons". I said wait, this is a wildly popular book, and so is the author. He said there is a doctrine of demons flowing around in the church. A deceiving spirit is operating and many are being caught up in his teachings.

This lead to a real search for real answers and I stumbled upon a website of a really popular Evangelical radio minster. I had done a search for "Deceiving Spirits" and his website was presented as one of the search results that had content regarding this subject. So I decided to read his sermon. This guy spewed venomous words filled with anger and hatred at those in the Faith and Charismatic movements. He said the most blasphemous things about the Holy Spirit; such as these groups do not worship Jesus they worship the Holy Spirit. And I thought dude, the Spirit of God is the Spirit of Jesus (see 2 Cor. 3:17)! He said Jesus is a spirit how can anyone feel a spirit? He said that he has never felt the Spirit of God, except in his heart. He went on and on about how they deny the faith because Charismatic guys say Jesus had to learn to be God! I read most of it and thought wow, this has no love in it all. I did not need to discern any spirits to see that he had no love for this group. It was that obvious. He obviously did not care to reach these people whom he assumed were lost. The Bible says, *"Wisdom from above is first pure then, PEACEABLE..."* (James 3:17) it also tells us not to argue about such things and that if we do, we should do so in a spirit of gentleness that we might impart grace to the hearers (see 2 Tim. 2:14). I thought to myself, this guy is clearly preaching in his flesh, but little did I know his sermon was inspired by something else far more dangerous.

After a few minutes of reading this spew of hatred for other Christians, I felt something pressing up against me and I started to get a headache. So I got off the site. Later that day as I driving home, my mind just went on and on about this site and I was becoming annoyed that it was still on my mind. It was also questioning things that I knew to be true about the Holy Spirit's activities in the life of the believer. The kicker for me occurred when I noticed that I did not appear to have any control over this voice that was ranting. It was ranting in the same way that this minister did in his sermon. As this went on I started to perceive that it was an evil spirit and so I demanded that it identify itself. Soon after, it named itself as a "religious spirit" then my eyes were opened and I saw it and I rebuked it and it left from my vehicle and the thoughts "immediately" stopped.

I was so shocked, to say the least, at this encounter. I finally knew for sure that there is such a thing as a "religious" demon. A religious spirit was the same spirit at work against Jesus in the persons of the Scribes and Pharisees. Interestingly this religious demon came from a well-known speaker who was in fact preaching on being deceived—and he was the one deceived. The religious spirit is deceptive because it comes as an angel with a form of godliness, but it denies the power.

Both the deceiving spirit and religious spirit have their roots in religious extremes. One works to deceive those intent on being fascinated by the supernatural and the other works to deceive those who are so vehemently against the supernatural that they risk blasphemy to deny the reality of an all powerful God.

This is why I stress over and over to people the necessity for *"balance"*. I say more on this in the chapter "Hindrances to Hearing". I have said over and over, God is both *"SUPERNATURAL"* and *"PRACTICAL"*. If you are really going to avoid being a victim of these two spirits you must accept this truth. If you resolve yourself to being fanatical you will open the door to deception via a super deceiver. Likewise if you insist on being self sufficient and answering your own prayers then blaming God for your lack of power, then you as well will find yourself in the clutches of deception via a religious spirit having a form of godliness but no real power to live victoriously. I find it to be very interesting that people only worry about being deceived by something that occurs in an obviously supernatural way. However, the reality is that you can be just as deceived by something that will restrict you to accepting death and hopelessness, sickness and disease, lack a life, and really boring Christianity, not having any real power.

Here is an example. Some years ago I was a part of a Bible study at my workplace run by a really nice Evangelical or Protestant teacher. He was a really good teacher and he and I became pretty cool friends even though we had opposing views on the reality of God's intimate involvement with people. He believed that we were to suffer through our experiences and I believed that we suffer but God gives us access to change the circumstances.

With this belief in mind he relegated himself to suffering without a car. He had a wife and three kids and one car and never asked God to change the situation. He believed that he was where God wanted him at that time because in God's sovereignty He had not changed the situation. I was also in a similar situation. I was not married at the time but the car I had was a lemon and I needed a new one. So one day after praying I felt led to get a new car and so I obeyed the voice of the Lord and He provided me a new car. There was nothing special about the way He gave it to me other than the fact that He gave me the resources to make the payments, all of which were paid on time with the exception of the one time I was furloughed.

At the following Tuesday workplace Bible study, I gave my testimony about God giving me a new car. This guy became angry and said, "Maybe God just wanted you to walk." He was so upset that God had given me what he needed but was unwilling to believe for. How special is my car?

I've had it twenty years and have only done required repairs. The clutch is the original from the purchased date 20 years ago! This is what I mean when I say that you can be so deceived by a religious spirit that you suffer unnecessarily for things that God would willingly give to you if you asked. I have even seen people die this way. They never ask to be healed because they are deceived into believing that if God wants to heal them He will do so by His sovereignty. Therefore they never asked to be healed. In fact I recently heard someone call cancer something God placed on his or her life. So it is absolutely important that you seek the balance.

As I said earlier Jesus demonstrates both. We can see this in Matthew 14:13-21 when our Lord feeds five thousand men and women with two fish and five loaves of bread. Notice that His access to the supernatural provision was also attached to a very practical idea. He showed us the power of a supernatural God to make supernatural provision. He also showed us that our supernatural God likes order. Jesus was not only able to get access to supernatural provision but He was also able to manage it! He sat them in groups of fifty before the supernatural provision was released. This was a practical way to handle the supernatural provision.

Do not be deceived by these two spirits. Purpose in your heart to find the balance and accept the "whole counsel" of the scriptures. Not just the ones that interest you and your point of view. Also, you will notice that I said the whole counsel of the scriptures!

Testing the Spirits Always

The other way that we can protect ourselves from these two spirits is to learn and accept the responsibility of testing the spirits…(see 1 John 4:1) and to test "all" things (see 1 Thess. 5:21). One of the reasons we are so vulnerable to these two spirits is the fact that we test the spirit of our favorite preacher and then we never test them again. We are in the habit of judging people and not prophecies and sermons. This is why we are often deceived by either extreme. Your pastor, teacher, prophet, apostle, and evangelist are all human and subject to error. You should test every message not just the person.

As I shared in my story above, this well-known minister was spewing forth hate-filled words fueled by a dark spirit on this occasion, but on other occasions he has spoken very helpful and God inspired words. So just because your favorite preacher was right this time does not automatically give him a pass excusing him or her from error. This is why so many people are led astray with preachers that once carried the word of the Lord in their mouths, but are now ministers of deception. This is how David Koresh and Daddy Grace and so many others are able to establish complete dominance over the lives of their followers. This is a form of "angel worship". When we hang on the words of people and forget that *"Man does not live by bread alone but by every word that PROCEEDS FROM THE MOUTH OF GOD."* The life giving words come from God alone, do not assume any man or woman of God has heard from God, but listen with the purpose of testing his or her words each time! This is what it means to be sober and vigilant. Why should we be sober and vigilant? This scripture goes on to tell us that our adversary the devil walks about as a roaring lion seeking whom he may devour (see 1 Pet. 5:8). It also tells us not to give him place or an opportunity (see Eph. 4:27). We give him an opportunity to deceive us every time we refuse to be discerning. The way we comply with the scriptures for our safety is to be responsible enough to test the spirits. This is the mark of real Christian maturity, learning to discern between good and evil (see Heb. 5:14). I would dare to say that this passage could be viewed two ways. The first is the obvious, distinguishing good from evil and right from wrong. The second is that it suggests that it is our responsibility to do so as we mature.

So many people right now are hoping they will not get a rock if they ask God for fish. However, the reality is that we are commanded to be discerning towards the supernatural, not voluntarily open for whatever happens. God expects this from us as we grow, so if someone is deceived it is not that God gave them a rock instead of a fish, but that they did not know the difference between the two because they were not being watchful!

A Vision vs. A Glimpse

The other thing that God showed me in Luke 4 about deception is that it always wants you to have a glimpse of something good. It is what we call a tease. In Luke 4:5 the devil supernaturally transports Jesus in the spirit to the top of a mountain and *"shows"* Him the kingdoms of the world *"in a moment of time"*.

This phrase "in a moment of time" is a key to discerning deception. God gives His people visions. Just look at any vision in the Bible. In every single one God allows the visionary time to clearly see what is in the vision. This "moment of time" is a glimpse that indicates something seen for a short time—it is temporary vision. When God gives us a vision He opens our eyes to see. His visions do not show us things that allow us to see for a moment of time but rather it allows us to permanently see from God's vantage point. The devil was teasing Jesus and denying Him a real opportunity to consider His offer. He was setting Him up with a glimpse of earthly goodies in exchange for his worship. What he was doing in this passage is the equivalence of the guy on the corner who flashes open a long overcoat filled with stolen goodies. He only opens it long enough to attract your attention. He never opens it long enough for you to see if what he has is real or counterfeit.

Let's put this into today's context. Imagine that you went to a church and standing in the pulpit is a prophet and he is prophesying homes, cars, land, and other earthly materials. Then he returns the next year and you are right there again hanging onto every word, and all he is talking about is the stuff God wants to give you. This is an example of a deceiving spirit at work. Sounds familiar doesn't it. I specifically asked God for an example of what He was telling me about the "glimpse" because I couldn't quite get the gist of what He was saying, and this was the example He gave me. This is what a deceiving spirit does to foster the worship of the person and the gift. This happens all the time, where we throw ourselves at men and women of God because they can give us a "glimpse of something". There is a movement of prophets doing this right now. They are set up as prophecy hotlines and some even use the word "physic". These are prophets who have set their minds on things of the earth.

One thing that we should understand about our God is that He gives us "visions" not glimpses. We should also understand that His visions for us are so much deeper than shallow material blessings. God's visions show us our destiny, our purpose, and our potential. He has His mind set of things above. God has more of a "teach a man to fish" mentality than "take a man fishing" mentality. He uses visions to show us what and how he designed us so that we can operate at a level where we can take care of ourselves. Does God give vehicles and wonderful material things? Sure He does. But is He more concerned about your new car than the fact that you cannot discern your future and His immense love for you. I doubt it!

One thing God is doing is raising up real prophetic ministries that really understand that the prophet is not one of God's elves delivering His multitude of gifts, but that he is one of God's tools to equip, build, and prepare the body of Christ for the work of ministry. If all you have been offered is a glimpse and that glimpse causes you to devote yourself to a human then you have just been "duped" by a deceiving spirit. Be careful not to worship any man and if the man does not reject your worship then you have just come face to face with an actual deceiving spirit.

The other thing to see in this passage is the contents of Jesus' vision. The Devil showed Jesus what he had to offer him in the now. God's vision is beyond the immediate view of life. He says in Jeremiah, *"I know the thoughts that I have towards you, thoughts of peace to give you a FUTURE and a hope…"*

The Matter of Interpretation

The last thing I want you to see about the spirit of deception is its desire to change or misinterpret the scriptures. Over the last few months I have enjoyed reading a few good books on seeing in the spirit and I have also had the pleasure of returning a few others on the same subject. I say pleasure because these authors attempted to explain their odd points of view by twisting scriptures to fit the idea they were promoting. In one of the books, the content was accurate. The author was spot on and biblical, but then for some reason he decided that he was going to make his point by forcing the subject. How did he do this? He started twisting and paraphrasing scriptures to make a point that the Bible clearly supported. Folks, he was teaching on the supernatural and what he was teaching was plainly presented in the Bible.

While I do not think that this guy was deceived, I do think that the practice of searching for hidden meaning in the scriptures has gone a little too far. It is borderline demonic and very similar to what Satan does to Jesus in Luke 4:9-10. This is a tactic of deceiving spirits. In Luke 4 Satan attempts to convince Jesus into doing his will based on his bad interpretation of scripture. He does the same to Eve in Genesis 3 when he asked her about God's instructions regarding the Tree of the Knowledge of Good and Evil. He says to her, *"Did God say that you should not eat of EVERY tree of the garden"* (Gen. 3:1). No, He did not say she could not eat of "every tree" in the garden, He only told her not to eat from the "one tree"! Her disobedience caused the death of mankind and if Jesus would have jumped from the temple He would have died as well and mankind would have died again!

What I also want to point out about this passage is the way Satan eludes to the supernatural. Throw yourself down and "angels" will save you. The religious spirit does this same type scripture twisting. Accept it uses the scriptures to convince people that God does not heal anymore or that God wants us to accept our death when it knocks as the door. Both of these spirits are deceptive and dangerous because they operate in religious circles. They operate in both the supernatural community and the conservative community, but they both have one agenda in mind—the death of your ministry, the death of your finances, the death of your soul, and the death of your body.

In all that I shared in this chapter, the one thing that I want you to know is that these two can only deceive those who are not watching and those who do not rely on the scriptures as the final authority. Last for the one-thousandth time, remember that *"The spirit of prophecy is THE TESTIMONY OF JESUS AS THE CHRIST!"*

Section 3
The Tools

Chapter Seven
Elements of Hearing

This is where we get into the heart of the subject of hearing God's voice. This will be the most important chapter in this book. Everything about hearing the voice of God, hinges on the concepts that I introduce in this chapter.

This chapter is going to challenge you in ways that will ask you to stretch your faith. It will call for a type of maturity that if obtained will release God's riches into your life. However, in all honesty, I find very few people who can smoothly incorporate these ideas into their lives. You may be saying to yourself, what kind of ideas are these? They are not new ideas. They are ideas that are so profound that most people find it very difficult to grasp. Likewise most preachers find them difficult to explain.

I can tell you this however, if you are willing to allow these two simple but complex ideas to take root in your life, you will have encounters with God that will blow your mind! You need to know that God is looking for someone before whom He may show Himself strong (see 2 Chron. 16:9). That someone could be you, and that someone should be you.

Stillness

I am going to start with the hardest concept to explain and work my way backwards. The concept that I have found to be the most difficult to explain and apply is "stillness". Stillness has two meanings. First it means that we position ourselves in such a way that we give God room to do what He wants to do.

The Bible says, *"Let Your will be done on Earth as it is in Heaven"* (Matt. 16:10). For most people this operates backwards. They make plans on Earth and then pray that Heaven will come into alignment with it eventually. When their plan is unsuccessful then it is customary to blame the failure of the plan on the devil. However, the Bible says that when we get a hold of God's plan and then execute it in the Earth, that the gates of hell cannot prevail against our works (see Matt. 16:18).

Stillness is our ability and responsibility to find out what the plan of Heaven is "before" we move forward. It is being in the place of dependency on God. It means that we have come to recognize our own limitations and are willing to acknowledge that He is limitless.

I cannot tell you how many people I have encountered that struggle unnecessarily because they are trying to help God fix a situation. There are a number of people who will leave their jobs because of turmoil and jump into a worst situation. I have seen the same in marriages. This kind of problem indicates that a person does not or will not practice the principle of stillness.

Hearing God is all about stillness. You cannot expect that God will be able to speak to you if you are never willing to give up the throne of your life. To really develop a true sense of intimacy with God you will have to do more than just call Him Lord. You will have to move into a place where you intentionally give Him the place of leadership. He must be the King in the realm of your life.

You may be saying, wow you sure are making a big deal about this! Yes, I am, and I can see why the scriptures say that not many noble and not many wise according to this world are called (see 1 Cor. 1:26). We know that it is His desire for all men to be saved, but this particular group has bewitched themselves into thinking that they are more intelligent than God. They have not come to the place of realizing their own nakedness and poverty. They are in their minds already full.

Understanding our lack is essential to hearing the voice of God. Have you ever noticed that the first four groups mentioned in the be-attitudes are those who are spiritually impoverished—those who are in need? We can even see this idea of lack in James 1:5. It declares that it is an attitude of lack that opens the mouth to God. It says "if we *lack* wisdom, we should ask for it and God freely gives it to those who come to him empty!" We must come to understand that God pours into empty vessels. If you can admit to God your own lack then God will fill you with His wisdom.

Paul in 2 Corinthians says that God allowed Him a buffer from Satan because of the abundance of revelations he was receiving. Then he provides us with a great truth about seeing the power of God active in our lives. He says, *"For this thing I pleaded with the Lord to take it away, but God said, My grace is sufficient for you. **For in weakness My strength is made perfect.*** Paul then says, *"I will glory or celebrate in my weakness that I may see God's power"* (2 Cor. 12:8-10). Paul has learned the power is stillness. He learned how to open God's hand and mouth by accepting a position and attitude of lack.

Stillness also, produces the conditions whereby we can hear the voice of God clearly. To hear the voice of God clearly you first must acknowledge your weakness and position yourself for bringing Heaven to Earth.

The second meaning for stillness is not an attitude but more of an action. It is learning to quiet your inner world. This actually becomes very easy to do if you can accept the first part of this truth that encourages an attitude of lack.

Your mind is a battlefield for voices. I know many would like to believe that God speaks to the inner man. This is just our desire to appear as deep, but the Bible is clear that spirits do warfare and communicate with our minds. Some have assumed that because the Bible specifically mentions the mind as the place that Satan attacks in 2 Corinthians 10:3-5, that the mind is a source of evil. In the latter chapters of this book I will explain the interaction between the mind and the spirit.

The Bible is just as clear in communicating that God wants to speak to our minds as well. Ephesians 1:17-18 says that Paul prayed for the Ephesians that the *"Jesus Christ would give to you the spirit of wisdom and revelation in the knowledge of Him, that they may know Him and that the eyes of their understanding would be enlightened."*

Not only does this passage support this idea, but we are also encouraged to "be renewed in the SPIRIT of our MIND" (Eph. 4:23). We are further commanded "renew in our minds that we may be able to recognize the good, acceptable, and perfect will of God" (see Rom. 12:2). I go further into detail on this subject in a latter chapter.

Your mind and your mental state are absolutely imperative to your ability to receive the spirit of wisdom and revelation. A wayward un-policed thought life is a sure way to find your self asking—is that God or is that me.

Wind and Waves Be Still

There is a popular story in the scriptures that I think helps to illustrate for us the power of stillness. In this story Jesus shows us the attitude and action of "stillness".

Jesus and the disciples were sailing to the other side of the sea when a great storm arose. The Bible says that the wind and the waves tossed the boat violently around in the water. While this raging storm was occurring, Jesus was in the lower part of the boat sleeping. After some time passes the disciples awaken Him in a panic and asked Him a question. They said, "Why are you sleeping, do you not care that we are about to die?" Jesus then responded by rebuking the winds and waves with a three small words— Peace Be Still (Mark 4:35-40).

What does this have to do with the mind? Everything! This story presents us with a few comparisons that are worth exploring. They present us with a very clear example of the power of stillness and hearing the voice of God.

First, we can see that both the disciples and Jesus were in the midst of a great storm, but only Jesus managed His turmoil differently. The disciples were in the storm working to save their own lives, while Jesus was in the storm resting. An observation of the text shows us that the obstacles and challenges facing the disciples were so overwhelming that they started "thinking" about what they should do to save themselves from destruction. Jesus however, did not take this approach even though we can see that He was caught in the midst of the very same storm. He somehow found the strength to rest when everyone else was restless. In the midst of clamor and chaos He shows us that His mind was "still".

How is it that they were all a part of the same storm but reacted differently to the same set of circumstances? Why are there some Christians who can go through absolute chaos on their jobs, family, homes, etc. peacefully while others completely unravel under the same pressure? The answer is "stillness".

When we allow ourselves to believe that God has only the best intentions for our lives then we can be like Jesus. He knew that His Father wanted Him to go to the other side. He knew heaven's plan and it produced in Him the ability to rest even though the situation was stressful.

The Bible says that Jesus only did what He heard and saw the Father saying and doing (see John 5:19). Even though the text does not say this, I believe that while He was sleeping God was giving Him directions for how He was to address this situation. This is a perfect illustration of stillness.

Stilling the mind is not emptying the mind, but it is bringing it into the heavenly reality of our Father's concern for our well-being. This is not a New Age Mystic concept but a biblical concept of looking to God for our resolve.

A Man After My Own Heart

The Bible is filled with other examples of stillness such as Numbers 9:8 when we see Moses say I will not make a decision without the counsel of God. Habakkuk 2:1, likewise, says I am going to wait to see what He will answer me.

We can even see stillness in the structure of the trinity. Genesis 1:2 says, *"For the Spirit of God hovered over the face of the waters, and the Lord said let there be light and there was."* We can see that within the Godhead that the

Spirit of God was waiting until He got the word to begin creating.

The greatest human example of stillness in my opinion is seen in the person of David. Many have heard it preached that David was a man after God's own heart (see 1 Sam. 13:14). I have heard many different interpretations of that passage. Some preachers and praise and worship leaders use it to teach that it was David's praise that God loved so much. While God certainly loves praise, I believe it was something even more valuable than David's praise that captured God's attention.

I believe it was David's unique ability to be still before God. It was the fact that he cared so deeply about what was in the heart of his Creator. David always and I do mean always sought to bring the vision of Heaven into the Earth.

David is an example of how we should approach our relationship with God. Just read through 1st and 2nd Samuel. You will see that David never assumed anything. Even when he was in situations where his next move seemed obvious, he honored God by seeking His counsel.

One such example occurs in 2 Samuel 24:14-18. David had been under attack by his former employer, King Saul, who was jealous of David's sudden success. The intensity of the attempts on David's life forces him to take shelter with Israel's enemy who is oppressing God's chosen people. The situation is so dire that when the King of the oppressive nation decides to go war with Israel, David lines up with them to fight against his own people. The kings comrades, however, see David as more of a threat and he is dismissed from the nation altogether.

When David and his men return to their camp they find that a band of raiders has taken their personal possessions, their women, and children. This unimaginable event understandably breaks the hearts of David's followers, and causes them such mental and emotional anguish that they decide that David should die. With all that was happening in the story, it seemed pretty apparent that if David wanted his stuff back then he should go and get it. This is how most of us would have approached this situation as well.

120

This however, is not David's attitude. He does not assume anything for himself, instead he turns to God for how *"and if"* he should respond. You will see this pattern over and over in the life of David. The one time he did not seek God's counsel is noted in his failure of impregnating a married woman named Bathsheba.

There is a stark contrast to this idea in the book of Joshua. In Joshua 9:1-27, Joshua is confronted by a band of servants that he thinks has come from a far place. It goes on to say that he enters into a covenant with them, but not before the passage says, *"But Joshua did not seek the counsel of the Lord."* This hasty decision on his part had costly consequences. His ability to obey all that God had commanded him was impeded by his rashness.

After making this decision it comes to pass that he discovers that these are not servants at all. They are kings of the land that Israel was supposed to destroy. The result was that Israel had to live with their enemies among them. And their gods eventually became a snare to God's people. All of this could have been avoided if Joshua had just stood still to find out what Heaven had in mind for this situation.

How many of you can relate to this situation? How many of you would be willing to acknowledge that most of your failures are at your own doing. Our failures occur because we have not learned to be poor in spirit. This is why not many noble, rich, and wise are called. Many of us make the assumption, that we can solve our own problems out of our wealth of resources. Those resources may be our strength, our money, our reputation and prestige, or any number of things that we exalt as our own ability to fix our own problems. But we need to realize that it is poverty of spirit that allows us to still ourselves within.

A Personal Example

Here is a personal example of stillness. It was the start of the 2015 Christmas season and I was seeking God in prayer. As I sought Him He spoke to me regarding purchasing a gift for someone less fortunate. At that time I had made the mistake of making Christmas all about my family. That being the case, His birthday became about my children. So I sought God in prayer for direction in finding a recipient. During our discussion He showed me a simple mental picture of a pink girl's coat. He said to take $50 and go to Marshall's and purchase the coat in a size 10-12. Upon finishing our discussion I relayed that exact information to my wife. When she arrived at the store and found the coat she called me to describe it. It appeared from the description that we had found our coat. She said, "By the way it is the only pink coat left and it is a size 10-12." But when she brought it home and I laid eyes on it I knew with certainty that it was the coat. It was exactly as God had shown it to me in the vision.

The next step was to get it to someone in need. Then it occurred to me that if God spent that much time to save a specific coat for a specific gender in a specific size, then He had a specific person in mind. Who was the question! This is where stillness is so valuable. My understanding of the coat was that it was meant to be a Christmas gift. Therefore I assumed God would show me the person by the time Christmas came around. But Christmas came and went. One week passed and we were entering into the second week past Christmas. I was wondering who the coat belonged to and my wife was starting to think I had missed God. I had passed up opportunities such as coat donation drives, a little girl who lost all of her clothing in a fire, and a woman who expressed the need for such a thing. I had many opportunities to give this coat away, but God had not shown me or released me to do so. I was being still until I received further instructions.

Then two weeks after Christmas my wife brought over a family member in a not-so desirable situation. While the girl was visiting, my wife started to express her frustrations about the girl's dire situation. One of the things she reported was that the girl had received nothing for Christmas. This was hard for us to digest, because she was the only one of her siblings that received no gift. The girl lives with her birth father and mother and three half siblings. And due to her father and mother being financially impoverished they could not afford to buy gifts for any of the children. The other children however received gifts from their birth fathers and their family. That meant that this young girl was the only child in the house that did not receive a gift.

One of the other things that came up in my discussion with my wife was that this young girl had come to the house without coat. Not because she forgot to bring one, but because she did not own one. I live in Maryland and this occurred in January. It gets really, really cold in Maryland in January. It was enough to break our hearts that she was the only child of four that did not receive a gift. But to know that she did not have a coat at the coldest time of the year crossed a line in our hearts. Then it occurred to me to inquire regarding her current coat size. My wife said, "Oh she's a big girl. That coat won't fit her". Then I said, "Have her try it on anyway". To our surprise the coat was a perfect fit. It was cut bigger than normal so what should have been too small, fit just right!. As she put the coat on a huge smile came over her face. God had made sure to keep her in mind and provided a coat for her as a Christmas gift from Him.

What if I had rushed to judgment regarding what to do with the coat? What if I had yielded the pressure in my own mind to give this coat to the many other valid opportunities that presented themselves? If I were not practicing stillness this young girl would have had a terrible Christmas. This is the value of knowing God as a commander. We never know how the decisions we make affect the lives of others. For this reason I encourage you let your actions take a back seat to your hearing so that you will be able to maximize God's intentions in any given situation in your life.

Expectation

Another really important element to embrace as you start your journey into learning to hear the voice of God is expectation. Expectation is the ability to look for something with a desired effect. If I had to compare expectation to something I would compare it to a dog that sees his owner coming up the street.

If you have a pet, a dog specifically, you know that once it senses that its owner is near, it will run back and forth between the front door and the window looking for the master. It is all done with such enthusiasm. We see this as the dog stands up in the window one second, get down runs in circles and then runs back to the window hoping to see its owner.

A similar scene is imagined in the child that has a promise from his dad to take him fishing. Just imagine with me this scenario. Imagine this little boy packing his lunch and preparing his fishing pole. Imagine him now going out the front door and setting his stuff on the curb. Now see him sitting on the curb going back and forth between looking down the street for his father's car and then back to the curb. One hour later he is still looking. Two hours later he is still looking. Then suddenly in the distance he sees two bright lights coming towards him. His little heart pounds faster and faster with excitement. Then the car passes by. He is a little disappointed but he is still hopeful. So He goes back to looking down the street for his father, and again he sees two headlights in the distance. As they get closer he can plainly see that it is his father. His heart's desire has been satisfied.

The story above is a great depiction of how to hear from God with expectation. Expectation is an element of faith, for *"Faith is the substance of things hoped for* or expected" (Heb. 11:1). You cannot think that you will just wake up one day and hear His voice. His voice is for those that are expecting to hear Him speaking. It is for those who are waiting and saying speak Lord for your servant hears.

The little boy in our story did some key things that show us how we should demonstrate our expectation to God.

The first thing I want to point out is that he prepared himself to be in a position to get what he was hoping to receive. Moses rose early every morning to meet with God at the tabernacle. The important thing is not that He sought God in the morning, although this is a good thing, but that he made preparations for God to speak to him. Moses met with God every morning because he was expecting God to speak to him. This action defines the latter part of Hebrews 11:2, *"...the substance of things hoped for."* Expectation is manifested in our preparations.

Next we see one of the most evident aspects of demonstrating expectation. That is the act of looking. If we want to hear the voice of God we must get in the habit of looking for God to speak to us.

The dog in our illustration above was waiting for his master by looking for him. We see the same with the young boy in our second illustration. He went back and forth between the curb and the street looking for his father.

Finally, our best example of expectation in the scriptures come from Samuel. Most people never consider why Samuel was so unsuccessful in recognizing the voice of God. We know that one obvious reason presented in the story was that Samuel did not yet know the Lord. (see I Sam. 3:1-10) But there was a more inconspicuous reason looming in the story. It is that of expectation or the lack there of.

It had not yet been communicated to Samuel that God would speak to Him and so he neglected to "look" for God to speak to him. Most people are same way. Most people do not pray and listen for God to speak because they are not really expecting to hear from God. Sometimes people don't pray at all because they do not expect God to answer their prayer. We see this lack of expectation in Samuel's story.

Notice that Samuel did not recognize and respond to the voice of God until Eli told Him that He should expect to hear God's voice. He said to Samuel, "When He calls you must say…" Notice the word *"when"* which is an indicator that the young man should live with an expectation toward hearing from God. The next time God called young Samuel he heard and responded because he was looking and expecting to hear.

You have to do the same if you are going to hear from God. After you make the preparation to hear, you need to start looking. Habakkuk in chapter 2 verse 1, says *"I will LOOK and SEE what He will say to me."* We can also see an example of looking for God in Numbers 9:8. It reads *"And Moses said be still that I may hear what the Lord will say concerning you."* Moses made the preparation, practiced stillness, and then he waited and looked for God to speak to him in the situation.

You should follow the examples of these great men. When you go to bed, look to have a dream or vision. If you do not get a dream or vision get up early and when you pray close your eyes and look for a vision. If you do not get one go throughout your day with your mind stayed on him and look for vision or listen for an answer in the thoughts of your heart. If that does not happen get a topical Bible and research the subject. But whatever you do, do not stop looking for an answer. This is what "looking" looks like for those of us who hear from God. We have learned to look and see.

125

If you are worried about how you will know that it is God that spoke to you, read the rest of the book. I have covered everything you need to know to look safely.

Finally, this little boy knew the character of his father. His father made him a promise and that is why he was looking for him. You should know that you have a promise from God as well. Your heavenly Father has also made a promise to speak to you. In Jeremiah 33:3, God says, *"Call to Me AND I WILL ANSWER and SHOW you great and mighty things which you do not know."*

Jeremiah sums it all up in this verse. 'Call to me' is what God expects of you. If you do, He will give you knowledge and wisdom. However, remember, to be in the position to hear you need to acknowledge your own spiritual poverty. The only people who do not expect to hear from God are the proud who say to themselves, I already know that!

If asked the secret to my insight I would tell you that it comes from my willingness to say to God, I don't know. It is because I know that I don't know, that He gives me answers. But He gives them to me because I "ask" for them!

I pray that I have been able to adequately explain these two foundational principles. I cannot emphasize their importance enough. You must learn to be still to know that He is God. It is your stillness that gives you access to the knowing within you. Likewise you must master expectation if you are to receive what He wants to say. The will of God becomes evident as we learn stillness.

Chapter Eight
Hindrances to Hearing

As you take on this journey into the world of hearing and seeing the voice of God you will have seasons where it seems as though you are not able to hear from God. But is God ever really silent, as it has been suggested by some theologians referring to the era when there was no open revelation between Malachi and Matthew.

Even when you look in 1 Samuel the Bible describes a time in which it refers to as having "no widespread revelation". So what makes such a thing possible? The Bible clearly demonstrates to us that God speaks. So what would make Him stop speaking? I would like to suggest that God does not stop speaking, but we stop listening or positioning ourselves to hear.

This chapter explores the various ways that I have found in the scripture that hinder our ability to hear from God.

We Do Not Recognize God's Voice

Imagine that you are a choir member who served faithfully for 20 years. Now imagine that you have just closed out a rehearsal session and the only people left in the building are you and the pastor. While you are busy gathering your things to go home you suddenly hear your name. So you run to the pastoral office and say, "yes, Pastor, what do you need?" The pastor looks at you with a puzzled look and says, "I didn't call you". You say, "Ok" and return to gather your things. Then again you hear a voice calling your name. So you return to the pastor and again he says, "I didn't call you". So you gather your things and you hear it again but this time you ignore it and leave.

This illustration, sums up the gist of the story in 1 Samuel, accept Samuel had a spiritual leader who was sensitive to the voice of the Lord. Some people find it hard to hear from God because of two reasons. One, they are not being properly mentored to recognize the voice of God. They may also be in ministries where the voice of God is not taught. Or sometimes leaders are not properly equipped to communicate the subject in an effective enough way that satisfies the student's curiosity. A lot times leaders use the "you just know" line as a principle.

Number two; improper mentoring leads to people serving or ministering before God that do not know Him. Please do not misunderstand my point. I am not referring to salvation. It is possible to be saved and not know God intimately. In fact, there are whole denominations filled with great spiritual teachers that do not believe that God speaks at all. These people are just as Samuel, ministering to God faithfully, but ignorant to the reality of His voice.

The first step to engaging God is to recognize that those who come to God must first believe that He is and that He is a rewarder of those who diligently "seek" Him (Heb. 11:6).

Being Double Minded

Doubt is another really big hindrance to hearing the voice of God. What is doubt? The word doubt means to have two minds. In other words doubt is double mindedness. Anytime you are struggling with doubt you are really struggling with seeing a situations two ways. For example we know that the Bible says that God speaks and that is one line of thought, but somehow we also believe that God does not speak. This is where our struggles manifest in our life. The word of God says one thing but your mind says another. The Bible says in James the result of this will be an inability to receive from God.

I use to read James 1:5 and interpret it the way most people do. I always read it to say that if a man wants wisdom from God that he only needs to ask and God would freely give it except in the case of the double-minded man. But upon really reading the verse I found that it actually implies that if you need to hear from God you only need to ask and *"He freely gives to all without reproach"*. It then says, *"But let him ask in faith doubting nothing for let not a double-minded man think that he will be able to receive anything."*

Just in case you do not see what I am saying, consider this illustration. When a quarterback has released the ball to an intended receiver it is already given to that receiver. It now becomes the responsibility of the receiver to catch what he was given the opportunity to receive. The same thing is happening in this verse. It says that God freely throws out the ball, but you must receive it. It is up to you to accept that God has spoken the answer to you. The problem most people have is that they are unwilling to accept and believe that they are the intended receiver. Most people fumble the ball because they are saying to themselves things such as "God wouldn't say that" or "maybe that wasn't God" or "God doesn't speak anymore" or "That's just my imagination".

This passage shows us that God freely gives his answer to us—we however, are not always willing to accept that answer.

A biblical example can be found in Matthew 14:22-23. In this popular story we can see that the disciples are on a boat that has been caught in a storm. While they are battling to row to safety they see Jesus walking towards them on the water and become afraid supposing it to be ghost. Then Jesus speaks to them and eventually Peter is allowed to go to Jesus walking on the water.

The interesting part of the story is that Peter was capable of walking on the water as long as He kept thinking on the word "come." But somewhere along the way he allowed the winds and the waves to change his mind and he began to sink. Then Jesus says to him, "Peter why did you doubt?" As if to say, "Why did you think again? Why did you accept another mind? I told you to come, so why did you think about my command to you another way?"

Peter was not alone, there are other biblical examples of doubt and how it affects our relationship with God. For example, Adam and Eve demonstrated doubt when they were speaking to the serpent. God gave them one way to see the Tree of the Knowledge of Good and Evil in the garden. Then the serpent presented to them another perspective that resulted in the downfall of their relationship with God.

Saul is another example when he is given the command to destroy the king of the Amalekites, his people, and all living things. He was given God's mind on the situation but he developed a second mind that said to keep the best of the sheep and oxen. This cost him his already strained relationship with God. God stopped speaking to him after this event and even replaced his anointing with a demon! (see 1 Sam. 15:1-35)

I bet you never thought about this as doubt. Most people see this passage as relating only to Saul's disobedience—and it does is part have to do with disobedience. But his disobedience is directly related to the second mind (idea) that he allowed to trump God's initial idea. It is a depiction of doubt!

So we can see that doubt, when it comes to the voice of God, is not about whether or not He will speak to you. If you ask Him a question He will give you an answer. The real question is are you going to receive what he has to say or are you going to allow another mind to steal his answer from your heart like we see in the parable of the sower and the seed (see Matt.14:12).

A Disobedient Lifestyle

One sure way to find yourself in a silent period is continued disobedience. We touched on this a little in our discussion on doubt when we referred to the story of Saul. Doubt will often lead to disobedience that can be innocent. Or it can lead to blatant disobedience.

Some people struggle with doubt because their faith just needs to be matured to a place where they trust God with their lives. This sounds strange but we can see this in the scriptures when we look at Israel's liberation from Egypt. They struggled to trust God because they were just getting to know God. Even the great Moses struggled to believe that the creator of the mouth could use him in spite of his speech impediment. These are instances that I consider to be innocent doubt due to lack of knowledge. The Bible says, "By

FAITH we UNDERSTAND..." (Heb. 11:3). Often when we have doubt we lack understanding.

Someone once used an illustration of a chair to demonstrate the idea of faith. The preacher went on to say that we sit in our chairs in faith. He also said that we do not know that the chair is going to hold us yet we sit in it anyway. He said that this was an example of faith. Well, that's just not true. We sit on chairs by faith because we understand some basic laws of physics. We know that 4 evenly spaced legs with a seat parallel to the floor equals balance. It is this understanding that makes us leery of standing on something such as a pogo stick or ladder.

By faith we *"understand"*. To resolve doubt and build faith you need to get an understanding of the subject you are struggling to overcome. Faith comes by hearing and hearing by the word of God.

Then there is blatant doubt that leads to blatant disobedience. Such was the case with Pharaoh, who in spite of clear evidence of a much stronger God, refused to comply with God's command. He was living in the kind of doubt that made him belligerent and it resulted in the worst imaginable outcome for his life and the lives of his loved ones.

Roman 1:28 says there is a group of persons whom resisted God's mind to the point that He just turned them over to their own mind. We call this reprobate.

A similar example is found in Daniel 4:12-23 when Nebuchadnezzar's disobedience resulted in him not only having the voice of God silenced in his life, but he also lost his mind.

The best example of this principle can be found in 1 Kings 19:12, the story of Elijah on at Mount Horeb. This story has been the base teaching for years for describing the voice of God as a "still small voice." However, if you really read and examine the story you will see that the sound of a still small voice is really a depiction of Elijah's disobedience.

131

In 1 Kings 19:12 you will find that there are three distinct terms used to describe Elijah's experience with the voice of God. They are "the word of the Lord", "a still small voice", and "sudden a voice".

In this passage we are presented with a scared and tired Elijah who has just received a threat against his life from Queen Jezebel. The threat takes place on the heels of one of the greatest demonstrations of God's power mentioned in the scriptures. Elijah now tired, fears for his life and seeks refuge in a cave. While he is in hiding he suddenly comes into an awareness of God speaking to him. This can be described as spontaneous thoughts that come to mind. It is also possible that it was a dream based on our understanding of how God speaks to prophets presented in Number 12:6-8. During this initial encounter God questions him as to why he is there. God also instructed him to go to the entrance of the cave. Elijah however, remains where he is. This is where we can see his disobedience. Everything else that follows happens on the heels of this information.

While he is in his disobedience, the Lord passes by the front of the cave and he sees at the entrance various experiences. One of these experiences was described as "a still small voice" for which we are not given any content. It was at this moment that Elijah obeyed God's initial instructions and went to the front of the cave. Upon arriving at the place he was initially commanded to be, he heard a voice whose content was identical to the "word of the Lord" which came to him in the cave. The still small voice which he heard while he was in his disobedience was now a clear audible voice, whose content was distinguishable.

What I am hoping is evident is the progression within the story. One, Elijah perceives that he needs to go to the front of the cave. Two, God is saying something that can only be described as a whisper. And three, as Elijah gets closer to where is supposed to be, he realizes that it is God speaking to him.

Hopefully, you can see how continued and/or blatant disobedience can cause quite the strain on your relationship with God. Hearing the voice of God and walking in fellowship with Him requires obedience.

Dulling of the Senses Through Lack of Exercise

Your spiritual senses can become dull. Hebrews 5:14 says: *But solid food belongs to those who are of full age, that is, those who by reason of use have their senses exercised to discern both good and evil.*

The earlier part of this passage says, *"...since you have become DULL of hearing."* And Matthew 15:13-15 says, *"For the heart of this people has grown DULL. Their ears are HARD of HEARING and their EYES they have closed..."*

I think it is important to note that these passages indicate that we have *"senses"* that get dull, not a *"sense"* that gets dull. It is also important to note that it does not say that these senses are totally deaf and/or blind, just dull. This tells us that there is some level of hearing and sight but not enough to discern a clear message or direction—a whispering still small voice.

So what causes dullness of the senses? Two things can cause dullness, disobedience and lack of exercise. Either one of these can result in a feeling where the voice of God seems far away.

In the previous section under #3, dullness of the senses, we discussed how Elijah's disobedience produced a dulling of the voice of God. His description of the still small voice was no more than another way of saying God I hear you saying something, I just don't know exactly what you're saying. Everyone with kids understands what I am saying. I often task my kids with assignments and sometimes I deceive myself into thinking I can scream my instructions over top of the sounds of the 3 other kids, two televisions and other sounds. It usually happens that if I really want them to understand the details of my instructions, that I must call them close and tell them face-to-face.

The same is true with God. He wants you to be close so that His instructions don't appear as a muffled whisper that you have to strain to hear. You can hear the voice of God clearly. I discuss this in detail in my book, *You Can Hear the Voice of God Clearly.*

The other way to dull the senses is simply an issue of lack of use. I can remember a time is my life when weight lifting was a very big part of my life. I would go into the gym for 2 hours at end of each workday. After some time I began to notice that my body was changing. It was adapting to the stress of the weight by building more muscle and toning the muscle that was already there. It felt and looked great. But I noticed that if I spent enough time away from the gym, that I was unable to perform at the same level. I was actually getting weaker and loosing muscle stamina.

Sometimes this happens to us spiritually as well. I am a witness that you can become so busy with life and the responsibilities that God has given you that you can inadvertently forget to spend the necessary time with God. Praying without ceasing becomes praying when needed. Likewise waiting before him just doesn't seem to fit in your schedule.

Seeking the face of God was easy when I was single. My first three years of seeking God, I spent every day and all day in my room with Him. I would come home from work, go in my room, and would not come out until the next day. One day I prayed for 8 straight hours.

Then I got married and had children and things got real tricky. This was definitely the case as my kids got older and became involved in school events and extra-curricular activities. This posed a great challenge to me and before I knew it I was giving God my spare time. This resulted in a dulling of my senses.

The beautiful part is that you can sharpen those senses again. If the dullness is a result of disobedience like Elijah, then you need to repent and start walking in obedience. Once Elijah got into position he heard the voice of God clearly again.

And if you are experiencing dullness due to lack of exercise, then you will need to re-purpose your day to accommodate time for God. Later in chapter 14 I discuss how to walk in the continued presence of God. One reason so many find it hard to make time for God is that we set times such as morning and before bed as prayer time. The solution to dullness is learning that you can walk in a continued consciousness of God's presence and prayer and worship can take place anywhere all day, every day.

Lack of Time in the Word

A very important issue to address in this chapter is a lack of time and or knowledge of the word. Investing time to learn what is in the Bible is absolutely critical to our ability to hear from God. I would dare to say that it is the basis from which all else will flow.

At one point in the development of my relationship with God I got so comfortable with hearing the voice of God that I actually began to neglect time in His word. As time went on I began to notice that God was not speaking to me as frequently as I was used to hearing. So I asked Him why He was silent. When He spoke, He instructed me to pick up my Bible and turn it to the side. When I did He said, "The covers of this Bible are My lips and the pages are My tongue. If you want to hear Me speak you only need to open the pages. I am always full of things to say within My word." This set the tone for the rest of our relationship, because God never speaks to me that much during my study time. Even the principles in this book are not the product of my study time in the word. When I read the Bible I am merely taking in information and studying the people, background and culture etc. But it is what happens after the reading and study time that is so important. Anywhere and everywhere, the Spirit of God brings the information together and presents a coherent teaching from all the scriptures gathered through my time of study.

It is very important that you understand that you cannot expect to confidently hear and obey God if you don't know what His overall will is for a particular area. The Bible is your first line of defense in discerning the voice of God. It is His revealed will and should be respected as such.

I remember once a friend of mine told me that God told her I was going to co-sign on a car for her. What she didn't know was that the night before God gave me Proverbs. 6:1 which states that you should not become surety (co-borrower) for any man. What if I didn't know the scriptures? I could have been deceived. She was more seasoned in the prophetic and I respected her as an instrument of God. I don't think she was trying to deceive me but she was obviously deceived herself.

Having a good knowledge of the word has also been very important and instrumental in getting me a promotion. My boss at the time was an elderly man who did not understand the promotion process. I had been working in an office for two years with two other employees. One was my supervisor and another employee that was my equal. We were all doing the same level work but my pay scale was one grade lower and it did not provide the option for me to earn what my counterparts were making. So I respectfully brought it to my supervisor's attention. He responded by saying let's wait, so that you can have my position when I retire. *(I'm writing this is five years after the promotion and he still had not retired!)* This was not the answer I wanted to hear and I really wanted to take it to the next level supervisor for resolution. Why didn't I? Because I know what the scriptures say about authority. I also knew that it was not the revealed will of God for me to usurp my authority.

Some time went by and I left it in the hands of God. After a while our office was re-organized and I was placed under the authority of a new boss. I sensed that God wanted me to pursue the issue with the new boss, which I did. He saw what was happening and understood it to be unfair, so he initiated a review process and worked out the promotion. One month after the promotion I was re-assigned back under my original boss. God literally moved my boss out of the way, did what He purposed to do, and then put me back and the whole time I didn't have to disobey the word to get what He wanted me to have.

Not only has He used His word to guide me in these types of miracles, but He often uses His word in my life in a very practical way. Often when my wife gets on my nerves I talk to God about what is happening, how I feel, and how I am planning to respond. This always prompts a scripture response from God such as "get the beam out of your eye before you attempt to get the splinter out of hers." I cannot tell you how many arguments I have avoided just by hearing God speaking scriptures to my heart. One of His other favorite verses that He spoke early in my marriage was Proverbs 3:1, *"Harsh words stir up anger, but a soft answer turns away wrath."*

136

I know the idea of God speaking in scriptures is not the most exciting thing in the world. I also understand that everyone wants to hear God speak his or her name or see glorious visions, and that might happen. I've had many such experiences, some of which I cannot begin to share. But there is no better foundation than that of the written word of God.

It is His word that protects you from deceiving spirits. I remember an instance when a guy, who called himself a prophet, deceived a female friend of mine. One day he told her that God had spoken to him that she was his wife. The problem with what he told her was that it was in direct conflict with the word. Why? She was already married! But in spite of the fact that this was a clear violation of the word she entered into an inappropriate relationship with this so-called prophet. She placed more value on his supernatural words of knowledge than she did the word of God. I wish I could tell you that this was the only time I've seen this type of thing happen. But it is not. I've seen many mistakes by people who placed an experience with the supernatural over the word of God. I have nothing against the supernatural; I've had enough supernatural encounters to write a book on those experiences alone. Nonetheless, we cannot allow these experiences to have a greater value than God's revealed will.

Again I say, if you are going to become proficient in hearing and following the rhema word of God, you will have to make His written word the primary source by which you weigh all voices. His word is so powerful as a foundation that the Bible says in Hebrews 11:3, we understand that the worlds were framed by the word of God. This foundation is sure to protect you from unnecessary pain.

Even in the course of writing this book I have heard God speaking scriptures to make His points. In fact, this point was not in the original layout for this chapter of the book. Once the Spirit of God spoke to me to add this point, I said Lord what scripture will I use. Immediately he brought to my mind John 14:26, *He will bring to your remembrance all things I said to you.* The implication is that He cannot bring back to your remembrance a word that you never read.

This passage communicates to us the very importance of study, reading, and meditation of His word. It is a very critical part of your development in learning to hear God's voice.

Faltering Between Opinions

This last one is particularly interesting to me. It came to me as an idea that God wanted to address. As I was taking out the trash one day, I asked Him what else needed to be included in this chapter. His response was, "Faulting between two opinions." Then He gave me the following:

"How long will you falter between two opinions? If God is God serve Him, and if Baal is god, then serve him" (I Kings 18:21).

Anytime there are multiple ideas put forth by religious factions seemingly at war with each other over the word of God, you can expect that it will stifle the hearing of young developing Christians. Today we have a war going on between the Evangelicals and the Charismatic groups. One group denies the validity of the supernatural and pursues the word of God for its practical value, while the other pursues the supernatural value of the scriptures.

Paul faced a similar problem in his day. *What I mean is this: One of you says, "I follow Paul"; another, "I follow Apollos"; another, "I follow Cephas"; still another, "I follow Christ." Is Christ divided? Was Paul crucified for you? Were you baptized in the name of Paul? I thank God that I did not baptize any of you except Crispus and Gaius, no one can say that you were baptized in my name. (1Corinthians 1:12-15)*

The Corinthians were forming groups and arguing about religious practices. Paul then corrected them regarding the value of the group. From his correction to them we got a great principle—the principle of one plants and another waters but God gives the increase (1 Corinthians 3:7).

Paul stresses to them that even though they are from the same source, they may find that you do not perform the same function. But at the end of the day it is God at work in both!

The same applies to the Evangelicals and the Charismatics groups. Just because they are used differently and have two opposing perspectives on how to approach life, doesn't mean that either is missing God. These types of unnecessary arguments provide great fuel to the enemy's camp. For Jesus said how can a house divided stand.

This ongoing feud communicates to me that neither group really understands the complexity that is the Church.

When I started this project my constant prayer to the Lord was, please help me to write this in such a way that I can show that You are both supernatural and practical.

I have in my twenty years plus experience, noticed that Evangelicals have great practical teaching. They teach on everyday subjects such as managing your finances and how to behave in the work place. Practical ways of meeting real needs. However I have often said that if I get sick in the Evangelical circle that I am are likely to die, because they lack any real understanding of how the supernatural works.

In contrast, the Charismatics seem almost fanatical about seeing God do the supernatural in seemingly unnecessary situations. They like to teach on ideas such as, how to gain supernatural increase. How to see in the spirit? How to operate in the gifts or how to do warfare in the spirit? I know I won't die if I can get with a group of Charismatics. They pray until God does something. However, they are sometimes overwhelmingly impractical.

For example, a woman confronted me one day regarding being "spiritual". I apparently was not spiritual enough based on my view of money. She attempted to make herself more spiritual by listing her "spiritual qualifications". Interestingly among the things she listed was that she had not been sick in years and did not need to go to the doctor. It all sounded great, but was an example of over the top charismatic thinking. This is what I mean, when I say the two groups are different. One is practical the other is supernatural.

However different they are, they are both from God. What saddens me however, is the fact that neither is willing to see that together they perform a most necessary function within their own sphere of operation.

Paul says it this way. Are all workers of miracles? Are all healers, are all prophets (1 Corinthians 12:29). No. That is the simple answer for this dilemma. All are not, but "some" are. Those that are not seem to be driven to the practical while the others are drawn to the supernatural.

The Bible says that we can see the invisible nature of God in what may be seen (Rom. 1:20). One such example can be seen in the medical field.

Most people have a primary care physician. Sometimes during our visits we may find that an issue arises that requires special attention from a doctor that specializes in that particular area. And even though they both studied medicine, they rely on their areas of special knowledge to assist in helping cure a patient. They usually do not conflict with each other but respect the knowledge and expertise of the other.

Even though we can see this kind of cooperation in the natural, we don't readily see this as an example with spiritual significance. Why can't we see that it takes people with various specialties to heal a person who has been taken captive? We are co-labors with one another in Christ. In fact, the scriptures say that we are His body, and the hand cannot say to the foot I don't need you (I Cor. 12:21).

With such clear teaching on how our differences make us a stronger whole, how can we then persecute our differences? Why do we not understand that the doctors of the body of Christ, (Apostles, Prophets, Pastors, Evangelist, Teachers) all specialize in a specific area in which God makes them experts?

You would not expect such from your own doctor. You would not expect your primary care physician to be an Ear, Nose, Throat specialist, a heart surgeon, an Optometrist, and an Oncologist. Why? We all understand that the body is far too complex of a machine for one person to comprehensively understand it. Then why would you expect one man or group to have all the answers to a God whom the Bible refers to as having manifold (many-sided) wisdom? (Eph. 3:10)

As you seek to hear the voice of God, I encourage you to get a balanced understanding of God. You need the Chuck Swindoll's and Charles Stanley's, as well as the other great voices displayed on WAVA. These are God's great practical researchers and they have God given insight into God's practical nature. But you have to be reasonable. These great men cannot tell you about the anointing, because that is not their specialty. And I say that respectfully. God has used these men to ground me in solid foundational principles of salvation. I shall forever admire their work.

Likewise, you need your Creflo Dollars, John Beveres, Kenneth Hagins, T. D. Jakes, and the likes. These are God's specialists in the supernatural. They can teach you how to walk in healing and power. They can teach you how to survive harsh life moments when all you have is your faith. But I would not expect them (other than Bishop Jakes) to give you a 6-point plan for how to balance a checkbook. That's not to say that they don't know how to do a checkbook, but that's not where God has gifted them.

My point is that, we cannot afford to be between two opinions. We must seek the *"whole"* counsel of God. I consider myself neither Evangelical nor Charismatic. I attend a Full Gospel Baptist church but one of my favorite television programs is, Sid Roth's It's Supernatural. I know how to study the word and I also know how to open my spiritual eyes and ears to receive divine revelation. And again I encourage you to find intimacy with God and explore both.

The principles laid out in this book are good for testing any voices that you hear, regardless of how it is received. They work whether you hear from God directly or via a human vessel. You are required to test the spirits (1 John 4:1) and that's what these principles are designed to assist you in doing.

If you make a habit of discerning the voice of God you won't need to fear being deceived by either side.

Examples of Practical and Supernatural from the Scriptures

A great example that supports the idea of God's practical and supernatural nature comes from the ministry of Jesus. We can see Jesus casting out devils in many places in the scriptures. In one particular place it says He cast them out with a word (Matt. 8:16). In other words when Jesus addressed a situation with His word alone He was able to bring deliverance. James says that if we submit to God we can resist the devil and he will flee.

This is a very practical way of addressing deliverance. I have personally seen the lives of many delivered from demonic oppression this way. Most of the time, all the individual had to do was apply their faith to and receive the word and it yielded fruit strong enough to eject the demonic forces from their lives. I have also, personally experienced this very practical approach to deliverance. Yes it takes longer and is more of a process than having it cast out through the laying on of hands. But nonetheless, submitting to God causes the devil to flee from you.

Yet I have also seen situations so severe and dire that only a supernatural intervention of God through the laying of hands would provide freedom. In fact, there are some sicknesses and conditions that can only be resolved by supernatural means.

Jesus also carried around money. We see this in the story of Mary Magdalene washing Jesus feet with her hair (John 12:6). This tells us that He had a practical way of handling money. Yet, when He needed to pay taxes for Himself and Peter, He tapped into the supernatural to pay what He owed (Matt. 17:27).

We can also see the practical nature of God in the story of Moses and his father-in-law (Exod. 18:13-27). Moses allowed the people to come to him with their drama all day, and he would seek God's counsel for each case. He was prophesying all day. Sound familiar! Then his father-in-law told him that what he was doing was not wise or practical. He then outlined for him a practical structure to handling the problem and it became a national standard.

Jesus again is a great example in that He clearly communicates to us that He expects for us be a church who is both supernatural and practical. In Matthew 10:1 He sent out the disciples to heal the sick, raise the dead, and cast out demons, this was supernatural ministry. However Matthew 25:35 reveals to us that He expects us to feed the hungry, visit the prisons, and visit the sick. This is an example of practical ministry.

Notice that He not only expects us to heal the sick, but to also visit with them. Sometimes we underestimate the power and value of good company. When my mother was dying, the one thing she most appreciated was having people around her as the Lord transitioned her to heaven. There were people who ministered to her practical needs and those who ministered to her spiritual needs. We need both.

I wonder what we could accomplish if we allowed the practical voice of God and supernatural voice of God to dwell together in harmony, working toward the one common goal.

For me this is an important and hard balance to maintain. Up until I met my wife I only bought clothes when I had permission from God. I would go years in the same clothes until they were so worn that I needed a miracle to replace them all. And because I needed a miracle, I got one.

On one such occasion I was given a vision of a blank check, on my way to lunch, and I was told to get what I needed. The problem was that the only money available to me was needed to pay my car note. So what did I do? I trusted God and went shopping. When I arrived back from lunch my job had been given me a bonus check. I also received a second one later that day. They covered my shopping spree and my car note.

This was my supernatural life in Christ. Then I got married and my practical wife gave me a practical suggestion. She said, "You know you don't have to wait until you have nothing. You can take a few dollars and get one shirt a month within your budget." The lights went on and I realized that God would prefer to save the supernatural for real needs not self-imposed needs.

My wife's practical suggestion is very scriptural. For Proverbs 6:6-8 says to consider the ways of the ant. It gathers in the summer for the winter. The ant saves for rainy days to prevent lack. That's practical.

My final thought on this subject is one of pleading. I plead with you to find the balance. You cannot think that the voice of God will only instruct you in how to live supernaturally. And you cannot think that the voice of God will only instruct you in practical matters. God wants to merge these two worlds and He would love it if He could start with you. You could be the first Evangelical Charismatic!

Section 4

Hearing His Voice

Chapter Nine
Preparing to Hear

Getting into Position

In Luke 19:1-10 we are presented with a story that is going to set up my subject for this section, of this chapter, which is position. In this story Jesus visits the city of Jericho. When word of His coming gets around, a crowd begins to gather, as was common. In the crowd there was man of short stature named Zacchaeus. The Bible says that he wanted to see Jesus but was not able to due to his short stature. So Zacchaeus decided that the best way to get a good view of Jesus was to climb up a sycamore tree. In his zeal to see Jesus, Zacchaeus changes his position to one that leans to his advantage.

When he changed his position He got Jesus' attention and Jesus requested to have a personal one-on-one with him. In hearing the voice of God we can take Zacchaeus as our example of how to get God's attention. In order to prepare ourselves for our encounter with God we must learn how to do the following: Get up, Get away, and Get down.

The Get Up Position

If it is your desire to have encounters with Jesus, you will need to learn how to get up. What do I mean by the term 'get up?' Getting up means that one must put forth intentional effort. Zacchaeus put forth an effort to get God's attention. His climbing the tree revealed his passion to see the savior.

For us today it means doing those things that get God's attention. Some of those things are things such as making an effort to get into a regular time of prayer and reading the word. It also, means taking the lead to initiate worship, for James says, *"Draw near to God and He will draw near to you"* (James 4:8). If you want to get God's attention you must go beyond the Sunday morning routine. It never amazes me that people go to their church on Sunday read, worship, and pray and won't do it again until the next Sunday or until a crisis arises.

This is not going to position you to hear the voice of God. The "hearing" position is first a "seeking" position. You need to show God that you are interested in Him. Also, it should be noted that the passage does not say that Zacchaeus wanted anything other than a view of Jesus. What about you? Are you seeking Him with the crowd to get your needs met or to have supernatural experiences. Or are you seeking Him because you really want nothing more than a view of His beauty? Are you seeking Him for no other reason than to know Him and understand His ways?

I have learned that any relationship built on the foundation of giving to get is sooner or later going to experience failure. That failure is sure to take place when the giver is not getting and the getter in not giving. Our relationship with God cannot be developed on the foundation that He is going to give us more stuff. Few things bother me more than prosperity prophets that only prophesy about houses, cars, land, jobs, etc. Real prophetic ministry draws us closer to Jesus for "the spirit of prophecy is the testimony of Jesus Christ" (see Rev. 19:10). At some point we have to come to a place of loving Him for who He is and because we have grasped the revelation of John 3:16. For God so loved that He gave! He sacrificed for us at the cross and we need to pursue Him for this reason alone.

The Get Away Position

The next position is the "get away" position. Zacchaeus changed his position by getting away from the crowd. This has two implications that are useful for this discussion.

The first is the idea that we are called to sanctify ourselves. You cannot expect God to take you seriously if you are not willing to live a sanctified, set apart life. We are called to Holiness and it is essential to walking with God. When Moses met God at the burning bush, the first thing He said to Moses was to take off his shoes; you are standing on holy ground (see ex 3:5). The reality is that developing your relationship with God will require sacrifice. You will not get holiness without it. If you are going to hear from God you are going to have to let go of some things. I had to let go of a lot of movies and televisions programs that were not a sin for me to watch, but just was not good for my soul. The Bible says to *"Set no evil thing before your eyes"* (Psalm 101:3). You are also going to have to let go of some friends and take heed to your conversations. You will definitely need to make Psalm 19:14 a scripture by which to live. It says *"Let the word of my mouth and the meditation of my heart be acceptable oh Lord..."*

Furthermore, we all know we are required to be holy because He is holy (see 1 Pet. 1:16). Lastly, the Bible says in Amos 3:3, *"How can two walk together unless they agree?"* So if you are serious about hearing the voice of God you need to learn how to get away from the crowd.

The second idea presented in the term "get away" is the idea of getting alone with God. Jesus in several places in the gospels got alone and prayed. I like to liken prayer and worship to sex. It is intimate and private, so much so that God says when you go into your closet to pray shut the door (see Matt. 6:6). Moses pitched a tent away from the camp. The Bible also says that God met him there everyday and spoke to him as a man speaking to his friend (see Exod. 33:11). Some people believe you should set a time to meet with God. I disagree and you will see why as you keep reading. The time is not important, but it is important that you learn to get alone with God so that you can get to know Him. Did you know that the word "know" in the Hebrew is the word "Yada", which means to know intimately? It is used in the verse be still and know that I am God (Psalm 46:10). It is also used in scriptures such as and Genesis 4:1, which reads *"Now Adam knew Eve his wife."* God invites us to be intimate with Him. He wants us to "yada" Him; to know him intimately.

So in learning the 'get up' and 'get away' positions you will need to walk in purity and make time to be alone with God. If you do you will begin to experience His presence and hear His voice.

The Get Down Position

Finally, we get to the "get down" position. Zacchaeus gets up and away from the crowd to see Jesus and when He finally has His encounter with Jesus He is told to get down. What does this mean to us? His getting down is a depiction of an act of submission. His obedience reminds us that we are called to submit to the Lordship of Jesus and the leadership of the Holy Spirit. The scriptures are clear that we are to humble ourselves under the mighty hand of God (see 1 Pet. 5:6).

I once had a conversation with God about why He did not seem to speak directly to so many of His people and this was His response to me. He said, "I cannot speak to them because they won't obey the written word. Why would I speak to them when they won't even follow my written instructions? If they don't do what they see, then how will they do what they hear?"

So the get down position is the position that calls us to obey the word/voice of God. Are you ready to obey what He tells you to do? Today there are a lot of people who want to see angels and who want to have fantastic visionary experiences. But I wonder if they are just as eager to position themselves for obedience. What about you? Are you ready to get down? Remember God resists the proud but offers assistance to the humble (see James 4:6).

I also want to inform you that after a while you will begin to see the part of the scripture "...*and He will draw near to you*" come to pass in your relationship. Once you learn to get away, the 'get down' principle will take effect. God will begin to initiate time with you.

Years ago when I started this journey I had a schedule of times to meet with God. As our relationship began to grow I started to notice that God would begin calling me to my room to spend time with Him. Can you imagine? He didn't have anything in particular to show me He just wanted to fellowship with me. He would also open my eyes to truths in His word.

150

Sometime later I decided that I would try to stay on a strict schedule and I was going to establish a meeting time with God. So one day I said God I am going to meet with you everyday at so and so hour. I assumed that He would be flattered by the effort I was making to set time apart for spending time with Him. His response caught me off guard. He responded to my proposal with, "No, come when I call." I tried presenting my case and again I heard, "No, come when I call". Finally, He said, "Kevin just come when I call you. How would you like it if I put my love for you on a schedule? How would you feel if I was only available to meet your needs between certain hours?" Then again He said, "Come when I call". Therefore, that is what I did and I am still doing.

This is another instance that really requires your obedience. Are you too busy to come at His beckoning? Or do you need to watch your favorite shows, or your game before you visit with the King? Are you willing to submit yourself to Him so that you can hear His voice?

One thing that I have come to realize is that many of God's people find prayer to be a difficult discipline. This seems to make it difficult to submit to His beckoning. But I would like to present a different perspective to how prayer should be viewed. Think of it in terms of a relationship. Is it hard for you to spend time with your spouse? Why not? You spend time with your spouse because you love them. No one has to keep you accountable to speaking to your spouse because you love your spouse. Can you imagine how it would sound if I were to tell you I was going to call you to help you remember to speak with your wife or husband. That sounds strange doesn't it? No one has to tell people in love to share time and energy with each other. Their love does that for them. Are you willing to get down? Are you willing to walk in obedience to hear the voice of God?

What to do Once in Position

Hopefully you understand the importance of getting into a position of seeking, sanctification, and submission. It really is the first step in the right direction to hearing the voice of God. This however, is just the beginning. Once you are in position to hear His voice, you will discover the necessity to incorporate some very valuable practices into your life. Notice I said practices and not disciplines. The things that we discuss going forward are not disciplines to me. Things such as prayer, worship, and meditation are a regular part of any relationship if it is put into the right context. Prayer is just talking to God, worship is simply expressing love to God, and meditation is nothing more than thinking about the one you love. Is it really that simple? Yes it is! And if you think about it you will see that these are all elements present in any relationship. Any couple that hopes to have a thriving healthy relationship understands the need to talk and listen to each other, express their love for each other, and love naturally produces a fascination that causes us to think deeply about each other. So as we move forward I want you to think of the elements presented from the position of relationship development. Trust me, your outlook will have an effect on the desired outcome. In fact these elements will become second nature.

Prayer

The first element that I would like to discuss as we prepare to hear the voice of God is the subject of prayer. What is prayer? Prayer is simply talking to God. It is seen all through the scriptures and it is presented to us as a fairly simple process. However, today prayer is presented as one of the things the church has made complicated and mystical. It's no wonder that so many people are so intimidated by the idea of talking to God. I remember growing up in church and hearing people pray. Their prayers were always filled with King James "thou's", "thee's", and large collegiate words. Their prayers were so poetic and eloquent. I remember thinking to myself, "I could never pray like that."

Then I grew up and it was my turn to talk to Jesus. And what did I do? I did what I saw as a child. One day I was going through my poetic prayer to God when He spoke to me and said, "Kevin stop. Just talk to Me." I said, Lord I'm praying, and again He said, "Kevin. Stop! Just talk to Me." What, just talk to you? What about the "thou's" and "thee's"? I discovered that day that attempting to pray like a deacon was a complete waste of time. God took away the intimidating element of prayer with a simple request, "Just talk to me." So that is what I did and have been doing from that moment till this day. My prayers also became so much more powerful because I was no longer praying with my head I was praying with my heart. I was able to have intimate real talks with Jesus because I allowed the issues of life to flow out of my heart, instead of being hindered by the legalism in my head.

Look at the simplicity of Peter's prayer in Matthew 14:30, when he is allowed to walk on the water to Jesus. When he got to the point where he was about to drown does he say, Lord thou art the great, deliverer. I pray thee now by the holy name of your Son Jesus Christ, that you would stretch forth thy grand arm and reach out and allow my frailty to touch your divinity. Reach out thou great God and save your servant from the very clutches of death. No! He says a simple prayer of his heart and screams out Lord, save me!

Can prayer be that simple? Yes. Look at Moses at the burning bush (see Exod. 3:1-22). Observe the simplicity of the conversation as God tries to encourage him about his calling. We can see that Moses is able to be completely transparent before a loving God.

Abraham is another good example (see Gen. 18:16-33). When God had decided that He was going to destroy Sodom and Gomorrah He stopped by to share His plan with Abraham. And again we see the transparency of the conversation. Abraham speaks to God with an ease and allows God true communion that flowed from his heart.

Prayer: Setting Our Mind on Him

One of the most important skills we can develop is listening. Listening is a very important factor in the development and sustaining health of any substantial relationship. It is reported that one of the most damaging things to marriages is the failure to master the art of communication. What is communication? It is the process of hearing, listening, and interpreting. People are pretty good at hearing—it's the other two areas of communication that causes the problems.

We said prayer is simply talking to God but it is also listening to God. You cannot really believe that you and God have the best relationship when you are the one doing all of the talking all of the time. For us to have an effective relationship with God we must learn the art of listening. Notice that I did not say hearing. It is possible to hear and not listen. Hearing is a by-product of

153

having ears. If you have ears that are functional you hear all kinds of sounds. It is the ability to focus and distinguish what you hear that is at the heart of listening. Listening is giving purposeful attention to what is heard.

Many married couples can attest to this truth. We have all at some point had a spouse decide to communicate something important to us during a favorite television program. What usually happens is that you hear them saying something. Then respond with by saying "ok." The next day you are sitting in the dark and your spouse is looking at you with contempt. What happened? Someone heard a sound but was not listening for the content.

You can hear words but never hear the content or context. I would dare to say that this has happens to many preachers on a Sunday morning with their congregations.

The story of Jesus visiting Mary and Martha in Luke 10:38-42 teaches us that there are those who choose to hear and those who choose to listen. Through this story we can see these ladies interacting with the presence of the Lord. One is listening and the other is hearing. First, we see Martha whom invited Jesus to her house but then ignored Him, because she was busy serving. She was in the presence of God and she would not be still to know Him. I'm sure she heard Him speaking. This goes back to our verse in Job. God speaks to man one way and another way but man does not perceive it. In other words, busy people hear the sound of God's voice but never stop to perceive or listen to His message.

Martha was in the presence of her God and He was speaking to her but she never heard a thing. This is amazing because Jesus never said anything trivial. This shows us her regard for what He had to say. What she wanted to do was more important in her mind than what God had to say! A good listener gives value to the character of the one speaking. Is what you have to do more important than what God has to say? If so then you will only hear his voice, but you will never hear His message.

Martha reminds me of the Samuel's of the church. In 1 Samuel, young Samuel was in the temple serving God but he did not know the Lord. How many people are serving a God they have not taken the time to get to know?

154

What happened? Samuel eventually heard God calling him, but He did not know that it was God. Therefore, he had to depend on someone who knew God to tell Him that it was God calling Him.

Second, there is Mary's example of interaction with Jesus, which recognizes that the Master is in the room and He is speaking. She decides that she is going to practice the principle of stillness and focuses on hearing the voice of God that is speaking to her. The Bible says she was sitting in His presence. We can also see a principle of resting in this passage.

Prayer: Tuning In

Mary shows us a key principle to listening, which is "focus." You cannot effectively listen to someone if you do not give that person your undivided attention. Also, if you are going to hear the voice of God, then you will have to learn to focus on God. The Bible says it this way in Isaiah 26:3, *"He will keep him in perfect peace whose mind is stayed or focused on Me."*

How do we focus on Him? If you were to look for a radio station what would you do? You would tune into a specific frequency. Tuning into God is much like tuning in to a radio station. Each radio station has its own channel or frequency. In order for the radio receiver to get that station the receiver must be programmed to that specific channel. The receiver must be focused to that specific frequency. If the receiver lands in an area outside of the frequency you can get static or a mixture of two channels broadcasting. Martha is an example of mixing channels. You hear but you don't hear clearly. Focus in prayer is essential to hearing. I deal with how to focus in to hear the voice of God in a latter chapter.

I have always been a creative person and I love the arts. I was a rapper, poet, dancer, and artist growing up. The one art I loved and excelled at was rap. I loved it and would study and practice for hours and days. After I became proficient at this art form I decided to pursue it as a career.

I loved it but I had one problem. I always ran dry—I suffered from writers block often. So I began to find inspiration in listening to music. That worked great for a time. Then the dryness returned. So I turned to listening to music and drudging up moments of anger from past hurts in my life. This really worked, but I began to notice that my work was taking on a really dark presence. It did work however so I kept it as a part of my creative process. I would sit on the floor and focus on my anger and wait for the first line to enter my thoughts then I wrote. Sometimes this inspiration lasted for days and I would write as much as seven songs in a day.

Once I gave my life to Christ and got filled with the Holy Spirit I began to notice that the Holy Spirit would move upon me the same way. I would sit reading the word and imagine that He was with me and suddenly there would be a rush of thoughts and images upon my mind. I always wrote them down. This was a revelation moment for me. I suddenly realized, that before my conversion, I had been allowing my self to be led and inspired by a demon of anger. While this was not the best news, I did learn that we could commune with God by allowing ourselves to get inspired by His flowing thoughts and images when we learn to focus.

In His book, *4 Keys to Hearing God*, Mark Vikler explains this as the flow of the Spirit. *"For out of your belly will flow rivers of living water, for this He spoke of the Holy Spirit"* (John 7:38). And that is exactly what it is. It is a flowing from within. Jesus said for the kingdom of God is in you (Luke 17:21). And meditation and focus allows for a release.

It's also worth mentioning that it is harder to get into God's presence when we are distracted. Going back to our story of Mary and Martha, we see that the scriptures say that Martha was distracted. Distractions can come from many sources. Sometimes we are distracted by the events of the day. Sometimes we are distracted by wayward emotions. Sometimes we are distracted because we allow darkness into our eyes. I said it earlier in the "get away" section that you will have to give up some things to really experience God the way He intends. You cannot watch and listen to all kinds of filth and expect to just pop into the position for hearing God's voice. You will find that as you attempt to meditate on Jesus that all that filth you took into your eye gates and ear gates will begin to come up and these wayward images in your mind will distract you from seeing Jesus. If you really want to hear God's voice "clearly", you will need to be transformed by the renewing of your mind. Why? It is where God will begin to show you the good, acceptable and perfect will of God. You cannot expect a mind that has not been transformed to recognize the mind of Christ at work within you. I deal with this subject extensively in the next two chapters.

Following the Flow

While writing this book God gave me an interesting perceptional vision. One day on my way to exit the bathroom I stopped to wash my hands. Our bathrooms at work had recently been upgraded to one of the fancy faucets with sensors. I had my hands lathered up with soap and as I proceeded to put my hands under the faucet the water was restricted. So I adjusted my hands up higher and still no water. Last, I moved my hands up and closer to the sensor and finally the water came forth. As the scenario was playing out I came into a sudden fascination with what was happening. I could see that the water flowed in proximity to my position to the sensor. Then I came into an awareness of God saying. Kevin, make the adjustment. You need to be closer to get the flow that I have for you.

Previous to this experience I had been having a grand worship experience. I mean the whole house was worshipping. Even my children experienced God and sensed the presence of the angels. It was grand. In the mornings I was awakened to worship songs in my spirit. So I decided to sing along and when the song changed I changed with it. What was so awesome about it all was that the more I focused on the music the more audible it became. When I say audible, I mean it was very loud and distinct—It was very clear. I could hear the voices of a choir of male singers singing popular worship songs. This went on for about two weeks where my days were filled with audible worship accompanied by a very tangible presence of God. This was all happening internally and the deeper in I went the more real it became. Finally, it all came to an end, well, it sort of came to an end.

What I begin to notice was that I still heard the worship songs but now they were at a normal volume level. However, after this experience normal sounded more like distant. This led me to explore this phenomenon by directing my attention to the song that was playing in my spirit. Once again the deeper I tuned in the louder the worship sounded.

God was teaching me a truth that I already knew, but did not completely comprehend. What was that truth? That truth was the reality that the kingdom of God is *"in"* me. A kingdom is place where a king reigns. Some would say its interpretation is "in the midst of you." Either way it is with you, and you have access to it. It is where God is and if you focus and follow the worship into the secret place you will find that the voice of God is loud and clear.

Prayer: Practicing the Presence

We often hear the statement that we are coming into the presence of God... Or the presence of God is here, but the reality is that God is always there; we however, are not always focused. Jesus said *I will be WITH YOU ALWAYS* (Matt. 28:20). It also says that the *Holy Spirit will be WITH you and IN you* (John 14:16-17).

So the issue then is not that God comes and manifest, but that we learn to step into His presence. I make it my goal to maintain an active awareness of God's presence all the time so I can hear His voice. I have recently discovered that I can go deeper into that presence when I need to speak with Him. The interesting thing has been, that the deeper my focus the louder and clearer the voice gets. All of a sudden it is not a whisper, it's an audible voice.

All of this leads to one conclusion. Listening is a choice and the experiences presented to you show you that there is so much more for the believer that is willing to listen. What about you? Are you too busy working when the Savior is speaking? Mary's example of stillness and focus ends in her being validated. For Jesus says, she has chosen what is good and it will not be taken away from her. Last, we can see an even greater reward in the life of Mary when contrasted to Martha. Martha worked when she should have rested, and Mary listened and in the end it was her to whom Jesus revealed Himself after the resurrection. Are you too busy talking in your prayer time? Try listening.

Worship

That leads me to the next subject of worship. Here is a scenario that I would like for you to consider. Imagine that you and your spouse are preparing for a night of intimate fellowship. The lights are dim and the fireplace is blazing. Maybe you have a glass of bubbly apple cider. The scented candles are lit. There's a nice dinner prepared and love is in the air. All that is needed to make the night a night to remember is a nice song. Your husband gets up and walks over to the IPod and suddenly you hear, *War, huh yeah, what it is it good for absolutely nothing, oh hoh, oh.* The mood is suddenly ruined by the wrong song choice. I use this illustration to show how important music is to setting a mood for something wonderful to happen.

You may not have ever really considered the idea that the Sunday morning worship is more than just a preliminary to the preaching. So many times we place such emphasis on getting the word from God that we ignore the very reality that worship is how we get our hearts ready to receive it.

The Bible puts a lot of emphasis on worship, but what is it. Worship means to give reverent adoration to: to bow down before. Worship is our expression of how much we adore and love God. It is the equivalent of a man serenading the woman he loves. How does it differ from praise? Praise thanks God for what He has done. It is talking *"about"* God's goodness, whereas, worship is talking *"to"* God and telling Him how great He is just because of who He is.

The Bible commands us to be filled with the Spirit and it says one of the manifestations is singing to God. Ephesians 5:19 says *"...And do not be drunk with wine, but be filled with the Spirit, speaking to yourselves in psalms, hymns, and spiritual songs, singing and making melody with your heart to the Lord. Always giving thanks for all things in the name of our Lord Jesus Christ to God, even the Father."*

Earlier I told you that the Holy Spirit would lead you into the plan of God. According to this verse one of the places He is leading you is into worship. And that worship is to flow out of your heart. Your heart is your mind (to include your imagination), will, and emotions; or your soul.

Do you realize that the scripture says that we are the temples of the Holy Spirit? Why didn't He say we are the house of the Holy Spirit? When Jesus refers to demons dwelling in people He calls the human body a house. But

159

when God is dwelling in a human body it is referred to as a temple. Are you wondering why? It is because temples were the places in ancient times that worship took place. The temple of David was a temple where Israel came to worship God. And now "we" are the temples of a God. We do not have to go anywhere to worship God. We can commune with and worship Him by following the songs that are going before God in our hearts. Jesus, when discussing the location of worship with the Samaritan woman says to her, *"God is a Spirit and those who worship Him must worship Him in Spirit and in truth"* (John 4:24).

Worship: The Power of Music

This leads us to the importance and role of music. I cannot caution you enough that hearing God's voice will require the guarding of your ears and eyes. Music is a spiritual force that has one purpose, and that is to create an atmosphere. Whether secular, demonic, or divine, it will create an atmosphere for inspiration. Have you ever noticed that many visual artists are also musicians or are connected to music in some way? All artists can tell you that one of the best sources of inspiration is music. Music is used to assist with stimulating the right hemisphere of the brain. Most artists will also tell you that they listen to the music that coincides with the type of images that they are creating. Rowdy artwork would be inspired by rowdy music. A hip-hop scene is usually created listening to hip hop music. Music sets the mood for inspiration.

How powerful is music as a force? In 1 Samuel 16 we see a young King Saul after God has told him that he is removing his anointing as king of Israel. Not only did God take Saul's anointing, but also He replaced it with an evil spirit that tormented Saul. As a remedy to the torment, Saul hired young David to play for him and in 1 Samuel 16:23 it says that when David played the harp that the evil spirit departed from Saul. This suggests that if there is a sound that drives an evil spirit away that there must also be a sound that calls them near.

What about God? Does He respond to music? Sure he does. In 2 Chronicles 5:13-14, there was a worship session that had a 120 member band behind it and it resulted in manifestation of the visible presence of God. It was so strong and awesome that the Bible says that the priest could not stand to minister.

We also see that God is responsive to music in 2 Kings 3:15. In this passage Elisha needs to get into the presence of God to hear the voice of God to provide a word of guidance to the kings. What he does next tells us a lot about the importance of music as a force that creates an atmosphere for the supernatural. When the harpist starts to play the hand of the Lord, or anointing (the power of God) comes upon Elisha and his ears open to hear the voice of God. This is interesting because when David played the harp for King Saul the evil spirit left, but when this unknown musician plays for Elisha the Spirit of God comes.

So we can see that music is a very important element that we can use to enhance our worship and prepare us for hearing and seeing the voice of God.

Worship: The imagination

There is so such material out right now about the imagination. One floating theory is that the imagination is the spirit realm. There is also another theory that says that it is the eye of the spirit. I personally do not believe that it is the spirit realm itself, but I do believe that it is a tool of our spirits that sees into and communicates within that realm. I go into much more detail about it in a latter chapter.

So what is the imagination and what role does it play in worship? As of now my understanding is that the imagination is a function of our mind that creates visual images from spiritual input. It is a property of our spirit as is the mind as a whole.

We are creatures with visible and invisible qualities or physical and non-physical qualities. We have a body and a brain and we have a spirit and a mind. We often assume that the mind is located in the brain, but there is no scientific proof that the mind is a tangible part of the body such as the brain. It is generally accepted by scientists and theologians, that there is no physical mind that can be handled through our five senses. All that science has been able observe is the affects of the mind on the brain. We all know that our bodies are controlled by our thought life. We are so much controlled by our thoughts that the Bible says that we are as we think. (Prov. 23:7). In other words our thoughts are linked to our character.

What has not been considered, however, is that the mind is a bridge between two worlds. We are spiritual beings in human vessels and our invisible mind is a property of our invisible spirit. One thing I have learned is that there is a spiritual and natural side to life. There are no in betweens. The invisible things belong to the invisible world and the visible things belong to the visible world. We were created in Gods image (Gen. 3:12) and God is a Spirit that has a mind. 1 Corinthians. 1:10 says, *"For, who among men knows the* **THOUGHTS** *of a man except* **the SPIRIT** *of the man which is in him? Even so the* **THOUGHTS of GOD** *no one knows* **except the Spirit of God....**" The Bible also says *"I (God) know* **the thoughts** *that I have towards you..."* And again in Isaiah we see *"For* **My THOUGHTS** *are not* **your thoughts**, *for as the heavens are higher than the earth so are* **My THOUGHTS** *higher than yours"* (Isa. 55:8).

We can also see an example of this in the story Jesus tells of the rich man and Lazarus in Luke 16:19-31.

19 "There was a rich man who was dressed in purple and fine linen and lived in luxury every day. 20 At his gate was laid a beggar named Lazarus, covered with sores 21 and longing to eat what fell from the rich man's table. Even the dogs came and licked his sores. 22 The time came when the beggar died and the angels carried him to Abraham's side. The rich man also died and was buried. 23 In Hades, where he was in torment, he looked up and saw Abraham far away, with Lazarus by his side. 24 So he called to him, 'Father Abraham, have pity on me and send Lazarus to dip the tip of his finger in water and cool my tongue, because I am in agony in this fire.' 25 But Abraham replied, 'Son, remember that in your lifetime you received your good things, while Lazarus received bad things, but now he is comforted here and you are in agony. 26 And besides all this, between us and you a great chasm has been set in place, so that those who want to go from here to you cannot, nor can anyone cross over from there to us.' 27 He answered, 'Then I beg you, father, send Lazarus to my family, 28 for I have five brothers. Let him warn them, so that they will not also come to this place of torment.' 29 Abraham replied, 'They have Moses and the Prophets; let them listen to them.' 30 'No, father Abraham,' he said, 'but if someone from the dead goes to them, they will repent.' 31 He said to him, 'If they do not listen to Moses and the Prophets, they will not be convinced even if someone rises from the dead."

In this story we can see that both the rich man and Lazarus have died and have gone to their spiritual homes. Lazarus is in heaven with Abraham while the rich ruler has opened his eyes in hell. What I want you to notice is that even though this rich ruler is in a spiritual form he still has his mind. His body along with his brain, as we know were left behind on Earth. But his mind has gone with his spirit. How do we know this? In verse 24 we can see that he has enough presence of mind to recognize Abraham and Lazarus. In fact he remembers that Lazarus was his servant and attempts to have Abraham send him to serve him. This tells us that he has his memory with him in hell. The memory is a product of the mind. He also demonstrates that he has memory in verse 27-28 when he begs Abraham to send Lazarus to his five brothers, who he clearly remembers. He clearly has a mind in the spiritual realm.

We can also look at the story in 1 Samuel 28:5-20. These verses tell the story of a fearful King Saul when he was under the threat of war. He needed a word from God but God had stopped speaking to him because of his continued disobedience. When Saul realized that God is not going to speak to him he decided to hire a medium to call up for him the spirit of the prophet Samuel. In verses 15-20 we read of the conversation between the two of them. In the conversation we can again see that the mind is clearly a spiritual property. Samuel recalled who Saul is, he even recalled the prophecy that he gave Saul about the destruction of Israel. He further went on to recall that David is to be the next king. These all demonstrate that the mind is the property of the spirit.

In fact when we really look at the scriptures we can see clearly that all spirits have minds. I once asked a woman who considered herself very spiritual the question, "Do demons have emotions?" She of course said, "No." I then said to her that the Bible says in James 2:19 that it is good that you believe, so do the demons believe and *"tremble"*. I also pointed out to her that they often fell before Jesus in fear of being tormented. Likewise we can see that angels have souls that include a mind, will, intellect, and emotions. This all tells us one thing. The soul is a part of our spiritual nature.

This is important for us to understand as we pursue the idea of worship because Jesus said that we worship God in spirit and in truth. To really understand this we must consider the reality that we are dual natured not triune natured though we may be composed of a body, soul, and spirit. We know that there are only two worlds in which we exist. There is a physical world, to which all physical things belong. Likewise there is a spiritual world in which all invisible things exist—Things such as the mind, thought and imagination.

Why am I bringing this into our discussion about worship? I believe we have been commanded to use all of our invisible faculties to worship God. Again, Jesus said, *"God is a Spirit and those who worship Him must do so in spirit and in truth."* We have read this passage several times in our life and I believe we have overlooked what He was really asking us to do. In fact we can see exactly what God is referring to in the first commandment where we are commanded to express our love for God with our invisible attributes. In Luke Jesus says that we are commanded to love the Lord our God with ALL our HEART (invisible), SOUL (invisible), and MIND (invisible thoughts and imagination) (see Matt: 22:37).

This is where the imagination is very important. We have written off our imaginations as evil because we wrongly interpret 2 Corinthians 10:5, which reads *"...pulling down imaginations and all thoughts that exalt itself against the knowledge of God"* We tend to interpret this verse as pulling down imaginations, and we overlook God's description of the type of imaginations we are to pull down—those that *"exalt"* themselves *"against"* the knowledge of God. Furthermore, the word "imaginations" is really interpreted in the original Greek as the word "arguments".

Even still, this verse is generally accepted by all as a reference to the faculties of the mind. It also challenges us to take every thought captive, but somehow we believe that we can separate the thoughts from the imagination when in fact they are one and the same. Imaginations are simply visual thoughts. I call them fraternal twins because like fraternal twins they come as a package but are very distinguishable. We can have thoughts without images, but we cannot have images without thoughts. So when we read this passage we should consider that we are to take every thought and imagination captive that comes against the knowledge of God. God is simply cautioning us that we need to be proactive in guarding both our auditory mental abilities as well as our visual mental ability. It is said another way in 1 Peter 1:13 which reads, *"Gird up the loins of your mind."* These are scriptures that caution us to guard our thought life, not abandon it. Likewise, we are encouraged to use it for good and not evil. Philippians 4:8, also says we are to meditate or to use our mental faculties to imagine whatever is noble, right, pure, lovely, admirable, anything excellent, and praiseworthy.

Earlier I said that the imagination is sensitive to spiritual input. If we go back to 2 Corinthians, we can see that our minds are receptors for spiritual forces—Spirit meaning breath or inspiration. You are a spirit; a breath; a source of inspiration. 1 Corinthians 2:10, *"For who among men knows the thoughts of a man except the **spirit of the man which is in him**?"* We can also see this in Ephesians 4:23, when we are instructed to be renewed in the ***"SPIRIT OF YOUR MIND"***. God created us with the ability to be inspired. That inspiration can come from within ourselves such as those who prophesy out of their own hearts, or we can be inspired by spiritual forces such as God or Satan. There are several places in the gospels where we see demons driving people, or inspiring evil actions. There are also a multitude of scriptures that validate that God inspired or drove people to action. We see several times the phrase "…and the hand of God came upon me and I prophesied…" We can also refer to the New Testament passage that clearly reads, Holy men of God spoke, as they were INSPIRED…

So what does this have to do with the imagination? When we worship God we also are commanded to "love". Love is an expression of the heart. You cannot say that you love your spouse and not express that love. You also cannot say that you love your wife with just actions. There should be some evidence of that love validated within your heart because we are beings capable of experiencing feelings of love.

God wants worship inspired by love. He wants you to express that love with "all" of your invisible attributes; your heart, soul, and mind. Most of us have learned what to do with our bodies. We have learned to lay prostrate before God, to bow down in reverence, and to dance and sing before Him. And all this is great, if it is done with all your heart, soul, and mind.

I have been in worship, at home and at church, with my hands raised while my mind was far from God. I think most of you can say the same. I believe that most people go to church to hear or sing a couple of songs so that they can get to the preached word. This means that it is easy for our worship to be filled with wayward thoughts. However in contrast, I have also been in worship with my invisible faculties, my heart and mind, engaged and worship became a glorious encounter with God.

So worship is to be done from the inside out. For "OUT OF YOU will flow rivers of living waters." "For the kingdom of God is WITHIN YOU!" When you are ready to engage God in worship allow the song that He places in your heart to guide you into His presence.

Meditation: Engaging the World Within

The first step to engaging the inner world is to recognize that there is an inner world. The Jesus said to His disciples in Matthew 10:18 that they were not to worry what they should speak for it would be given them what they should speak that hour. It goes on to say that it will be the Spirit of your Father speaking "IN" you. Ephesians likewise says that it is God who works "IN" you—the key word being "IN".

This is important to establish because when you engage God in the inner world, you may come into experiences: experiences such as various types and levels of visions. This is not an endorsement to seek out experiences, rather it is meant to inform you that while engaging God you may be granted one.

For instance consider the fact that God says if there is a prophet among you, I the Lord speaks to him "IN" a vision. I make myself known to him "IN" a dream. We also see that He spoke to many such as Abraham "IN" a

166

dream of the night. Daniel in 2:9 **says,** *"As for you oh king, **thoughts came to your mind** while on your bed about what would come to pass after this.* **Daniel 4:13** says, *"I saw in the visions **of my head**, while on my bed..."* **Daniel 7:1 says,** *"In the first year of Belshazzar king of Babylon, Daniel had a **dream and visions of his head** while on his bed. Then he wrote down the dream, telling the main facts."* Lastly, **Daniel 7:15** "I, Daniel, was grieved in my spirit within *my* body, and the ***visions of my head*** troubled me." The NIV actually says, "...and the fantasies of my head."

What I am hoping is evident is the many references to "IN" and that the location of these meetings with God and angels occur in the inner world of the imagination. Notice that there was sight and sound in that place. I said it earlier that there is a physical world and a spiritual world. Likewise, the physical part of you has eyes and ears, sight and sound. Likewise your inner man has sight and sound. It is your imagination that assists with facilitating the process of seeing and hearing in the inner world. These inner sights and sounds are known as visions and dreams.

The passages in Daniel are so revealing and helpful in de-mystifying the phenomenon of visions. We would like to believe that they occur in the spirit realm and to a degree they do, because our minds are property of our spirit. However the reality is that they happen when our imaginations are overwhelmed by the influence of the Holy Spirit. It's important to also notice that they can occur while we are sleeping or while we are awake and may occur in various levels of consciousness. Some may experience a vision while fully conscious, such as mental images that may appear as flash images or lengthy movie like images that fade slowly. While others may experience a vision that happens on a subconscious level such as daydreams and trances. Others may experience visions on the deepest level of unconsciousness as dreams or what Daniel calls night vision. Finally, some will have out of body experiences like Ezekiel. These are higher-level encounters with the spiritual realm.

Regardless of how they occur we can be certain that God has used the faculty of the imagination to communicate to us a truth. You should also be aware that 2 Corinthians warns us that God is not the only force capable of inspiring and communicating with us via imagination. There are evil spirits around and waiting as roaring lions for those who are or refuse to be discerning (see 1 Pet. 5:8). This is why we cannot afford to convince ourselves that what we take into our ears and eyes has no effect on our inner lives.

Taking the Inner World Seriously

A few years ago I made the decision that I was a strong enough Christian to start watching horror movies again. I had grown up on horror movies. They never bothered me and I really assumed that my connection to Christ was strong enough that if anything demonic popped up that I would just rebuke it and keep going. So after watching about a year or two of horror movies, old and new, I started to notice that I was becoming afraid of the dark.

Can you imagine! I was a grown 40-year-old man turning on the lights before I went into a room. I remember very specifically after watching Halloween, which I had seen several times, that as I was walking up the stairs in the dark I could see in my mind a projected image of Michael Myers in my house. I quickly realized that I had invited a spirit to utilize my imagination by my open communion with the kingdom of darkness. So I repented and it took a few months to get rid of the spirit of fear.

What about the ear gates? Some time thereafter, when I was courting my wife I again thought it would be okay to listen to a little secular music. What's the worst thing that could happen, right! While I was enjoying my romance with secular music I came across an Aaliyah song called, '*I Don't Wanna*' that would later torment me.

My girlfriend, now wife, broke up with me for some reason. We were always on and off. However this particular time occurred during my romance with the world. When we broke up the words of that Aaliyah song played so loudly in my head over and over and over again. All I heard was the music and the words, "I don't wanna be without you, I don't wanna live without you, I don't wanna be alone." It tormented me so, so, so bad that I put my pillow over my head and pleaded with God to make it stop. Needless to say, I had to ride it out and I realized that day the importance of feeding my spirit and mind healthy food! It was such a surreal experience.

I hope that you noticed that with each situation that it was my imagination that became the source of my torment and allowed these wicked beings to communicate with me. Likewise, I can say with 100% certainty that your impure imagination is the problem with your ability to commune with God also. You must narrow the way if you want to make it easier to discern the mind of Christ.

I would like to encourage you to use this great gift of forming mental images we call the imagination during your worship to engage the Spirit of God. You may find that He will respond to you in a visual and or audible way.

Entering In: Going Boldly Before Him

The next subject to address under this chapter has to do with entering into the presence of God. So far I have addressed topics that allow you to prepare yourself to go before God. We have covered the need to get into a position of seeking, sanctification, solitude, and submission. We have also discussed the importance and role of prayer, meditation, worship and the imagination. Now we're going to deal with an area that I have found deters most people from pressing into the presence of God. That is the idea of "guilt". It is very important for you to understand how to remove guilt as you prepare to hear from God.

I have always heard preachers say that the closer you get to God the more you see your own wretchedness. Personally, I have not found this to be true. In fact, the closer I get to God, the more confident I become in the finished work of the cross. When I come before God I don't feel shame or guilt, but in contrast I feel the most accepting and wonderful love - the kind of love that is accepting, welcoming, comforting, exhorting, and edifying. I feel this way because even though I know I am wretched, He still welcomes me with open arms.

So where does this idea originate? I believe it is derived from Isaiah chapter six, when Isaiah receives his prophetic calling from God. In verses

5-7 we are allowed to see Isaiah's reaction as he stands before the Holy God of Israel. *"Woe unto me, for I am a man of unclean lips"*, he cries out in the presence of God. When Isaiah comes into his first encounter with God he is immediately overwhelmed by his own guilt. It is this passage that I believe has been the backbone of the idea that our own disgusting nature is highlighted in the presence of the Holy One. The fruit of this statement, however, has proven to cause more harm than good. Who wants to be in the presence of someone that reminds them that they are filthy? This idea nullifies the work of the cross so that people are afraid to approach the holy and loving God.

What preachers fail to communicate is the redemptive aspect of the story. If you keep reading you will see that redemptive quality is displayed when God sends an angel to touch Isaiah's tongue with hot coal as a symbol of the purging of his sins. God cleansed from him the guilt that made him feel so uncomfortable in His presence. As a result we are never again presented with the idea of Isaiah's guilt before God again. How would he have ever been able to stand in the counsel of God to hear the report of the Lord if his mind was overwhelmed with thoughts of shame?

When we read this passage we always focus on Isaiah's reaction, but what about God's reaction? Let's see God's reaction for what it was. As we said earlier, God addresses the need. He removes the dividing wall, which in reality, is only in Isaiah's mind. The reality is that God brought Isaiah into His home to speak with him, but His guest was so overwhelmed that it was stressing their communion. So God had to do something to make Isaiah comfortable in His home. Are you seeing it yet? God wanted Isaiah to be comfortable in His presence. It was not His desire for him to feel guilt and shame. Therefore He made a loving gesture to help ease Isaiah's mind. God did not do this for Himself. It was done for Isaiah.

The Bible says that the blood of goats and bulls could not remove the stain of sin (see Heb. 10:4). For it reminded the Israelites every year that they were sinners. But Christ was offered up once for all. Why? It was for the purging of the conscience (see Heb. 9:14). Christ is the realization of the hot coal used to ease the guilty conscience of Isaiah.

170

In other words, God does the same thing in Christ that He did for Isaiah. He has sent out an invitation for all mankind to come and commune with Him. However, we are often like Isaiah, undone and focused on our own wretchedness. You should recognize, however, that just as God went the extra mile to make Isaiah comfortable in His presence, so has He gone the extra mile for you. *"For God so loved the world that He gave His only begotten Son"* (John 3:16). God wants you to come into His presence boldly and you need not worry about your guilt. He has already done the work to prove to you that He really wants to fellowship with you.

If you struggle with guilt and shame, there is a remedy. First you need to recognize that the voice that is oppressing you is Satan's. Second you need to understand that the deliverance you need is in the presence of God, *"For where the Spirit of the Lord is there is liberty" (FREEDOM, DELIVERANCE) (2 Cor. 3:17)*. So do not run from God but run to Him. Third you need to understand that Satan is no longer in the position to enforce his plan of guilt and shame. He has boundaries. One reason Satan is so effective in keeping us out of the presence of God is because we don't know that he no longer has the right to oppress the believer.

You have a legal right that you can enforce against him when he tries to oppress your conscience. Earlier I showed you that God did the work to cleanse your conscience according to Hebrews. So why are you still struggling with these awful feelings?

In Revelations there is a vision depicting the Devil as a Dragon. It talks about how he drew away one-third of the heavenly host and fought against God. The vision tells us that he lost his battle and was cast down to the Earth. When he arrives on Earth he goes after Israel, because she gave birth to Jesus Christ.

Then it says this. *"And there was no more place found for him in heaven. For the accuser of the brethren that accused them day and night has been throw down..."* (Rev. 12:7-12). Also it says *"They overcame the devil by the blood of the Lamb and the word of their testimony."*

This is really a subject for another book, but in short you need to realize

171

that you cannot be held captive by your conscience without choosing to do so. The Bible says *"Do not give place to the Devil."* What place can you give the Devil? The place of accuser, which place he no longer has a right to! The Devil no longer has a place in heaven for accusing you of your sin. God has redeemed you by the blood of the Lamb and your testimony. So the next time you are being attacked by guilt and shame, plead the blood. Pleading the blood is similar to pleading the Fifth Amendment in a courtroom. It does not mean that you are innocent, but it means that you are protected by the law from incriminating yourself. Likewise, when Satan tries to play the role of prosecutor, you can plead the blood of Jesus to remind him that you have been forgiven and that he can no longer enforce the power of guilt and shame over your life. Remind him that you have been exonerated. I can promise you that if you learn this principle you will have far less trouble warding off those nasty feelings of condemnation and shame. Since God has taught me this I never struggle with guilt and shame.

How to Encounter God

The hardest part of sharing this type of information is finding a way to make such a difficult subject practical. I'm sure you are wondering how to make use of this information. Therefore, I am going to use as an illustration the same thing God used to explain the process to me.

I am a father of four beautiful children and my love for them is something that I cannot put into words. One of my children in particular has become my heart. She is my last child whom I had late in life. She is the fulfillment of a vision God gave me 20 plus years prior, while I was single, about the number of children I would have. After having three children and one miscarriage, my wife and I decided that we wanted one more child but we were really pushing the envelope when it came to age. We also had two boys and one girl and we had discussed that if we had another child that we really wanted another girl. We both felt that God was giving us a desire for another child but we considered ourselves too old. We would only do it again if we could have another girl. So I expressed to God my concerns and He said nothing.

As time went by we started to notice that God had made the decision for us and we were expecting our fourth child. Nine months later we gave birth to a beautiful baby girl. She was just what we wanted. Because of these circumstances I have found that I have a real appreciation for her because she symbolizes to me answered prayer, and that God really will give you the desires of your heart.

I cannot explain my feelings for her. No, I do not love her or express more love for her than I do for my other kids. It's just that she is a reminder of God's goodness. Therefore, I hug and kiss her all the time. One particular hug was very special. It was special because as I closed my eyes and hugged her I felt the warmest feeling as I thought about how much I loved her. It was in that moment that God made the principle of loving God with all my heart, soul, and mind a revelation.

In that moment I realized that I could engage God in the same way. I had already been engaging God but I could not explain it to others. That was until this incredible hug with my daughter. I also realized that when God commands us to love Him with your heart that what He is asking you to do is to engage Him with your emotions.

That's right, you will find that it is easy to engage God when you use you mind to include your thoughts and imagination along with your emotions and feelings to express love for God. When I worship I like to follow the song that God inspires in my innermost being. Once I hear that song I sing it considering what the lyrics of the song say and I allow my emotions to stir my feelings of love for God. It is at this moment that you will find a very real awareness of God's presence and it is the most likely atmosphere for you to hear and see the voice of God.

I can remember years ago when I would worship in church that I would get so lost that I completely forgot about the people around me. Often after service people would come up to me and tell me that they enjoyed watching me worship. They said it was so beautiful to watch and that they could really see my love for God. I thought nothing of it; in fact, I didn't even notice anyone watching.

While I was lost in worship I engaged God will all my emotions and mind. On a couple of occasions He responded by giving me visions. One such vision that occurred during my worship was a vision of a tidal wave moving towards the front of the church. After that vision the next couple of Sundays exploded in new salvation conversions. It went from 8 to 9 people saved a Sunday to 12-20 per Sunday. And the church began to experience tremendous growth that has continued until this day.

Why am I sharing this particular vision? I shared this story as an example of how God speaks to those who are willing to engage Him with their invisible attributes.

The beautiful thing about this concept is that it is not limited to church. I sing songs to God most of the day. While I am sitting at my desk I am singing worship to God. When I am walking down the hall, or riding in my car I am engaging God with my entire person. The result of spending so much time with God will absolutely blow your mind. Spending time in the continued presence of God not only benefits you, but it benefits others as well. For the Bible says that *"Where the Spirit of the Lord is there is Liberty." (see 2 Cor. 3:17)*

Here is an example. Earlier I said that I am in constant worship and always engaging the presence of God. One day as I was walking down the hallway on my job I was singing as I often do. Being filled with the fruit of joy, I stopped by the secretary's desk and just shook her hand and said hello. When I did, she looked at me with a gaze. I thought nothing of it at the time. I just went to my desk and continued to do my work. Later that day as I was coming out of the office this lady called me over to her desk and began to explain to me why she looked at me so strange earlier in the day.

She said that she had been having a really bad day and was experiencing an unshakable feeling of heaviness. She went on to explain that the moment I shook her hand she felt something lift up off of her and she immediately felt better. This became a perfect situation for me to share my faith and that's what I did. She did not get saved at that moment, but she had an encounter with God that she will always have with her. And it was all because I was willing to walk with the Deliverer.

Imagine how many lives could be changed by you allowing yourself to love a lovable God. Even the scriptures provide a good example of what happens when we express love for God and how that encounter with Him may impact those persons around you.

In Acts 16:16-40 Paul and Silas were in jail and while they are being held in shackles, they began to sing psalms and hymns to God. After some time of singing to the Lord the prison shook and the doors swung open, and the shackles fell off of everyone!

The story goes on to say that the jailer responsible for watching the prisoners that night assumed the worst and was about to commit suicide. Paul however, having this revealed to him, stopped him, and as a result the jailer and his whole house was saved.

How wonderful is that, and it all started with worship. Hearing the voice of God is accomplished when we remember that He is a person just like you. Except much stronger, bigger, and greater, but nonetheless, He is a person. If you are going to enjoy the fruit of the relationship with Him you must learn to treat Him as such. Learn to get into position - get alone with Him, seek after Him, and submit to Him. Lastly, worship and adore Him. Dare to engage Him with ALL your person and I promise you that He will reciprocate and speak to you with His entire person. If you get into position you will hear the voice of God in your life.

Chapter Ten
The Sound of His Voice

The Most Important Question

Well we have finally arrived at the chapter that will answer the most important questions. The questions that are most likely on your mind such as what does the voice of God sound like? What am I to look for when He speaks? How am I going to hear Him? Am I listening with my ears? Am I listening with my spirit and if so how? How will He speak to me?

One thing that I hope to communicate in this chapter is the practical way that God speaks to us. Some people say that God speaks to our spirits. Some say God speaks to our hearts. But think about it for second. Where do you direct your attention to hear what God is saying, in your spirit or your heart? While this may have the appearance of being a "deep" question, it is also not very practical for teaching purposes. Again, most people cannot identify their heart or spirit. Also, I want you to consider that while this has been passed down from generation to generation in the church, it is not explicitly mentioned in the Bible. That's right, there is no clear mention of God speaking to our spirit or our heart.

I think that this idea of God speaking to our spirit and heart is rooted in the passage Hebrews 3:15, *"Today if you hear his voice, harden not your hearts as you did in the rebellion."* Or from John 12:40, *"He has blinded their eyes and hardened their hearts, so they can neither see with their eyes, nor understand with their hearts, and turn, so that I should heal them."* When we examine these passages we must keep in mind that the scriptures are referring to our overall attitude towards God. It is not so much that our hearts are capable of hearing as much as the conditions of our heart allow us to receive the voice of God.

We see natural examples of this all the time. I frequently minister to people who have unresolved conflict and unforgiveness in their hearts towards family members, friends, or coworkers. As such, I witness rather often how a hardened heart towards another person deafens the ears of the offended person. You have more than likely witnessed this as well in your own personal life. I am sure that you can attest to the reality that it is really difficult to hear or receive any kind of loving gesture from someone with whom you have an ongoing conflict. If you are married you definitely understand what I am saying. The same is true with God. It is not that our heart hears the voice of God, but the condition of our heart affects how we receive the voice of God.

Likewise people use 1 Corinthians 2:11, to teach that God speaks to our spirit. It reads, *"For what man knoweth the things of a man, save the spirit of man which is in him? Even so the things of God knoweth no man, but the Spirit of God."*

If you read the passage you will notice a subtle but very revealing fact. That fact is that the Spirit of God searches the things (the mind) of God for information to bring to us. It likewise says that our spirit knows our thoughts. Most of us are conditioned to believe that we receive in our spirits and interpret what we receive in our minds. So we lightly regard anything in our minds. But, the passage shows us that our spirit interacts with our mind. The word "likewise" is the key in this passage. It tells us that as creatures made in God's image that we function the same way. This begins to establish what God revealed to me as the "from" "to" concept. It lets us know that our minds are valuable in the process of hearing the voice of God. It establishes the idea that God is not speaking to our spirits but "from" our spirits.

There is also biblical evidence of God interacting with our spirit to lead us, but we are not examining being led by the Spirit, we are examining how to hear His voice. There is a difference between the two. Sometimes God leads us and sometimes He speaks to us. I covered some of this in the chapter *"Ways God Speaks"* and we looked at scriptures that showed God speaking in an audible voice that was internal and external. We likewise looked at scriptures that showed us that God sometimes stirs, and impresses direction into our spirit. I cover the leading of the spirit in the "The Voice and the Unction", a chapter in the next section of this book.

So what does the Bible have to show us about where we can listen to hear God speaking to us? Again, it teaches us that God does not speak to our hearts or inner man (spirit), but He speaks from our inner man and that spiritual communication is perceived with our mind. The voice of God shows up as inspired or spontaneous thoughts in the mind.

In this chapter we are going to explore what the Bible actually reveals about God speaking to our minds and where the source of that voice originates. By the time this chapter concludes you will also understand that your mind is a tool with faculties that engage the invisible world in general. You will also understand that you are a spirit and that you exist in the spirit world. Lastly, you will come to understand that learning to discern is of the utter most value because as a spiritual beings we are constantly engaging other spiritual beings.

God Speaks from Our Heart to Our Minds

If the scriptures do not support the idea of God speaking to our spirit but from our spirit, what do the scriptures actually say? Job 32:8 says, *"There is a spirit in man and the inspiration of the Almighty gives him understanding."* This passage tells us that God "inspires" understanding. There are two words in particular that are of interest, the word *"inspiration"* and the word *"understanding"*. If we look at the passage we see that the word inspiration is used in direct relationship to our spirit. Inspiration as we have defined many times means to be moved by wind (to be inspired). In the passage it tells us that God blows on our spirit and creates a sense of spontaneity. It also tells us that this sense of spontaneous flow results in understanding. Understanding is a function of the mind. Likewise Job 38:36 says, *"Who has put wisdom in our inward parts? Or who has given understanding?"* Here again we see a relationship between the inner man and understanding. There is a clear line of "from" and "to" taking place in which our spirit is inspired by God and perceived with the mind.

God told me that the "from/to" relationship is a very critical part of understanding how to have a strong sense of "knowing" or certainty. But we are examining this method of operation from the Old Testament's point of view. In the Old Testament the Spirit of God would come upon men and women for a purpose and He would inspire or move upon their spirit and that inspiration would show up in their minds. After He had accomplished His task He would then leave or lift off of them until He was ready to move again. In the New Testament, however, and under the better covenant, He does something similar but different. In the New Testament the Holy Spirit resides permanently in us. Therefore, He inspires us from within our beings. If He resides in us, where in us does he reside? He resides in our spirit.

John 7:38 Says, "*He who believes in Me, as the Scripture said, 'FROM HIS INNERMOST BEING will flow rivers of living water.' But THIS HE SPOKE OF THE SPIRIT, whom those who believed in Him were to receive...*"

Notice that it says that the flow or inspiration would flow *"from"*, so there must be a *"to"*. Also, take note of the fact that it says that this flow will come "out of" a place. The passage says that the place of origin is out of "our spirit"! Lastly, this passage is very clear in revealing to us that the flow coming out of our spirit is the "Holy Spirit!" In an effort to help you visualize this idea I want you to imagine a one-piece HAZMAT suit hanging in the closet. As it hangs there it is absolutely lifeless. However it will all of a sudden spring to life the minute you step inside of that suit. This is how the Spirit of God indwells us. He comes into our lifeless spirits and inspires it with life and causes it to live, move, and have being or meaningful existence (Acts 17:28). Ezekiel 36:27 says, "*For I will put My Spirit in you and CAUSE you to walk in my ways...*" The only difference between you and the HAZMAT suit is that you have a will that can resist or quench the Holy Spirit's activity. In the next chapter on "Transforming Your Eyes and Ears to Hear" I actually show you how to transform your mind so that the life and voice of the Holy Spirit can flow freely from within you to your mind.

The movement that you feel in your innermost parts to go this way or that way or the deep urging and nudging is literally the Spirit of God moving in a particular direction. This is the leading of the spirit, and if you can imagine yourself as this HAZMAT suit and Him as the person inside of you, it will create in you the ability to better sense His movements with more accuracy. Under the section "Impressions" in the chapter "Ways God Speaks, I showed you multiple ways that the scriptures show God moving upon our spirits. It is this understanding that creates what we call a witness in our spirits or a strong sense of "knowing" deep within. *"For His Spirit bears WITNESS WITH OUR SPIRITS..." (Rom. 8:16).* In the chapter, "Ways God Speaks" I also spoke of the witness as a filling up. This might be pictured as a balloon being filled with helium. It rises as the air is forced into it. Either way, both the filling up and the movement of your spirit will give you a great sense of certainty in knowing who is speaking. They are best felt when we learn the principle of stillness.

In the Old Testament there is another word of interest to this conversation. That word is the word *"prophecy"*. In the Hebrew it is the word "Nabi" and it means to bubble up or bubble forth. This provides us with yet more insight into this subject because it gives us a description of what the great prophets experienced when they heard a word from God. It also gives us a great view of how they were able to speak with such accuracy and certainty. This word "Nabi" confirms for us that the voice of God comes to us by inspiration within us. It also shows us that, while it may start from within, it moves up. Again, it means to bubble UP or FORTH. This could be pictured as a geyser that has had a rock removed from its opening. So here again we see the idea of moving "from" and "to. To where is it bubbling up or forth? Remember Job said the inspiration of God gives us *"understanding"*. The bubbling up and forth is moving towards our minds.

One example of this is found in Daniel 4:19. In this chapter Daniel is being requested to interpret Nebuchadnezzar's second dream. As the interpretation is downloading, the Bible says *"And the thoughts of his mind troubled him."* God was downloading or should I say uploading the answer to Daniel's mind.

Locating the Flow

Okay, so now we know that God speaks from our inner man to our minds, but exactly where is the inner man. This is an interesting question, because Jesus said the Spirit flows out of "your inner most being", but the King James Version says it flows out of "your belly". This seems like a gross misinterpretation, but it is really a God inspired incident. Why would I say that? I do not believe in a God limited by man's errors. I believe that God sits outside of time and He knew way ahead of time that this question would arise. With that in mind He carefully orchestrated the answer. I don't know for sure if the spirit is in the belly region, but I do know that when you engage your spirit or even when you speak in tongues, that there is a flowing and pulling felt deep within around the belly region. Many of you know exactly what I am saying. Even in prayer you can tell the difference between praying with your head and praying with your spirit by that tugging in the gut region. We also get a sense that this may be true from the most popular clichés, "I got a gut feeling" or "I feel it deep in my gut" or "my gut is telling me".

This may not seem important to you, but trust me it really is very important information to know. Later in the chapter I will provide more insight into why this is important to know.

How It All Starts

When the inspiration of God starts, how will it happen? Remember I told you that the bubbling forth is like a geyser that has had a rock removed from its opening. This is a great example because the first thing God does before He speaks is get your attention. How does He do this? He stirs your inner man, which may literally feel like a bubbling up inside of you around the belly region. In "Signs of His Voice" I spoke of God filling us up as one of the signs that we experience in our encounter with God. I used as an example the story of Elizabeth coming into the presence of Mary. I showed you that when the baby John the Baptist heard the sound of Mary's voice that the Bible says that he (the baby John) leaped within her and she was filled and spoke.

This is a very common process seen in the New Testament as well. One of Jesus' instructions to the disciples before His ascension was to take no thought regarding what they would say, but that the Holy Spirit would give them the words to say in that hour (see Matt. 10:18). Then in Acts we see this process at work. In Acts 2:1-6 we see the disciples sitting in prayer in the upper room waiting on the promise of the Holy Spirit. When He finally arrives they are *"filled"* and then they *"spoke"*. Again we see this process in Acts 4:31 when the disciples are beaten and have been overcome with fear. In their fear they prayed to God and asked Him for boldness and the Bible says that they were *"filled"* and the place where they were gathered was shaken and they went out and *"spoke"*. Ephesians 5:19 says be *"filled"* with the Spirit *"speaking"*... Hopefully you see the connection. Jesus said that they should take no thought for what they would say and that the Holy Spirit would give them the words to say in that hour. As we observe these passages we can see that He did just that. But before He gave them words to speak He first filled them or "Nabi" bubbles up and forth.

This is important to see because this is the process. Some of you have heard people say that God has many ways of speaking to people. While this may be true in part, the Bible also teaches us that God has a way of doing things that we can see and identify as Him at work. *"He says your thoughts are not My thoughts, your ways are not My ways."* (Isa: 55:8) God has ways of doing things! If we study the scriptures closely we will see these patterns. Uniformity is a concept that you will see with any real military. In fact they use uniforms to symbolize the idea that they are one unit with a certain way. This is important to understand because it allows God to show us how He operates and to give us truth that we can pass along to others. This lack of understanding is why we always see things such as seven different doctrines on one subject that all contradict each other. The truth is found in learning His *"WAY"* of doing things. Moses says to God in Exodus 33:13, *"Teach me Your ways that I might know you..."* The key to the knowing is found first in learning His way. Not doing so is why there are so many rendered useless by doubt. We have taught people that God is like a buffet and that He will not be boxed in. However, the reality is that these many conflicting opinions only kill the faith of those who are really interested in being used by God. Narrowing the way is how we kill the spirit of doubt. Learn the narrow way.

Jesus said *"Narrow is the WAY..."* He also says *"I am THE WAY..."* God has a way and hopefully I have been able to show you that way scripturally, as He has shown me. Furthermore, I guarantee you that if you learn His way you will find unimaginable peace in your fellowship with God. You will also drastically decrease the constant questioning as to whose voice you are hearing.

The Mechanics of the Process

Genesis 2 shows us what I would call the mechanics of the process. If you are wondering why I am going into this type of detail, it is because understanding how God has designed us to operate in our bodies makes it easier for you to identify the inspired process of hearing the voice of God.

Genesis 2:7 says, *"God breathed into Man the breath of life and he became a living soul."* Adam had a body but no spirit and soul. What is interesting is the fact that he did not become a living-animated soul until God breathed (inspired) on him. It was the inspiration of God that made him a creature capable of thinking, feeling or emoting, and making decisions. In other words Adam became a living soul, which consists of the mind, will, and emotions.

What we see is that there is a very clear connection between the soul and spirit. In fact Ephesians 4:23 shows us that there is an even clearer connection between the spirit and the mind. For it tells us to be renewed in the *"spirit of our minds"*. This is important because what it teaches us is that it is our spirit that moves upon our souls. Also, if you search the scriptures you will see that the spirit or heart and mind are mentioned several times together. This further strengthens the idea of a connection between the two. Likewise I showed you at the beginning of this chapter in 1 Corinthians 2:11 that there is a spirit to mind connection.

So what is the connection between the two? The mind is the gateway to the soul. It is your mind that allows access to your emotions and will. What happens is your spirit moves upon your mind to inspire thoughts, those thoughts affect your emotions, and this information leads to a decision or chosen course of action.

We can see this process in the scriptures in the life of Jesus. In Matthew 14:14, Jesus looks up and has a "perceptual vision" in which He sees Israel as sheep that have no shepherd. Then it says He was moved with compassion. So His thoughts led to emotions and finally those emotions led to a choice of action. Compassion moved Him to heal.

This happens again in the ministry of Jesus. In Matthew 21:12 He enters the temple and sees that business is being conducted in church and this leads to inspired thoughts. These inspired thoughts lead to Him being angry and finally the anger lead to a chosen course of action. For it says that he turned over the tables and beat them out of the temple.

Acts 13 tells us a story of Paul's encounter with Simon the sorcerer. It says that this sorcerer resisted Paul's message and attempted to turn the audience away from Paul's message of the Gospel. Then it says that He was filled (inspired) by the Holy Spirit. This led to inspired thoughts, which Paul's actions reveal. Paul made the inspired thoughts known by what he said and then in holy anger he cursed the sorcerer.

This is such a powerful truth that we often see God using His word to change a person's mind to affect their behavior. The scriptures also present us with a negative view of this process in the life of Moses. In Exodus, God attempts to change Moses mind about his speech impediment because Moses is trapped in feelings of inadequacy. These feelings clearly hindered Moses from moving into action. God then attempted to remedy his feelings by offering Moses another thought or way of thinking. Why? God knew that if He could change Moses' thinking, He could change his feelings, and changing his feelings would free him to action. So this process is invaluable.

I could go on and on showing you this process. It is all through the scriptures. In the Old Testament, God would come upon someone and they would be inspired through this same process. This is because this is how we are designed. You can even see this in your personal life. When you are in love you have thoughts of love that lead to feelings of love that lead to actions reflecting that love. The same is true with anger and any other emotion. The difference is that it does not come from deep inside of you and it is a passing wind that fades with time. God however comes to abide and so we experience Him deep within us. When He inspires us it is a stirring from deep within that leads to inspired thoughts that produce confidence and certainty.

This is important to know because there is a term used today in the church to judge the activity of other Christians. That term is "soulish". It is used to describe people who are dancing or praising God out of their emotions instead of their spirit. Those who use such terms really do not understand that one cannot do anything outside of their spirit. Your spirit is the part of you that gives your soul life. Spirit flows into the soul and this leads to action in the body. This is why we have the gift of discerning of spirits. This gift does not determine whether we are moving in our soul or spirit, but whether the source inspiring our soul is human, demonic, or divine. Therefore, we see Jesus being inspired by His spirit with compassion, which is an emotion.

So take that term out of your vocabulary. It is not term found in the Bible and it's also not consistent with the scripture. There is no such thing as "soulish" activity—just human, demonic, or divine spiritual activity. In fact we are commanded to "love" the Lord our God with all our "Heart", which includes our emotions!

The Mind

So if the mind is the gateway to all of this activity then we should understand as much about it as possible. This is what I hope to accomplish from here forward. In fact in the next chapter I tell you how you can transform it into something that is capable of releasing the Divine Inspiration. I have discovered that some people know how to receive the divine inspiration, but are not able to move beyond the emotional stage to allow it to turn into action. This is what is called *"quenching the Spirit"*. This is how I came to this understanding. I was a person that was experiencing deep rumblings in my spirit and I couldn't figure out what was happening on the inside of me. I was constantly asking God, "Lord, what is that feeling of eruption and why can't I release it". Then finally He said, "Kevin, get in the flow." Then He said, "Align your mind with your heart." The moment I did as I was instructed, the Holy Spirit poured out of my being with a fiery anointing.

It was literally a feeling of fire all over my being. Revelation also began to pour forth and the voice of God was clear and audible. Furthermore, the conversation between us flowed naturally and He spoke in words and images flowing to my mind.

Since that day I have learned exactly what I am telling you. I learned to recognize the rumblings and sensation of being filled with inspiration from deep in my being in the belly region. This is the same inspiration that I write with. It is the Holy Spirit fulfilling Jesus' words, He will teach you what you should say in that hour. I learned that He *"fills"* and *"flows"*. Remember that, for it is the process.

I also learned the importance of having a transformed mind. Lucky for me, I know how to hear the voice of God because I long ago transformed that part of my understanding. So it was easy for God to give me those life-changing words. But for some of you transforming the mind is a consideration that must be acknowledged if you are going to recognize the voice of God. Why? The word "transform" in Romans 12:2 means to renovate. Renovation is the process of tearing down and cleaning out old structures. You may be wondering what structures are in the mind? Your mind is full of strongholds fortified by reasoning and ungodly philosophy. There are things that you believe that exalt themselves against the knowledge of God. Things such as, God doesn't speak anymore, or I can get divorced if this doesn't work out. Even thoughts such as my Pastor is a man just like any other man, I don't owe him any respect. These are just a few, but your mind is full of contrary ideas about God ways. Your thoughts are definitely not His but He wants to change that for you and in the next chapter I deal with *"how"* in great detail.

Faculties of the Mind

If God fills our spirit and then flows upon our minds then what happens in the mind, or what faculties of the mind does God use to accomplish this process? God uses three important faculties in the mind to communicate with us. In order for us to understand these faculties we must first understand that we are spirits that live in bodies. **YOU ARE A SPIRIT** that lives in a body. You are not a body that has a spirit. This is very important to understand because your mind is a spiritual tool that connects you to both the supernatural and the physical realms. It maintains an active presence in both realms even though you are only aware of one—so you think! The reality is that you that you are engaging the invisible realm all the time. The faculties that allow such to take place are in the mind. They are the conscience, intuition, and the imagination. These are all spiritual tools by which we interact knowingly or unknowingly with the spiritual realm.

Conscience

The conscience is the spiritual part of us that allows us to sense right from wrong. Likewise, it is a tool that is often subject to much spiritual activity. How is the true? The devil uses it against us to produce guilt and shame. He attacks humans by producing thoughts attacking their conscience. In fact the Bible calls him the accuser that accused us before God day and night. Notice I said accused. He no longer has a place to do this in heaven. However those who do not understand the finished work of Christ and who do not know that he has no place for this behavior are his victims. Likewise, the scriptures show us that the Holy Spirit uses the conscience as well. He uses it to help us know when we are right and wrong. Paul said, *"I tell the truth in Christ I am not lying, the Holy Spirit bearing me witness in my conscience."* (Rom. 9:1)

Intuition

Then there is the obvious intuition. Intuition is perception. It is the part of us that feels, senses, and perceives spiritually. We see this in the life of Jesus often as the scriptures uses the phrase, *"...Jesus perceived in His spirit..."* (Mark 2:8) Paul perceived that they were going to shipwreck in the book of Acts. These are instances of perception or intuition. It is the part of us that senses knowledge beyond the five natural senses. Many people call this the sixth sense.

Imagination

Last there is the imagination. This has been the topic of a lot of discussion lately. It has been called a spiritual realm, the eye of the spirit, and a doorway

188

into the invisible world. I do believe that it is connected to the spiritual realm and is a way of seeing into the spiritual realm, but I do not believe it is in itself is the spiritual realm. It is also, a doorway by which some enter into the invisible world. While this may be the case, my goal is to share with you how the Holy Spirit uses this mental faculty to communicate with us not to teach you how to use it to intrude into the invisible realm.

Your imagination is a screen and God uses it as well as many other spirits as a visual communication tool. It has sight and sound, or at least mine does. In the next chapter I deal with the way God uses this faculty and how we are to use it as well. I also deal with how it relates to the heart in that chapter.

So when we feel the bubbling up and the sensation of God filling us, and we yield to what He wants to do, we will be inspired with perception. Perception is intuition and imagination. Intuition is the revelation knowledge flowing into our minds and the imaginations will be visual images that God shows our mind to communicate truth to us. This is one of the ways we receive visions from God. In short, perception may appear as concepts and ideas. It can happen suddenly. In which case you will instantly know something. Or it may come as daydreaming.

Another Way God Speaks from Our Spirit

There is another way that God speaks to us. When God speaks to us with mental perception, it is revelation gifts at work in us; Gifts such as word of wisdom, word of knowledge, and discerning of spirits. These occur when the Holy Spirit bubbles up and then we start to perceive knowledge. There is, however, another way that God moves upon us. It is by the gift of *prophecy*. We already learned that this means to bubble up or forth and this is when God inspires utterance. It is literally our spirit speaking. It may appear as your inner voice.

I can remember when this first began to happen in my life. I would get filled with the Holy Spirit and then I would start preaching to myself and as I was preaching to myself God would pour out supernatural knowledge. In this process your mind and your spirit are working together. Your mind perceives revelation and your spirit is speaking it out. Why am I noting this as a distinct method by which we receive the voice of God? I am noting this because even when you do not open your mouth and preach, the words are heard and felt as impressions in your spirit as it is speaking. This is a very audible way that God speaks to us but it is still Him moving or inspiring us to speak to us. The Bible says it this way, Holy Men of God spoke as they were moved or inspired by the Holy Spirit. They felt and heard the bubbling up on the inside of them and they felt compelled to do something. Remember God fills us then He flows.

This is more than likely what most people are talking about when they say God is speaking to their spirit, but what is really happening is that He is breathing on them and they are feeling that inspiration as it manifests in their own spirit. Remember, He dwells in our spirit and from there He flows out. When God speaks this way it feels like words breathed into your spirit.

Some of you will understand these analogies God gave me and some of you will not. The first example He gave me to describe this is an image of someone breathing on the back of someone's neck. Not blowing but breathing where you feel the pulse of each breath. The second image was an image of someone speaking words and breathing on your neck. If you don't know what I am talking about, have someone stand close behind you and speak. You will notice that with every word you will feel breath on your neck as you hear the words. This is how it feels to get impressions in your spirit from God.

Quenching the Spirit

Sometimes when God starts to flow we may find that He seems restricted. If you feel that this is the case it is because you are quenching the spirit. As I said earlier, I had this problem. As a resolution to the problem God gave me a vision of a lid being placed over top of a fire. The placement of the lid smothered the fire until it was completely extinguished. This is how He explained to me what it means to quench the Spirit.

What was I doing that was causing this quenching sensation? God had explained something to me days before that I was struggling to accept —I doubted what He taught me. I told you in "Hindrances to Hearing" that doubt is one of the hindrances to hearing the voice of God. I further explained that

190

the word doubt means to have two minds. Lastly, I told you that if you have double-mindedness that you position yourself to miss the answer that God has freely given to you. Well this was the case with me. God showed me that doubt is like a fork in the road. He said it divides the prophetic stream and makes it difficult to receive.

So what is the answer for doubt? Is it faith? I have always been taught that the opposite of doubt is faith. But God said the opposite of doubt is peace. Peace means unison. It is single-mindedness. It is what happens when our spirit aligns with our mind. This is why God says let the "peace" of God guard your heart and mind (Phil. 4:7). It also says be anxious for nothing. What is God guarding our hearts and minds from? His peace guards from anxiousness, which is worry, the spawn of doubt—double-mindedness. It also protects us from an evil heart of unbelief (see Heb. 3:12). Keeping these two in unison or at peace keeps us in a position to be in a place of faith.

This is important because faith sees God. *"For faith is the substance of things hoped for, the evidence of things not seen"* (Heb. 11:1). This simply says that faith allows us to see the invisible and experience the intangible reality of God. Faith connects us to God *"For with the heart one believes!"* (Rom. 10:10)

Faith directly affects prophetic flow. The Bible says let him who prophesies do so according to his faith (Rom. 12:6). It is the alignment of the heart and mind that positions us to operate in faith and experience the free fill and flow of the Holy Spirit.

Stirring Him Up

Music and Worship

Can we make God speak to us? I think the Bible suggest that we cannot make Him do anything, but it also suggest that we can make the request. It also reveals to us that He is usually more than willing to speak to us if we ask. In Jeremiah He says, *"Call to Me and I WILL ANSWER"* (Jer. 33:3). He also says *"If any man lack wisdom or needs guidance let him ask of God WHO FREELY GIVES TO ALL..."* In fact I challenge anyone reading

191

to search the scriptures regarding this idea. You will find that God never resisted answering a question. He is always seen responding to those who sought Him. Sometimes it was by voice, by dream, by sign, by an angel, or by a prophet. But He always answered. The only time he didn't answer was seen in the life of King Saul. We can also see in 2 Kings 3:1-15, that when Elisha needs to request a meeting with God that he is able to provoke a response from God. So how do we stir Him up?

As we discussed in *"Preparing to Hear"* God responds to music. He is drawn to melodious sounds. Some of you may be thinking that I am referring worship music, but I'm not. I am speaking of music in general. I discovered this one day as I put on a CD of just music and ocean sounds. After seconds of this CD playing the anointing of God started coming upon me. It was very strange to me that He was responding at all to this type of music. Not only did He respond, but He also responded with an overwhelming anointing that moved over me in waves—waves that I could both feel and hear.

Now I want to ask the real question. Did God respond to Elisha's harpist or was there more to the story. I have discovered that it was not an issue regarding whether or not God would respond. It was an issue of Elisha's heart. The music allowed Elisha to come into a place of peace. As I have already stated, it is when your spirit and mind are one that you will experience a release of flowing inspiration. I believe that Elisha was brought into a place of peace. How do I know that he was not in a place of peace before the musician began to play? I know this because he had a resistant attitude towards one of the kings. He did not want to prophesy or seek God on behalf of that particular king (see 2 Kings 3:14). He only did so because as he said, he regarded the presence of King Jehoshaphat. In other words his mind was not in tune with his spirit. He was not in a place spiritually to allow His gifting to flow. The music was not used in worship to God. It was used to get Elisha's mind and spirit aligned so that the hand of God could come upon him, and he could fulfill the will of God.

This is why I value so much a really good worship leader that understands the power of a good song. One thing that I do often is listen to really good worship music. Some of it has lyrical content and some of it is instrumental. If you learn to value real worship music and soaking in music you will position yourself as Elisha did to encounter the voice of God.

Praying in Tongues

Another way to align yourself to receive from God is to pray in your prayer language. This small gift has the strange capacity to align us with God. The Bible compares the tongue to a boat rudder (see James 3:3-5). On a boat the rudder is a small part that determines the direction the boat flows. Speaking in tongues seem to have the same effect. It directs us into the flow where we can get into position for "the flow."

Accepting the Inner Reality

In a previous chapter I made reference to the idea that we have an inner world as well as an outer world. This is important as we move forward, because hearing the voice of God is about learning about your inner world. You have eyes that see outwardly and you have eyes that see inwardly. Your outward looking eyes (physical eyes) see tables, chairs, cars, people, light, etc. Likewise you have eyes that see the inner world. With your inner eyes you can see your thoughts, your memories, ideas and inventions, desires and fantasies. The same is true of your ears. You can hear outwardly things such as voices, television, people etc. You also have inner ears that perceive your personal inner voice and sometimes, unbeknown to you, other voices. You can even mix the two senses and have experiences with memory that involve seeing and hearing. We all know this to be true.

If you can accept this as truth, the things I share going forward will be easier to understand and embrace. As a reminder, I again point out to you that God spoke to Abraham and many others "IN" a dream or vision not "by" a dream or vision (see Num. 12:5-8). Likewise Jesus said in Matthew 10:20 that you would experience the Spirit of your Father speaking "IN" you. Last, I just showed you that the Holy Spirit is coming "out" of your spirit which means that He is "IN" you. Lastly, as I've shared multiple times the Kingdom of God is "IN" you. This all means that you must come to value your inner world because that invisible, intangible, and immaterial part of you is a part of the spiritual world and it engages that reality.

Stirring up the voice of God in you requires that you accept and understand the spiritual reality that you are a spirit. In fact we can see our lack of understanding in this area when we pray. Have you ever noticed that when you pray with your eyes open that you look up, but when you pray with your eyes closed you look inward? This is because our physical eyes keep us grounded in the physical reality. If, however, you take away natural sight you are prone to looking inward where God really dwells. I have had to train myself to look inward even when my eyes are open. This allows me to see visions even with my eyes wide open. This is the result of being spiritual minded. Spiritually minded people have accepted the idea that we are spirits living in bodies and this is the perspective from which we view life. This is why we can see things that others cannot. The spiritually minded person sees the spiritual things in life as they relate to the natural things. *"For we look not at those things which are seen but at those thing which are not seen"* (2 Cor. 4:18). *"Moses endured seeing Him who is invisible"* (Heb. 11:27). *"Seeing afar off they confessed that they were pilgrims"* (Heb. 11:13). If you read through the faith chapter you will see one common thread—all of them saw something invisible. This is the spiritual mind at work giving us sight beyond sight. This is what faith does. It sees.

The Power of Revelatory Truth

So far we have discussed the sound of God's voice and how the Holy Spirit bubbles up to create a flow between mind and spirit. But what can we expect to be the affect of the sound of His voice in our lives.

Have you ever wondered how Adam was able to be in the Garden of Eden and never notice his beautiful naked wife? I did and God showed me something interesting in the passage. In the Garden of Eden we see a very interesting and familiar term. That term is "their **EYES** were **OPENED**" (Gen. 3:7). This term is fascinating to me because we see it used in other places in scripture.

When the Syrian army surrounded Elisha and his servant he prayed to God to *"OPEN HIS EYES"*, referring to his servant (see 2 Kings 6:18). A few passages later, we see him praying that the Syrian army would be blinded. Then he led them to the king of Israel.

194

For years I thought to myself, how was it possible to lead such a large group if they were physically blind? Then one day the Lord opened up a very profound truth about this passage. When Elisha's servant's eyes were opened, he was able to see the real truth in the situation. He saw that there were more angels with them than there were demons with the Syrians.

This is truth that is revelatory in nature. And when we ask God for truth His flow from within us will enlighten our thoughts. The bubbling up of thoughts occurring in your mind will result in the spirit of wisdom and revelation. God uses this process to give us vision.

The opposite happens with the Syrians. When God blinds them He blinds their minds to the truth. You see this in the story, as Elisha is able to persuade them that he was not the man they were looking for, even though he was standing there in front of their faces. This is called blindness because they were blind to the truth. The situation became direr for them when they arrived in the midst of the Israeli King and his army. At which point Elisha prays for God to open their eyes (verse 20). Once their eyes were opened and they saw the truth.

There is another place in the scriptures that provide a fascinating insight into this idea of blindness and vision. It is found in the story of Samuel's first encounter with God. In the story the young boy finds himself in quite the dilemma. He is hearing a voice but he does not recognize the speaker. Once he has received guidance regarding who it was speaking to him and how he should respond, he finds himself positioned to hear God's message. But what makes this story interesting to me is the fact that even though we are not told of any visual occurrences during this encounter, it was called a vision. Suddenly we can see that this story is not only about Samuel's hearing problem, but also his seeing problem.

For it says that after Eli told him how to respond to the voice of God, that the Lord came and stood *"as at other times"* (see 1 Sam. 3:10). The Lord was there each time and He called Samuel's name and Samuel did not see Him until he received the word. Samuel was blind. The story tells us that he did not know or was unable to recognize the Lord. Also, it was God's word that opened Samuel's eyes and gave him vision. Psalm 119:105 says, *"Your*

WORD is a LAMP unto my feet a LIGHT unto my path. " 2 Peter 1:19 likewise says, *"We also have the prophetic message as something completely reliable, and you will do well to pay attention to it as to a LIGHT SHINING in a dark place, until the day dawns and the morning star rises in your hearts."* This simply says that the voice of God is light in our hearts. It opens our eyes.

It is also interesting that the Bible says, "If our gospel is hidden, it is *hidden from those who's MINDS the god of this age has BLINDED.*" It further says *"For it is the God who commanded LIGHT to shine out of darkness, who has shone in our hearts to give light of the KNOWLEDGE of the glory of God in the face of Jesus Christ."*

Ephesians 1:17-18 also alludes to the fact that our minds are a primary way that God communicates with us. For it reads, *"...that the God of our Lord Jesus Christ, the Father of Glory, may give to you the spirit of WISDOM and REVELATION in the KNOWLEDGE of Him, the EYES OF YOUR UNDERSTANDING being enlightened, that you may KNOW."*

What I am hoping is evident is the many references to the descriptions of the mind such as wisdom, knowledge, and understanding. I am also hoping that you will see that familiar term again referring to the "eyes opening".

The Mind is a Bridge Between Realities

So what does this have to do with Adam and Eve? In the last chapter I introduced the idea that your mind is a property of your spirit. We saw a few scriptures that proved to us that this is a fact. In each case that we viewed, the rich ruler and Lazarus, Samuel when he was brought up from the dead, we see that they are aware of their spiritual surroundings. They were conscious of their surrounding in the spirit realm and they had all the faculties of their mind.

Earlier in the chapter I stated that knowing from where God flows within you was very important. It is important because your mind is a receptive place for voices and spiritual communication. God is not the only person that speaks to your mind. Demons also communicate with the mind as well. So what is the difference? God's thoughts flow from within us to our minds

196

and again this is why we can have such a strong sense of knowing about something. Demons speak to the mind from outside the spirit. So even though they may speak it does not register deep within us as something we can hang out hats on. God told me that this was very important for us to understand. Demons do not inspire Christians from deep within. Only God can inspire the believer to action and this is why He can say so emphatically, *"MY SHEEP, KNOW MY VOICE and a strangers voice THEY WILL NOT FOLLOW.*

It is also very important that you accept the fact that you are a spirit, living in a physical case…the body. Your body contacts the natural realm and your spirit makes contact with the spiritual realm, whether you realize it or not. Your mind is constantly engaging the two realities and this is why learning how to discern is so vitally important.

Again your mind is connected to both realms and we sense God and the spiritual realm with the perceptual faculties of the mind, the conscience, intuition, and imagination. This is one of the reasons why it is possible to have all kinds of experiences while we are sleeping. Our minds do not sleep. It is always in a state of working even though we may not always be conscious of it at work. In fact dreaming is nothing more than our minds at work engaging the inner world at the spiritual level. Our subconscious level of the mind is really just our awareness of our spiritual man.

Let's look at a scripture you have seen many times throughout this writing. Job 33:14-18, which says that *"God speaks in one way or another way yet man does not perceive it. In a dream, in a vision of the night, when deep sleep falls upon men, while slumbering in their beds, then He opens the ears of men and seals their instruction in their hearts."*

This passage simply says that the best time for God to speak to mankind is in their sleep. Notice that He is perceived by the mind in dreams and visions—the language of the inner world. Why is it however, that we cannot perceive the voice of God while we are awake? Why does the passage suggest that is it easier for God to speak to us while we are asleep? It is because, as I pointed out earlier, when our eyes are closed there is a natural tendency to look inward. It occurs when our physical eyes that ground our conscious minds in the reality of the physical world do not distract us. It is only when we close our eyes to the outer reality that we intuitively look inward toward the subconscious or spirit at which point man is available to hear His voice.

I know that this is a hard truth for some of you to digest, but the subconscious mind is the spiritual part of the human being. This is why when God decides that he needs to change Peter's mind, he put him into a trance. He needed Peter to be totally blind to his physical reality and natural perceptions and stigmas that his eyes would not allow him to ignore. The same happens to Paul in his conversion experience. God closes his physical eyes to open his spiritual eyes.

Adam and Eve were likewise blind to the physical reality of the conscious mind that made them aware of the world around them. So it is possible that they did not know that they were naked because they only perceived their spiritual reality. They understood that they were spirits and were likely more aware of this reality than the reality that they were experiencing a physical reality. This is completely opposite for us. We are aware of the physical reality, but blind to the spiritual reality. We struggle to see that we are not alone and that there are other beings such as demons, angels and a very loving God who desires fellowship with us. This is why Adam and Eve were able to have such experiences as hearing God walking in the cool of the day, and hearing Him audibly.

But once their "eyes were opened" by the **"knowledge"** of good and evil, they became mentally or consciously aware of the world around them and for the first time they **"knew"** that they were naked.

Being in the Right State of Mind

Being in the right state of mind is important because the Bible says that the things of the spirit are "spiritually" discerned. It also says that the carnal minded person cannot receive spiritual things. Again, the carnal mind is not a reference to the "mind" but it refers to the state of mind. The carnal mind is the state of the mind that only perceives the world through the physical senses. Most of people think that it is a reference to a sinful mind. However, in reality it is referring to a mind that is disconnected from the spiritual reality. It has to do with having a spiritual perspective. A spiritually minded person as Romans 8:6 calls them, is a person who sees or has a perspective like Elisha. They see that we wrestle not against flesh and blood. They are able to distinguish between facts and truth. The fact was that they were out numbered and out gunned. However, the reality or truth was that they were in great company and well protected. The carnal minded person sees like Elisha's servant. They only see the world in front of their five senses. They see the facts!

This is why we are encouraged to be renewed in the spirit of our mind. This is also why we are further encouraged to be transformed by the renewing of our mind. For it is with the mind that we recognize the good, acceptable, and perfect will of God. A transformed mind is able to perceive the mind of Christ when it starts to flow upon us, which mind all believers have, *"For who has known the mind of the Lord that he may instruct Him? But we HAVE the MIND of CHRIST."*

If we have the mind of Christ, then why can't we access it? It is because your mind has not been transformed to recognize when God's thoughts are flowing through it. What you know really does matter when it comes to being able to not only hear, but also release the voice or mind of God in your life. Again, this is what the scriptures refer to as "spiritual minded".

There is a teaching that uses Romans 8:7 which says that *"...the carnal mind is enmity against God and cannot be subject to the law of God"*, as a base teaching to discredit any dependency on the mind. Likewise, 1 Corinthians 2:14-15 is used to further this idea. These are erroneous interpretations of scriptures. To really get the context of the Apostle Paul's statements you must read the previous verses which set the proper foundation for understanding his statement. In Romans 8 the previous verses say, *"For those who live according **to the flesh set their minds on the things of the flesh**, but those who live according to the Spirit the things of the Spirit. For to be carnally minded is death, but to be spiritually minded is life and peace." (Rom. 8:4-6)* Likewise, 1 Corinthians 2:15, says, *"But he **that is** spiritual..."* Paul makes a clear distinction regarding the type of person. As you can also see in Romans,

Paul is not referring to our mind, but he is referring to the perspective, focus, and condition of our mind. He is trying to encourage the church to live with a mind submitted to the Holy Spirit's flow.

One of the things that will help you not only hear the voice of God but even move into the gifts of the Spirit is the transformation of your mind to understand spiritual things. A spiritually minded person is person who has a mind trained to understand spiritual things. This is why it is important for you to get into a strong teaching ministry. Proverbs 4:7 says, *"Wisdom is the principle thing; Therefore get wisdom. And in all your getting, get understanding."* At the minimum you should at least purchase books, CD's, mp3's and mp4's, etc. regarding spiritual things. The more you understand the ways of God the more you will be able to yield into the things of God without your mind fighting you. The only reason your mind is opposing you in any given area is because it is untrained in that area. Training makes the mind submit to the law of God. This is why I said earlier that some people can hear Him fine, but can never seem to master obedience because they get stuck at the fork in the road. The fork of doubt, that presents us with two minds or two paths to take. The informed believer who knows the word of God and has transformed his mind finds it easier to know which path to choose.

Adam and Eve had this mind in them and they chose a path that started the process of dimming and closing their eyes to the spiritual mind when their eyes were opened to carnality. Likewise, as I pointed out in chapter one, we see man slowly forgetting about God, *"And even as they did not like to retain God in their knowledge..."* (Rom. 1:28) Just think about the reality of this for a second. Mankind went from walking in the Garden and hearing the audible voice of God to a time in which we see people who do not believe He even exist! That is a pretty extreme opposite.

This is why the Bible is so emphatic about the mind. It is essential to the battle and that is why we have a helmet of salvation. It is also the reason we are told to gird up the loins of our minds *(to protect it)*, and to take every thought captive. Your mind is a battlefield for control and it is the gateway to your soul. Satan wants you to make the same mistake that Adam and Eve made. He wants you to make blind decisions based on fleshly perception.

200

He wants you to do things because of the lust of your flesh, eyes, and pride. Allow God to enlighten the eyes of your understanding and you will see life with a discerning eye.

Staying in the Flow: Mind Stayed on Him

Now that we understand that the voice of God bubbles up from within and registers in our minds, how can we stay in the place of this blessed communion. We do so by keeping our minds stayed on Him. (see Isa. 26:3) We have the ability to tune in to both the natural world and the spiritual world. It is a simple matter of awareness. Awareness meaning, we decide to focus our attention on Christ. We are commanded to set our minds on things above, where Christ is seated in the heavenly places (see Eph. 2:6). This is simply a diagram as to how to get us into a position to hear His voice. As stated before your mind is a key asset in the hearing process. As we also discussed earlier in "Preparing to Hear", your mind is a faculty of your spirit. As such, you can use it to perceive spiritual realities. God is a Spirit and those that worship Him must worship Him in spirit and truth. This passage tells us plainly that to have contact with God, spirit must engage spirit. So how does this happen? This happens the same way that you perceive the physical world around you. You must acknowledge the reality of the spiritual realm; accept the truth that God wants to speak to you, and purpose to be aware of both realities. You must set you mind; your thoughts and imaginations on HIM. You must learn to look within yourself, really listening and looking. We must learn to be attentive to what enters into our mind, which is encouraged. You are commanded to take "every thought" captive (2 Cor. 10:5). You are the border patrol agent in your mind. If we are careful in our inspection we will find that God is speaking to us through our thoughts. *(In the next chapter I go into this in much greater detail)*

A Lengthy Word About the Imagination

First let me start by telling you that you will need to really understand how to use the witness of the Holy Spirit to grasp the idea that I am presenting on the imagination. This subject caused me the most grief and I really struggled to accept and understand this particular faculty of the mind. It is so much more than even I admit to understanding. What I am attempting to do here is to give you what God has shown me in the word (of course), what I understand so far, and reluctantly what I have experienced.

The imagination is a fascinating faculty of the mind to which we give very little consideration. In fact we use such dismissive phrases as "Oh, that was just my imagination" or "My mind is playing tricks on me." We dismiss it because we do not fully understand what it is or what function it serves. The Bible says some things about it plainly, and in other places it is more elusive. Such as 2 Corinthians 4:18, which says, *"We look not at those things which are seen, but at the things which are not seen: for the things which are seen are temporary, but the things not seen are eternal."* In fact, the very colorful nature of the vocabulary of the Bible, suggests quite an involvement in the imagination by the many different authors. Lastly, the many dreams and visions are also a clear indication of the imagination at work.

So far what we do understand about the imagination is that it is the heart of creation and at the center of our ability to form mental images. The imagination is the part of us that gives our mind eyes to see the dreams we have at night. It is also the function by which we create images and solve problems. It is absolutely fascinating, but it is also very (and I do mean very) spiritual. As I stated earlier invisible things belong to the invisible realm.

Understanding that the imagination is spiritual is very important. The King James Version of the Bible actually says we are to cast down ungodly imaginations. However in the New King James Version and in the original Greek the word "imagination" is translated as the word *"arguments"*. Again this is one of those gross misinterpretations that is the work of our sovereign God. Notice that God allows this to occur in the passage that talks about spiritual warfare in the mind. This misinterpretation allows us to link the reality of thought and imagination. 1 Chronicles 29:18, connects the two by using the phrase "the imagination of the thoughts". This reaffirms for us that the mind's components are thoughts (auditory data) and imagination (visual data).

With this understanding now we can see that the spirit realm has access to us by our minds, as I have already said, and that the communication functions are our thoughts and imaginations. The real question is why do we only acknowledge the reality of the auditory part of our minds as being engaged in the spiritual realm? We willingly accept the idea that a person can get an idea from a demon or that demons speak to the minds of mankind. Yet most people do not acknowledge the reality of the things that they see in their imaginations. In fact we use casting down imaginations as a way to dismiss what we see. The passage, however, is clear that nothing in the mind should be dismissed or ignored. We are commanded to monitor our minds sounds and images and to take captive anything that does not line up with God's revelation of Christ's character.

So what is the goal here? My goal is to help you to live a biblical life of embracing and policing your minds thoughts and imaginations. What does this have to do with the voice of God? It has everything to do with the voice of God! As I said, the voice of God starts as inspiration in our inner man and then flows up and forth to our minds. When the voice of God is speaking you will hear the thoughts of God's mind and you will also see the images that He uses to communicate with you. And it will spring forth from deep within in you.

That is how the imagination is used in communion with God, but there is another function. It is a truth that is very hard to swallow. The imagination's connection to the spiritual realm is more real than just images in your mind where you assume that intangible means not real. We cannot touch what we imagine with our physical bodies, but we are more engaged in that reality than you are aware. Every time you do something in the natural it has an effect in the spiritual. The reality is that it really works backward. You are a creature of inspiration. As stated earlier you have a spirit and "it" drives and inspires you. You work from the invisible to manifest in the visible. The Bible says it this way. *"So that the things which are made are not made of things which do exist..."*(Heb. 11:3) It likewise says, *"God breathed into Adam AND THEN HE BECAME ALIVE..."*(Gen. 2:7) It was what happened in the invisible that determined what manifested in the natural. For example, everything invented started from an invisible place inside of the inventor. It existed in the inner world, before it reached what we call reality. It is created in our spirit and manifested by our bodies. This is why I am stressing to you that this is very, very important for you to understand that you are a spirit. As a spirit you have an impact on the natural as well as the spiritual realm.

You have the ability to have contact with both realms. It is your design, *"For God is a SPIRIT and those that worship God MUST DO SO IN SPIRIT and in truth"*. Again spirit must and does engage spiritual realities.

Most people are undiscerning and never really consider the reality of angels and demons and the impact that they have on us as humans. The Bible clearly warns us about demons and the war they wage on our minds. It likewise clearly teaches us that we engage angels often and that they are with us all the time. The Bible says that they encamp or live around those who fear God (see Psalm 34:7). It also says that they interact with us by ministering to us as heirs of salvation (see Heb. 1:14). Last, we see that they gird us up in their arms lest we hurt ourselves (see Psalm 91:12). As you can see we are constantly in an atmosphere of the invisible and we are not aware of the reality that we are spirits just like them. They are aware of both the natural and spiritual realms and we should be as well. This is the heart of any real teaching on spiritual warfare. No one can successfully teach on real spiritual warfare without accepting this truth.

What does this have to do with the imagination? The Bible says in Exodus 20:4, *"You shall have no other gods before Me. You shall not make for yourself an idol, or any likeness of what is in heaven above or on the earth beneath or in the water under the earth. You shall not worship them or serve them; for I, the LORD your God, am a jealous God, visiting the iniquity of the fathers on the children, on the third and the fourth generations of those who hate Me..."*

The imagination is not just a tool that thinks up great designs but it is also a part of our inner world that perceives or sees into the spiritual realm. The unknowing bring into reality graven images of those things seen there. This is why we have an overwhelming number of horror, occult, and violent movies in the theatre. Those who are creative are very sensitive to this invisible realm but like most people are very dismissive about the validity of what they see in their imaginations. And because this is the attitude about the imagination in general we willingly put ourselves into positions for demons to speak to us.

The passage above is all about imagination and worship. It tells us first not to make an *"image"*. This means that God is speaking to them about the creative process. He is referring to what we do with our imaginations. He further goes on to tell us not to make images of the following:

1). Things in the heavens
2). Things in the earth beneath
3.) Things in the water under the Earth.

This is an interesting list. We know that the things on the earth are animals, plants, and rocks. We sort of know that things in the water refer to fish and probably the ancient serpent leviathan. We also understand that things in the heavens refer to the sun, moon, and stars, right! Now keep this in context. We have seen what is on the earth and some of what is in the waters beneath. But what do the sun, moon, and stars look like to the ancient world (without our technology)? From the earth, without a telescope it appears as lights and the larger more visible bodies appear as spheres. Have you ever seen a picture of a sun God that was a sphere? No, you haven't. The visuals created to represent idols are man's interpretation of what is seen in the imagination. Now I want you to consider who inspires false god worship. Hell is the source of the worship of false gods and the images are supplied by Hell itself. I Corinthians 10:19-20 clearly tells us that idol worship is demonic. It reads, *"What am I saying then? That an idol is anything, or what is offered to idols is anything? Rather, that the things which the Gentiles sacrifice **they sacrifice to demons.**"*

The images we see created for false gods are sometimes revelations of actual demons. The images the artisans see are real, though they were imagined they are not imaginary. This is also true of the angelic images that we see. Sometimes, though not always, but sometimes what you think is just your imagination is a real encounter with what is happening in the spiritual realm. So, this passage also refers to the artisans not making physical replications of the angels and demons that they see in their imaginations. This is also why tattooing was outlawed in the scriptures. Everyone involved in deliverance knows that those who get tattoos of demons are getting tattoos of real spiritual forces that use tattooing as a sign of allegiance. This opens the door for demonic affliction. It's not just an imaginary figure on your body. It is a stamp of ownership by an actual demon! This is why God gives us clear instructions for taking what we see in our imagination seriously.

I need to be clear that I am not saying that you cannot create art with such images. That is not what this passage is saying, as some have suggested. It instructs and warns us not to create images of the unknown for the purpose of worshipping them. There is a difference between creating a story with these beings represented to tell a story that glorifies God, and creating a story in which these beings are represented as the stars or heroes. Jesus the only begotten Son of God is the only hero in our story. Everyone else is a co-star and villain!

This is important as you pursue your relationship with God because demons do speak; they do so the same way all communication happens in the spiritual realm, thoughts and images. Some people are teaching that the imagination is a spiritual realm. I don't believe that the imagination itself is a spiritual realm, but that it definitely connects us to the spiritual realm and that it is very much like the spiritual realm. They both have qualities that are not bound by the rules of the natural world. I believe that while they may interact that they are different because God tells us that we can speak vain visions and delusions from *our own mind!* "Delusion" is a key word in the passage. The word delusions means, a belief held in strong convictions despite the fact that the evidence is clearly contrary.

This definition of delusional is very important in helping us to recognize the spirits of deception I speak of in "Voice of Deception." This is because God has the power to overwhelm our imagination and pull us into experiences such as Peter's encounter with the great sheet and Ezekiel in his many visionary experiences. Or consider what He says in Number 12. He says, *"If there is a prophet among you I the Lord speak to him "IN" a vision…"* not by a vision. I believe the "IN" refers to God meeting us in the place of imagination. In fact we see that he speaks to many in dreams. Science has proven that dreams occur in our imagination. So God uses this faculty as a tool of communication but so does Satan. And with his people and the undiscerning he will attempt to pull humans into experiences. However, recognizing his communication boils down to delusion. He (Satan) is a liar and the truth is not in him to tell. This means that anything he says will result in delusion. An example of delusion is seen as the prophets in the book of Jeremiah have visionary encounters in which they see peace for Israel even though they are clearly worshipping other Gods. This clearly violates the Book of the Law in Deuteronomy 28:15-68. Jeremiah's revelation of captivity was not a new revelation. God told them in advance what the penalty would be for their harlotry. Any prophesy contradicting God's initial revelation was delusional.

Today it appears in those who only see angels. Why is this delusional? Jesus had more recorded encounters with demons than angels. Why you might ask? Jesus had more encounters with demons because He came to set the captives free! He came to confront the evil that kept you bound. Angels are not holding humans captive. When we see them in scriptures they are working along side the man of God to accomplish his task of setting captives free. Jesus saw what was at the root of captivity and His presence alone drew them out of darkness into the light. If you are really walking in the light you will find some dark ones. Real light brings them out of hiding, that I can promise you. And that's okay, God allows us to see them to expose them and cast them out.

My Encounters

I remember when God first started to open up the reality of the spiritual realm to me. At first I was horrified by what was happening. Then I learned about my authority in Christ. I also learned to use what God revealed to set captives free. After a while I became so accustomed to seeing behind the veil that I began to handle the revelations casually.

Then one day at work my eyes opened and I saw a dark cloud of demons running down the hall into my office. I had assumed that they were going to meet me there in an attempt to wreak havoc. By this time it was normal for me to see them and I knew how to use the authority of Christ to bind them and get rid of them. So I lightly regarded them. I just allowed them to go about their business. A few minutes later one of my dear co-workers started to violently vomit and she "suddenly" developed a very high fever. When she arrived at work there were no signs of illness, it just happened "suddenly". In fact, no one else got sick that day or any day after. So she was immediately rushed to the hospital and almost died. I felt absolutely horrible about having this information and doing nothing to prevent them from terrorizing this woman. I repented and told God I would never again ignore the things that He allowed me to see. But this was not seen via imagination. This vision I saw with my own two eyes as I had always seen them.

Then there was another occasion that occurred with my imagination. It was this experience that caused me to seek the face of God about the subject of imagination. In fact I had seen many static visions in my imagination and I understood God using it this way, but that was all. Then I had this experience and it just threw me for a loop. I just didn't know what to make of it.

I know a couple that is going through serious marital issues and they are on the brink of a divorce. They both have issues, but the husband had some serious issues going on in his life. They are the kind of issues that sort of lead to a clear indication that something was really going wrong in his spiritual life. So being the good Christian and intercessor that I am, I decided that I would intercede for him. And so I did. I have interceded for many and have had many unusual experiences but this one was most different. As I was praying, I started seeing a picture in my mind of this guy, but it was projected out in front of me. It was like looking through a window, or at least that's how I would describe it. As I looked I saw that he was tied up in a chair and three demons surrounded him as if they were protecting him. So thinking that this was a vision from God directing me in how to intercede for him, I started praying a prayer of binding and loosing. Then all of a sudden one of the demons turned around and looked in my direction as if he could hear me. I thought to myself "hummm" that's a bit strange I didn't imagine him turning around. Why is he turning around? Then in a flash this thing was in my face. Not my physical face, but in my mind's eye in front of me as if standing in my face. It was not a fleeting image. It was literally an animated image held in my face. I was shocked to say the least but I kept praying. Then this thing named himself. He said, "I am the destroyer." At which point I ignored him and kept praying. From that moment on I saw him in my house and he was doing all he could to create an atmosphere of havoc between my wife and I. My wife at this point does not see like I do and I did not know how to proceed to get this thing exposed and out of our life. I knew that telling her what was really happening was a risk. I was afraid that she would think I had lost my mind. I told her before we were married that sometimes

God allows me to see behind the veil but she had never seen me used this way. This thing literally tried to destroy my marriage in the short time that it was operating.

At first I thought maybe it was just my imagination. I really struggled to believe what was happening because I was used to seeing them with my physical eyes not in my imagination. So I started praying in the kitchen early one morning because I could see this thing at night in my bedroom whispering in the ear of my wife. So I decided enough is enough and that it was worth confronting. So I called it out by name and said spirit of the destroyer! Next I saw an image in my mind of him coming from my bedroom moving quickly down the steps. As I pondered the reality of what was happening, my son, with a confused look on his 9 year old face, said, "Daddy, who's coming down the steps? Someone is coming down the steps." Then my inner man's peace went off. So I finally exposed him, bound him, and sent him out of my life and immediately our life returned to normal.

I told God that I did not want to tell these stories. In fact until this book I have never shared them with anyone. However He insisted that I tell them so that you would have an understanding of the reality that exists in the imagination and so that you would know not to use your imagination for angel worship or any other type of false deity worship. Lastly, so that you will know that what you see is real and God uses it to expose darkness so that you can set the captives free.

The last point I made is of uttermost importance, because this is the discerning of spirits at work. I find it very strange that people say they are operating in this gift and all they see is angels. The word "discern" means to distinguish. How can you distinguish between spirits if you only see angles? Also, discerning of spirits is not a gift of seeing the obvious in the spiritual realm. It is an ability to know the difference between things in the spirit realm. I have seen things in the spiritual realm that are godly, but do not look like what you would expect a godly creature to look like. Likewise, Isaiah's description of the Seraphim leads you to believe they are more weird in appearance than beautiful. So pretty does not equate to a creature of God and ugly does not equate to demonic. Demons do not always appear as demons. The Bible says that they can transform into angels of light. Like I said above, the spiritual realm is not limited to the same rules of physics as the natural realm. In that realm anything is possible. In Daniel 10:1-20 the prophet has a vision of the mighty Arch Angel Gabriel and he was so terrified at his presence that his strength left his body. So the angel changes his form to a human form that would better help Daniel to hear his message (see Dan. 10:16). Read the story it says *"And **suddenly** one having the likeness of the sons of men touched me."* As you keep reading you will notice that the man that suddenly appeared is the same Arch Angel Gabriel. The Bible also tells us that we entertain angels unknowingly (see Heb. 13:2). So do not assume that the angel you see is from the Lord. Test him to be sure.

So discerning of spirits is not the gift of seeing angels and demons, but it is the ability to know the difference between the demonic and the divine. As I have said elsewhere, if you are only seeing angels, one of them is a spirit of deception. If you expose him he will reveal his true nature to you. Then you can get rid of him.

Why is this important to know? It's important because some people believe that God would not allow us to be deceived. This is true, but this does not mean that He does so apart from your participation in the process. He protects us by informing us with everything we need to know so that we can discern. That is why we have the Bible and the supernatural gift of discerning of spirits. It should also be noted that the Bible is full of Christians that were deceived. *"O foolish Galatians, who has bewitched you* (Gal. 3:1)..." *"Keeping the faith and a good conscience, which some have rejected and suffered shipwreck in regard to their faith* (1 Tim. 1:20)..." *"Some have already turned away to follow Satan* (2 Tim. 5:15)..." As you can see it is very possible to be deceived.

As you can see it is very important to learn how to be watchful and learn how to discern. I said it in *"Voices of Deception"* it's not about whether or not God gives you a rock or a fish. It's about you knowing the difference between the two! So learn to be watchful as the Bible says. I told you this spiritual stuff that people dabble in is not a playground. Things can get really serious for the undiscerning and immature quickly!

210

God told me one day, that He was not offended` by me asking and checking to discern that it was Him speaking to me. He said that He expects that and teaches that. It is what we are expected to do. Furthermore, it is also what you are expected to do as well. Demand any angel to confess that Jesus Christ came in the flesh and that He is Lord. The Bible says that this can only happen by the Spirit of God.

Without a doubt this idea of the imagination is going to draw some criticism, but I challenge you to read your Bible and consider that Daniel and many others encountered supernatural beings in their dreams and visions—Dreams and visions, which Daniel clearly states are occurring in his mind. In Daniel chapter 10, which you read earlier, he says that all of the vision was happening while he was on his face on the ground in a deep sleep. The Angelic being seen in Daniel's dream that is obviously occurring in his imagination was real. Read it for yourself, it can be easily verified in the word. In fact read all of Daniel, it is quite a revelation on the subject.

Moving Forward

As you go on in your journey to encountering God, you need to know that His voice bubbles up from inside of you and flows to your mind in thoughts and images. Therefore, write them down and discern them. It will take you some time to mature in your discernment, but journaling will help you grow in learning the voice of God.

Also remember that you may hear His voice as perception (intuition, conscience, imagination) or you may hear His voice as an utterance coming out of your spirit.

Don't ignore your imagination. When God uses it, the encounters are real. Also I hope that you understand that hell uses it as well. In fact sometimes you are more aware of demonic voices than God's voice initially. This happens because you are familiar with the works of the flesh and God's ways are strange us. This is why we study to learn His way so that our minds are transformed into a place that recognizes Him at work in our lives.

Protecting What You Hear

Something that still appears to be difficult for us as Christians to accept is the reality that we are in a spiritual war. Whether we know it or not spiritual warfare is being waged against every human being. Hearing the voice of God makes you a prime target for real spiritual warfare because your enemy is not interested in allowing you to change your mind. He will do everything possible to resist your efforts to transform your mind into the mind of Christ. He does this because the more you understand about Christ, the more of His nature you will be able to reveal. It is like opening a door slightly to allow light into a dark room. The more you open the door the more light pours into the room. To demons light is agitating, they are spirits that dwell in the shadows. This is why they are referred to as thieves and not robbers. Robbers move boldly in the light to steal, but a thief comes in stealthily to take from those that are sleeping. Jesus wants you to be watchful so that the things that He speaks to you are not stolen from you; things such as your future, your dignity, your integrity, and finally your witness.

One thing you will come to know as you hear the voice of God is that His word to us is a seed that takes root. It is with proper care and watering that you will find that His word produces growth in you. Remember I told you that God's voice edifies, comforts, and encourages us. It takes us to the next level.

Matthew 13:1-18, reaffirms to us the reality that the word God speaks to us is a seed planted inside of us. It is also clear in this passage that it produces fruit. It tells us that our hearts must be in a certain condition for the seed to produce growth. This is what our main passage in Job tells us as well, when it says that the inspiration of God leads to understanding. This is very important because the first thing that Satan tries to do in the passage is to steal the word from those to whom it was given. It says they hear the word from God's mouth, but do not understand what they heard. So it's not enough to hear the word from God, we must also seek to understand it if it is to produce real fruit in us.

This is something that I understand all too well. When God first started dealing with me about the reality of some of the beings we see in our imagination I struggled really hard to understand what He was saying. This led to a roller coaster ride of seeing visions and then going mentally blind. God would speak a particular truth to me regarding the imagination and I would accept it and would immediately start moving in it. Then that second voice (doubt) would arise and steal it from my heart. Finally, I realized that God's "ok" regarding the use of imagination was not enough to settle my heart. I needed to understand what and how the imagination worked. It was at this point that God poured understanding into me from the scriptures and opened my eyes. Once I understood, nothing Satan tried to do prevailed against me.

You should know that this is going to happen to you too! Everything in this book that you fail to understand is going to be subject to being stolen from your heart. And it will impact your experience. As I said earlier, you will not get this for free. Your adversary is going to do all he can to limit your progression in hearing the voice of God. Therefore, you need to understand the process that the word of God goes through to become understanding in your heart.

Every word or seed from God goes through three phases to become understanding.

Revelation

First there is the revelation. Revelation is what this book is all about. It is the moment that you hear the voice of God and He deposits a word in your life. It could be as simple as a word saying you are special to God. It is revelation because it is something in the heart of God that you didn't know until He told you. It is His word and it is a seed in your life. It is destined to produce fruit in you.

Incubation

Then there is the most important phase. This is the phase where we are challenged with doubts. Things such as, *did God really say... If you are...*

How can someone like you be special? It is the season when the word of God is tried (see Psalm 18:30, Prov. 30:5). In the Bible it is depicted as the wilderness.

This phase is important, because it will sort your soul from your spirit. What I mean is, if you really believe you have a word from God, you will study and seek after the knowledge you need to reach the next phase, which is activation. I said it in the chapter, "Hindrances to Hearing" under the section titled doubt that we understand by faith. In other words, some of the things you struggle to walk in are a struggle because you lack the depth of understanding needed to walk in that word. Seeking clarity is the answer to such a problem.

Activation

Then there is the activation phase. In this phase the word of God has passed through the fire and has produced in you a light that allows you to walk in truth. It is the "ah ha" moment or the moment when the light comes on. The beauty of reaching the activation phase is that understanding leads to application. Once you understand something you will find that you have the wisdom to apply what you know.

So in the revelation phase you will suddenly "know" something. In the incubation phase you are tested on what you heard. It is the questioning phase and it is very important. Lastly, there is the activation phase, which is the phase in which you understand what you know and you are able to use that knowledge.

Example of the Process

Here are some biblical examples of those who had words that followed this process.

Israel

Israel heard a word from God regarding going to the promise land. That was the revelation. Then they got stuck in the wilderness. But prior to the wilderness their word was tested when they saw the giants in the land. That was the incubation of the revelation. Then 40 years later the word arose in their heart and they took the land. That was the activation of the revelation.

Moses

Moses is another example. He knew that God wanted to use him to deliver Israel from Egypt (see Acts 7:22). That was the revelation. Then his illegal actions drove him into the wilderness where He was until He saw a burning bush. I'm sure the dream died in him over those 40 years. This was the period of incubation. Then God sent him to do what was in his heart 40 years prior. This was the moment of activation.

Abraham

Abraham had a revelation from God of a promised child that would become a great nation. Then time passed and he and his wife in their attempt to try to understand how God would bring such a thing to pass created their own version of the plan of God. This waiting period is the word going through the incubation period. Then finally God gave them the promised child and they cast out what they created by their own understanding and walked in the promise. This is the activation period.

Jesus

Lastly, we see this in Jesus Himself. He is baptized and the Father speaks to Him from Heaven saying, "You are my beloved Son in whom I am well pleased." Then the Holy Spirit drives Him into the wilderness and there His truth is tested as Satan repeatedly questions His knowledge of His identity. *"If you are the Son of God,"* he says. This challenge in the wilderness is the word going through the incubation period. Then last, Jesus comes out of the wilderness and straightaway goes into the temple and declares who He is (see Luke 4:7). It is the moment where the revelation He received at the baptismal pool became understanding. This understanding activated Him and from that point forward we see Him walking in that truth. He heard something, it was tested, and then He understood it and walked in that knowledge.

As I said above, this is going to happen to you as well. It is not enough to hear the voice of God. You need to understand what you know if you are to really be able to use what you heard. If you do not learn to pursue the understanding you will be overwhelmed when doubt comes to test the word.

Going from Incubation to Activation

Building on the previous idea of revelation, incubation, and activation, how do we move through this process to allow or assist with getting to a place of understanding?

Paul in 2 Timothy 2:7 provides us with some insight into how we get an understanding of the word we received. He says to the young pastor, *"Reflect on what I am saying, for the Lord will give you insight into all this"*. In other words Paul tells Timothy to meditate on what he is hearing and he says that this process leads to God turning on the lights. He says that reflection leads of understanding.

Later in the next chapter I go into greater detail on how the process of pondering not only plants the word in your heart, but also transforms the mind. In this chapter I am merely attempting to help you understand what to do with the word the Lord has given you. But one understanding does not a transformed mind make. It is only when we allow what we understand to change how we think, that we start the process of transforming the mind.

The other reason it is necessary for you to reflect on the word you hear from God to ensure you get an understanding, is so that you understand the timing of the event. God says to Jeremiah, *"What do you see? He says I see a rod of an almond tree."* Then God says you have seen well, now I am ready to bring my word to pass. Seeing clearly is a symbol of understanding in this passage. It is only when you can see clearly that you can really begin to walk in your word.

I see this all the time with preachers. God calls them on Monday and by the next Sunday they are ready to preach. This is because they do not understand the process of revelation, incubation, and activation. Most of them never get to the activation part but die in the incubation part of the process. Why? They die because they don't see clearly or don't really understand what God really wants them to do. They only have a revelation. However, if you want to get to the activation part of your word from God then you need to reflect on the revelation until He gives you the insight you need to walk that revelation out.

Here is another example of this idea at work. In Ezekiel 37, the prophet is carried away by the Spirit of God into a vision, and in that vision he saw a valley that was full of dry bones. From the outset it appears that this is a vision of nothingness. The Bible describes the bones as dry, disconnected, and scattered in the valley. But once God causes all of the bones to partner with the right bones and causes sinew and flesh to come upon them we see a clear picture of an army. What I want you to see is the fact that the army and all that was necessary for the army to exist was always there in the vision. Ezekiel, however, could not see this army until God brought the things or the understanding of the things in the vision together. Here we can plainly see the importance of allowing God to clear up our vision so that we can walk in understanding. You should know that it might take 40 years as it did with Moses and Israel. Or it may take 40 days as it did with Jesus.

Manifestations of the Voice

Now I want to deal with the subject of manifestations of the voice of God. In the chapter titled *"Fruit of His Voice"* we talk about the effects of hearing the voice of God, but in this part of this chapter I want to deal with what the voice of God produces contextually. Fruit deals with the feelings produced, but manifestation deals with the end product. It is what we see.

So the question is what might the voice of God look like when all is said and done? To answer that question we must look at the revelation gifts in 1 Corinthians 12. They are Word of Wisdom, Word of Knowledge, and Prophecy. Most people say that there are three revelation gifts but for this purpose I am including prophecy as the fourth because of what type of information it produces. Discerning of spirits is also a revelation gift but for this discussion you won't need to understand this one. The other three impart to us information for the purpose of communion. Discerning of spirits is not a communion gift per se, but more useful as an atmospheric thermometer. It tells us what is in the spiritual atmosphere around us. It is a very, very, very powerful and necessary gift, but when it is just you and God you will know it is Him—or at least you should.

So what about theses revelation gifts? These gifts have been traditionally taught from the prophetic point of view. The prophetic point of view is a very limited view of these gifts and how they manifest. It is important to see that the Bible says that there are twelve gifts but they can have differences in operation. This means that they can manifest differently depending on the need that is present. So what may operate one way in one ministry may operate differently in another ministry. Some of the confusion about this subject is due to the fact that a lot of people want to be prophets and apostles. They hear the glamorous stories about the dreams and visions, but they do not often hear the not so glamorous stories about the loneliness, being misunderstood, the embarrassment, or the not so pleasant encounters with dark forces. Either way, you need to understand what they are because the voice of God is going to produce one of these three manifestations.

Word of Knowledge

The first manifestation that I want to discuss is the gift of the word of knowledge. It has always been taught as the divine revelation of facts about people and places past and present. For example, if you were standing in line at the grocery store and suddenly you got a revelation about the person standing in front of you. It might be something such as a vision or random thought showing them holding three kids. This is supernatural knowledge communicating to you the number of kids this woman has. It is supernatural knowledge. This gift however is not limited to knowledge of facts about people and places.

It is called the word of knowledge. It is a manifestation of supernatural knowledge. It is when God tells you something or imparts to you knowledge that you did not learn through natural means. I know this challenges the traditional view of this gift, but you must remember that these revelation gifts as well as the utterance gifts must be defined considering the climate of that time.

When you consider the climate of the early church you must remember that there was not a Bible or any other written document regarding Christianity. Christianity was a completely new concept that was literally being defined as it grew. This is where the revelation gifts are best seen in operation. They were literally used by God to impart doctrine and teaching regarding the foundations of the faith. With this understanding we can now see that the word of knowledge was not just a manifestation of facts about people, places, and events, past and present, but was a manifestation and a heavenly impartation of divinely inspired knowledge.

This may be the reason that people think God stopped speaking (He has not). I have heard people say that there is no new revelation to add to the Bible. This is true, but as you can see, there are thousands of doctrines that can be extracted from the Bible. However, the meaty and deep things can only be given to you by the Holy Spirit. He searches the deep things of God, and brings them back to us. There are so many things to understand, why would God stop teaching us what we need to know. This is how it operated then and this is how it should be operating now. This is why we need the gift of the word of knowledge in operation.

The most prolific person to operate in the word of knowledge is seen in the person of the Apostle Paul. How else do you think that he had knowledge that the kingdom of darkness is divided into principalities, powers, and rulers of the darkness of this age? Or how else do you think that he had such deep understandings of grace, faith, the laying on of hands, and baptisms (plural). He did not get this information from a book it was imparted to him through the word of knowledge at work in his ministry.

We see this happening more and more today. God is giving people supernatural knowledge of things such as deliverance and healing, body, soul, and spirit. There is supernatural knowledge about money and how the kingdom works. Even this book is the result of the word of knowledge. My understanding of this subject did not come out of my study time. It was all spoken to me by the Holy Spirit at various times and in different ways. It is supernaturally imparted knowledge.

Word of Wisdom

This is probably the most misunderstood manifestation of the group. The word of wisdom is taught as being a word about the future. This is incorrect. Wisdom is defined as insight and understanding. It differs from knowledge because you can know something and not understand it. For instance, you can know where the engine is in your car but not understand how it works. From a spiritual standpoint you can have a dream and know that it is from God, but not understand its meaning. So the word of wisdom is a supernatural the ability to receive understanding and give counsel. It is seen in the interpretation of Joseph's dream. It is also seen in the ministry of Daniel who was renowned for his wisdom in interpreting dreams. (see Daniel 1:17)

In Genesis 37 Joseph sees a dream of twelve sheaves bowing down to his sheaf. He immediately knows that this refers to him. That is the manifestation of knowledge, but the interpretation and understanding of the dream is the word of wisdom. It can also manifest as a word of counsel as it did in Ahithophel. 2 Samuel 16:23 says that Ahithophel's counsel was as if one had inquired of the oracles of God. In other words his wisdom was so great that it was like talking to God. He was gifted to speak words of wisdom.

Today this is best seen in the ministry of Bishop T.D. Jakes. I don't think anyone, saved or unsaved can argue with the fact that he has an extraordinary sense of wisdom. This is why people hang onto the words that he speaks. It is the supernatural manifestation of the word of wisdom at work in his life and ministry.

I know that someone is going to disagree with this definition because it has been taught for so long that it was the gift of foreknowledge. But if you consider Solomon, who was considered the wisest man in history, you will see that with all of his wisdom, he was not known for foreknowing. He was known for his profound understanding of the many subjects of life. The book of proverbs, which is Solomon's writings, does not contain foreknowledge.

Then there is Ephesians 1:18, in which Paul prays for the spirit of wisdom and revelation... He is not praying for them to have a spirit of foreknowledge, but that the eyes of their "understanding" would be enlightened. In fact, wisdom is only taught as foreknowledge in reference to 1 Corinthians 12. It is not thought of in this manner by any Bible scholar or in any other place in scripture. You will never hear someone teach on wisdom in connection to knowing the future in any other part of the Bible. This fails our "scriptural test". Truth is parallel!

So the word of wisdom is not a foreknowing gift. It is a word of supernatural understanding. In fact when Solomon receives wisdom from God it is called an understanding heart (see 1 Kings 4:29). Now, having an understanding heart may affect how you handle the future in terms of making wiser decisions, but it will not tell you the events of the future.

Prophecy

Now we get to the gift that is most earnestly desired. The gift that Paul says all should seek, prophecy (see 1 Cor. 14:1). In traditional teachings regarding prophecy it has really been limited to edification, exhortation, and comfort. These however, are descriptions of its function. These are words that describe how we feel or the effect a prophecy has on us, but they do not define prophecy. So what is prophecy? It is the gift or manifestation of foretelling and or forth telling. It is a speaking forth of the mind, plans, or intentions of God. It may be predictive or it may not. When a word does not contain predictive elements it is simply a forth telling. This is what most people call basic prophesying. It can be as simple as God telling a person that He loves them and has so much more in store for them if they would just give him the pain that they are harboring in their heart. That is basic prophecy. Then there is a deeper level or stream of prophecy that is predictive. Both may contain words of knowledge and or wisdom, but they are most evident with the predictive element of prophecy. For example, God may tell someone that He loves them and has so much more for them if they would let him heal the pain in their heart. And that tomorrow a particular bookstore will receive a shipment of a particular book that God is going to use to give them an understanding of how He heals the hurting heart. And when all is said and done that information is going to be used in ministry to many women across the globe. And that the pain is just a set up for the future ministry!

Can you see the difference? One is shallow and the other is a little more in depth. Sometimes people judge the depth of a prophecy by the amount of words of knowledge proceeding even though in the end the prophecy may not say anything more than God loves you. However, the deeper end of the prophetic stream sees afar off and may contain little in terms of words of knowledge.

For example, sometime ago as I was entering the cafeteria at work and I saw a young lady from my noonday Bible study. When I saw her, the Spirit of God came upon me so I engaged her in conversation. As we were talking I noticed that she was pregnant and in that moment the Lord spoke to me about the child. He told me the child's name and that the child would do some great things. This stunned the young lady because the name that God had given me was the name she had chosen for her child. This word of knowledge opened up the deeper flow. It was just one word of knowledge but it led to a deeper predictive flow. Now this child is grown and has already been in the newspaper for her athletic abilities.

This story is a perfect example of how prophecy leads to comfort, edification, and exhortation. One piece of information I omitted from the story is that this woman was not married. This child was not conceived in the perfect will of God, but yet in His mercy He spoke to her about the child. He edified, comforted, and exhorted her by allowing her to know that even though she was in the wrong, that she was not forgotten by her Savior.

We can see examples of this in almost every book in the Bible. In fact, we see it in all the books of the prophets. You will also notice while reading through the prophetic books that there are not a lot of words of knowledge or wisdom. They are pure prophecy. It is just forth telling and foretelling of the mind of God.

The Anointing and the Voice

One of the phrases seen most often in the Old Testament in relation to the prophetic voice of God is the *'hand of God.'* In Ezekiel 37 the prophet uses the term to describe what he experienced prior to God bringing him into a vision of a valley full of dry bones. Likewise, we see a similar thing occur when Elijah asked for a harpist to play for him so that he could prophesy the will of God to the kings. (see 2 Kings 3:15) It was not until the hand of the Lord came upon him that entering the realm of the supernatural was possible. Lastly, we see this in the life of Elijah when the Bible says that the hand of God came upon him and he outran King Ahab's horse drawn chariots. (see 1 Kings 18:46)

So what exactly is the hand of the Lord? The hand of God is the tangible anointing or empowering of the Holy Spirit that comes upon us to accomplish a specific task. It is not the presence of God but the power of God. What is the difference you may ask? Let's consider a police officer. He has presence that comes with being a police officer. The presence is his authority. He also has a gun, a taser, a club, and handcuffs to enforce His authority. These give him power. This is a natural truth with spiritual significance. God can be seen speaking from His presence in his encounters with Moses at the burning bush and with Abraham in his many encounters with God. But when God needed to demonstrate the power of His voice you will see that the hand of God was involved. Some may say that you don't see this in every situation. That is because God often provides us with examples of His process. So we are allowed to see in the instances of Elisha, Elijah, and Ezekiel the process in various situations. Elisha's example demonstrates to us that the hand of God enabled him to prophesy. Elijah's example demonstrates that the hand of God empowered him to do the physically impossible. Again, in Ezekiel's example demonstrates to us that it was the hand of God that empowered him to have visions. While these situations are all different they all share a common thread of truth. That truth is that God's hand empowers us to do the supernatural.

To really get a clear understanding of the anointing as the hand of God, we need to understand the term *"hand."* The term *"hand"* is a reference to God's assistance. The popular cliché, "Can you give him or her a hand with that?" would be a depiction of the way the word "hand" in used in reference to the hand of God. This idea of a helping hand is what we see in each of these stories presented. We see God helping men do the impossible.

In the Old Testament God used prophets to visually depict the hand of God coming upon a life by the anointing of that person with oil. So we see a pouring on of the anointing. However in the New Testament we do not see this term "hand of God" coming upon individuals. What we see however is that the hand of God came upon the church. This is what we call the Baptism of the Holy Spirit. It is seen several times in the book of Acts. The difference is that the hand of God came upon men in the Old Testament and lifted. However in the New Testament it comes upon us and fills us. So there is one baptism of fire but multiple fills. Remember, God fills and flows upon us.

This means that if you are a believer, God's hand will come upon you and then when God is ready to move He will fill or inspire you to do His will. When this happens you will feel a tangible power spring up out of your person and overflow onto your body. For me this feels like a warm liquid fire or larva. In fact when it comes upon me it starts at my core and increases in intensity depending on what God wants to accomplish. Sometimes it appears as a light as warmth on my back and at other times it goes from my head to my toes. My point to you is that it is very tangible power. Again, it feels like liquid fire or electricity—it has weight, and can sometimes be heard as it moves over the body in waves.

God also uses it to separate His thoughts from mine in matters where He needs me to do something important. When I want to operate on a supernatural plane He will anoint a particular thought or He will give me a thought that stirs the anointing.

This has two purposes—one, to empower me to know what He is asking me to do and two, to reaffirm or create a witness to me that what He has asked me to do is His will. In other words it is a sign of His agreement. The Bible says, *"If any two of you touch and agree on Earth concerning anything that you ask it will be done for you. "* (Matt. 18:19). We always assume that this passage is restricted to humans, but the Holy Spirit is also on Earth. That being the case, He will touch you to create a sense of agreement with you to accomplish His will. If I pray for someone and the anointing does not manifest, I know I don't have divine agreement. Sometimes this simply means that the miracle is going to have to be accomplished by faith in the promises of God. But if I pray and the hand of God comes upon me it creates an agreement with God that means it is surely going to be done on Earth as it is in Heaven!

So what does this have to do with the voice of God? Hearing the voice of God is eventually going to lead to ministering the voice of God. In fact, the Bible tells us plainly to desire to prophesy (see 1 Cor. 14:1). It also says for *"all"* may prophesy (see 1 Cor. 14:31). So eventually as you develop your spiritual hearing and sight you will more than likely be used of God to speak on His behalf to edify, comfort, and exhort someone from time to time. When this happens, not only will prophecy become activated, but you may find that God will call upon you to operate in other manifestation gifts of the Spirit. As this begins to occur, you will need to understand what the anointing is, how it works, and what it does. This tidbit of information that I am attempting to deposit should help start you on the way so that you can not only develop a beautiful relationship with God but will also understand how to move with Him in the gifts. For more understanding of this subject I recommend reading Kenneth Hagan's books on the subject.

As it relates to the gifts operating in my life, often when I am in conversation with someone and God wants to speak to them He will bring the anointing upon me to let me know that He wants to speak to the individual. When it starts to come upon me it is usually attached to either a spontaneous thought or some subject that arose during the conversation. It is my sign to partner with God to do something special for the person. Sometimes I will reveal to the person that the Lord wants to speak to them about the issue. Other times I will just allow Him to speak freely through me. It is always funny to me that the person will say at the conclusion of the conversation, "That's so weird, I was just praying about that this morning. You don't know that God was using you to speak to me." I just laugh because I always know when God is using me to speak to others because He comes upon me to let me know

225

He is going to do so. So why do I not always take the "Thus saith the Lord" approach. I don't always take that approach because it is not about my Glory. It is about His glory and the edification of the individual. The important thing is not that I am seen, but that I recognize God's opportunity to speak into someone's life, tune in, and yield to allow Him to do His will.

Someone may be wondering whether or not I am concerned with making sure the person knows that the word given is from the Lord. The funny thing about the anointing is that you do not have to make people listen to you when God is speaking. Remember His word burns in our heart as He is speaking to us. He is not easy to ignore and if you really have a word from God the recipient is really the only person who can verify that word.

I also want to point out to you that the way this particular anointing manifests on me is how it operates in the manifestation of the revelation and utterance gifts. God manifests the anointing with a slight difference when it comes to operating in the power gifts. For instance, the "gifts of healings" will often manifest all over my being but my hands will feel as if I am wearing gloves or oven mitts. But in general it is still a feeling of liquid fire or electricity, except it is felt in my hands.

I suspect that God has led me into this discussion because many of you will begin to experience the anointing coming upon you as you are reading this book. If you feel a sudden warming sensation coming upon you it is God verifying and validating your faith. You will also begin to notice that it will manifest when certain thoughts pass through your mind.

Some people have said that feeling the anointing is just a starting point for the immature. But it has been 20 plus years for me and God still chooses to manifest this way and it always produces results. Also, you will see examples of this in the scriptures as a way of God operating. In the Old Testament era it came upon the saints and in the New Testament era and dispensation if fills us and flows out of us. So ignore those who tell you to operate in the supernatural without it. Again it is God's helping hand that allows you to easily accomplish His desired will.

Chapter Eleven
Transforming Your Eyes and Ears

Don't Start Here

In the last chapter we discussed the sound of God's voice. We also discussed the process whereby we come to receive divine communication. One of the things presented in that chapter is the reality and or importance of the mind in the process of hearing the voice of God. I hope I was clear in communicating the necessity of transforming our minds into a place that not only hears, but recognizes God. This chapter is dedicated to explaining the mind in more detail. It is also my goal in this chapter to help you to understand what role faith and meditation play in the transformation process. You may be wondering why I would write a book about the voice of God and add a chapter about the mind. But as the title suggest this book is not only about hearing the voice of God. I have in my many years of walking with God come to thoroughly understand that people are not struggling to hear the voice of God. They are struggling to distinguish it from the others.

I have also come to realize that the main cause of such a problem often boils down to people not knowing the character or mind of God. In fact, as I was writing this book, I came into contact with a person that was certain she was hearing from God. Even though she got a contrary result, she still held to the position that it was God who spoke to her. Not only did she hold to this position, she actually proceeded to chastise God for not keeping His end of the deal. This all communicates to me one very profound truth. People really do not know the mind of God.

The other problem that clues me into this reality is the fact that people can say that they are hearing from God and yet their lives remain defeated and unproductive. In the last chapter I told you that the voice of God produces words that God uses as seeds to cause change in us. I also told you that in the process of God turning the inspired thoughts into understanding, that it must go through three phases; revelation, incubation, and activation. This process is very important if we are going to transform our minds. It is not enough to have a revelation. The revelation must be incubated and finally activated so that it will transform that part of your understanding. You will find that with each new understanding gained, that you are changing and growing. You will become productive and see the effect He is really after. That is, that you are changed into replicas of Christ.

As we proceed onward in this chapter I must tell you that this is not a starting point. If you are like me then you have a tendency to read through the table of contents and start reading at the chapter you feel answers your immediate questions. Please do not attempt to start at this chapter. This chapter builds upon ideas and concepts about the mind established in previous chapters. In this chapter I am going into some deep places about the mind and imagination as tools of transformation. Some of what you read will challenge you to see differently about the role of the imagination, and its usefulness in the process. I will also attempt to explain how this incredible perceptual faculty impacts our faith.

Two Minds, One Person

The starting point for this discussion is the understanding that you are not the only person living in your body. In the last chapter we read how the Holy Spirit lives in our spirit. And guess what? He also has a *"mind"*! Yes, the Holy Spirit has a mind. I pointed this out in the previous chapters that the Bible says He has thoughts. We also see He is creative which means, He has an imagination.

This is very important for you to understand if you are to clearly hear the sound of God's voice. God has a mind to which He refers as the **MIND OF CHRIST**, which we all have (present tense) (see 1 Cor. 2:16). That mind, although it is His, is resident in each of us. I have also, stated several times now, that we recognize His thoughts by transforming our mind to mirror His mind. His mind reveals the good, acceptable, and perfect will of God to us. As God was sharing this with me I could see a mind with thoughts running through it and His thoughts were distinguished by glowing thoughts. Yes, His thoughts were glowing in the mind. They lit up the mind so that it had light. This was the visual He gave me to demonstrate His point.

This is important because wrong theology creates a wrong practice. Some people believe that God uses our imagination and I understand what these people are innocently trying to communicate. I also initially believed that God was using my imagination to communicate with me as well. And He does to a degree. Your mind engages His mind in communication. However, I always noticed that there was a slight difference between my imagination and the visions I was seeing. They always seemed like my imaginations, but were somehow different, and I could notice this difference. I said it in the last chapter that my visions appeared as if I was peering through a window. This also explains the spontaneous nature of the thoughts and images. I did not know or understand how this was happening. I only knew that I was seeing something somewhere else outside of my mind but somehow it was in my mind. I know that sounds confusing, but it is the best way that I can explain it. Now I understand that I have a mind with thoughts and images, and God has a mind with thoughts and images and we both reside in the same vessel. Likewise, because we are roommates, He allows me access to His room (thoughts) so that I can see and hear what He is thinking towards me.

Jeremiah says I know the thoughts that I think *"towards"* you, not about you. There again is the "from" and "to" concept. It is very important to notice the difference because this means that God's thoughts come to us from His mind. Therefore we see such phrases in the Bible as, *"For He sent His word..."* and *"For the word of the Lord came to me..."* The same is true with His imaginations, or visions. This means they are spontaneous and not under our control. Remember that they bubble up and forth and flow to us from within. We cannot make God speak to us in a vision or dream, we must wait until He speaks and when He does so our heavenly roommate will do so spontaneously. He will always do so at His own choosing. In fact Jesus said that the Holy Spirit does not speak of His own, but He speaks only what He hears (see John 16:13). This means that He is not someone that is rambling on and on, that we tune in to hear speaking, but to the contrary He speaks when He hears from the Father. Our job is to tune in and wait for Him to speak, which may or may not happen at that moment.

The Imagination and the Heart

One of the other things that is happening today is that people are using Proverbs 23:7, *"As man thinks in his heart so is he"*, as a springboard to foster the idea of positive thinking as a creative force. In other words, the teaching is that what you see in your imagination will create a reality for you. This is partially true, but only partially.

This is what God has taught me about this verse. First He showed me that while the imagination is used to create and invent, it does not perform the same function in relation to the heart. When this passage says as a man thinks in his heart, it is not referring to the imagination. It is referring to the very essence of the person. It is the inner character of the person. In this situation the imagination acts as a mirror or reflection of the heart. The images you see of yourself in your mind's eye of you scared, angry, insecure, and proud are really a reflection of who you are at your core. This is why God says He does not see like man sees, man looks at the outside but God sees the heart. (see 1 Sam. 16:7) He sees who you really are at your core—the person you see in your own imagination. This is also how demons make use of our weakness. The Bible says that Jesus said, Satan has nothing in me (see John 14:30). It also says of humans that there is nothing good dwelling in our flesh (see Rom.7:8). This "nothing good" to which Paul refers is what Satan uses against us. It is the basis for what we see in our imagination.

A few years ago I remember having an image in my mind of myself curled up in a fetal position in a corner. At the time I thought it was a vision from God, but what God has shown me is that it was my own imagination reflecting my inner man's condition. It was a reflection of my timidity and hurt manifesting in my imagination. God uses the imagination to reflect the inner man hidden in your heart.

In fact I can also recall recently having a stare down with a stranger. He had stepped out into the street as my vehicle was approaching so I slowed down.

230

And as I slowed down to allow him time to cross the street he proceeded to stare me down like I was the one who stepped out in front of a moving vehicle. So in a moment of weakness I returned fire and proceeded to stare him down. I know I was wrong, but this guy was pushing the ego button. As I drove off my imagination proceeded to show me images of me beating the crap out of this guy. I fell into the process and my spirit stirred with anger, I got inspired angry thoughts, and that anger led to an action. Was it the work of a demon? No! It was the hidden man in my heart being revealed through my imagination. It was my pride, the real source of my anger, taking visual form.

The Hidden Man of the Heart

I know what you're thinking, what hidden man in my heart? Yes, there is a hidden person in your heart (see 1 Pet. 3:4) and your imagination reveals him to you. Job 15:27, says *"...the IMAGINATIONS of their heart run riot."* What I want you to see here is the connection between the imagination and the heart. In this passage the imagination is a revelation of the heart. Genesis 6:5 again supports this idea for it says, *"Then the Lord saw that the wickedness of man was great on the earth and that every IMAGINATION OF HIS HEART was evil continually."* The imagination in this passage was clearly a reflection of man's heart. It was a clear indication of "his intent", his hidden person.

Likewise, when Jesus tells us that we commit adultery by lusting in our hearts, He is not saying that we do so in our imagination. He is saying that our imagination reveals the adulterer hiding and living in our inner man. It is very, very, very important that you make the distinction. Your imagination is a vital tool in the process of transforming your mind. Do not ignore the images that your heart reveals to your mind's eye. It will show you your flaws, hurts, and failures. It will also reveal to you your strengths. I gave the same advice on dreams in "Ways God Speaks". Your heart will reveal the hidden man of the heart to your imagination while you are asleep and anything else about yourself that you need to know. Please get this, so that you don't prophesy out of your own heart or deceive your self with your own imagination. People do it all the time. This is why we must learn to discern between good and evil.

A great example of the hidden man is found in John 1:48. In the passage Jesus sees Phillip afar off under a tree and as Phillip approached Jesus, He said, *"Behold an Israelite indeed in whom there is found no guile."* Jesus saw the hidden man that revealed the truth about Phillip. Peter sees this way as well by the gift of discerning of spirits when Simon tried to purchase the gift of imparting the Holy Spirit through the laying on of hands. Peter tells him, "I see that you are poisoned by bitterness." He saw the hidden man of Simon's heart.

Keeping all of this in mind, I want you to consider what was said earlier. I established earlier that God also has an imagination, mind, and heart as well and guess what? When His imagination reveals His heart to you, you will see a reflection of what is in His heart about you and others. This is what prophecy is at its core. It is the imagination of God revealing God's heart to us about people, places, and events in time. It is when we are allowed access to the mind of Christ.

I also want to point out that this is also true with the demonic. When someone is filled with a demonic spirit that spirit will communicate with the individual its thoughts and imaginations. This is why people struggle to make the thoughts and images stop playing in their minds. The struggle is rooted in the reality that it is not that person's mind at work. It is the mind of another being.

Getting the Right Image from the Right Source

Remember earlier I stated that the teaching regarding the use of positive imagery as a creative force was partially true. It is partially true because God never intended for you to purpose to think positive thoughts about yourself. He does not want you to exclude Him from the process of building a better you. He does, however want you to think the right things about yourself. So how are you to get these positive ideas? You get them from God. God wants you to seek His heart so that He can give you His reflected image of you. He wants you to see yourself the way He sees you and it can only come from Him. Later when I deal with the role of faith in this process I will explain how to use what God shows you to develop this hidden person.

If you don't believe me just look as Jesus in Luke 3:22, when he comes up from the water His Father tells Him the thoughts that He has towards Him, "*You are my beloved Son in whom I am well pleased.*" Look a Paul in Acts 9:16, Jesus says, "I will show Him…" What will He show Paul? He is going to show Paul His thoughts towards him—His view of Paul. Look at Gideon, the Angel of the Lord says, "You mighty man of valor." These are all instances where God reveals His heart to show people how He sees them. He sends His thoughts towards them. We see the same with Jeremiah, it reads, "*Before I formed you in the womb I knew you, before you were born I sanctified you and I ordained you a prophet*" (Jer. 1:5). These are God's thoughts given to the prophet. They are not the result of self-willed positive thinking. God has a heavenly perspective that He would like to give you about yourself. He does not want you to create images of yourself. This is the same trick Adam and Eve fell for in the garden. Satan wanted them to imagine themselves as wise like God. Did they achieve it? Yes they did, but at what cost? We should not consider the New Agers practices valid, just because they seem to have experienced some success with their methods of positive thinking. Some have stated that it is just faith bringing the invisible into the visible. What it is, however, is the garden all over again. It is Satan once again convincing humans that they really do not need God to get the things they desire. It is self-dependency. These ideas came from their master not ours. His way always encourages people to think highly of themselves, but in contrast the mind of Christ is that of a servant of others. It is a mind that esteems others better than himself (Phil. 2:3). These are the reflections of Gods heart.

Furthermore we must be careful not to adopt this self-dependent ideology because self-dependency leads to us being alienated from God. This is what happened to Adam and Eve and it results in the darkening of the mind.

The Different States of Minds

The Darkened Mind

That being said, I want to move forward in our discussion of transforming the mind to deal with the different types of minds or states of mind presented in the scriptures.

Your mind as I have said before is a very important part of your spiritual journey into hearing the voice of God. One of the things the Bible says about the mind is that it can be darkened, veiled or blinded. Ephesians 4:17-24, says *"This I say, therefore, and testify in the Lord, that you should no longer walk as the rest of the Gentiles walk, in the futility of their mind, having their UNDERSTANDING DARKENED, being alienated from the life of God, because of the ignorance that is in them, because of the BLINDNESS of THEIR HEART."* 2 Corinthians 4:4 also says, *"If our gospel is hidden,* it is *hidden from those who's MINDS the god of this age has BLINDED."* It further says, *"For it is the God who commanded light to shine out of DARKNESS, who has shone in OUR HEARTS to give light ..."*

As you can see from these passages, our minds can be darkened. This can happen to believers as well as non-believers. In the passage above in Ephesians, we can even see that Paul in speaking to believers, when he encourages them not to walk in a darkened mind. We dealt with this issue in "The Sound of His Voice" when I shared that spiritual blindness and spiritual sight have everything to do with what you believe. Lies and sin darken the mind's eye but truth opens up the mind to see clearly. John 3:21 says it this way, *"But he who practices the TRUTH comes to the LIGHT..."* Truth produces light.

It is hard for a darkened mind to recognize the mind of Christ because darkness alienates us from the reality of His presence *"...being alienated from the life of God, because of the ignorance that is in them"* (Eph. 4:18). A key word in this verse is *ignorance*. Often it is what we do not know that causes us such hardship. Hosea 4:6 says, *"For My people perish for lack of KNOWLEDGE".* When it comes to hearing the voice of God, if you have never been told that you can hear His voice, and if it has not been taught to you from the scriptures, then its not likely that your darkness will turn to light. But once you know the truth, the truth will make you free (see John 8:32). You need to know something before you can see it.

Heavenly Minded

Hearing the voice of God means hearing the will of God for the earth. Jesus in what is called the Lord's Prayer makes a profound statement at the end of the prayer. He says, *"For Yours is the Kingdom, the power, and the glory forever amen."* The key to this prayer is summed up in the phrase "Yours is the Kingdom". Another way to say it is 'for this is Your Kingdom, this is Your power, this is Your glory.' In other words, He was saying this is what your kingdom is all about. What Jesus does in this simple prayer is offer us a perspective of the Kingdom of Heaven and what that kingdom offers.

Why is this important to understand? It's important because Hebrews 12:25 says that He speaks from Heaven. *"See that ye refuse not him that speaks. For if they escaped not who refused him that spoke on earth, much more shall not we escape, if we turn away from him that speaks from heaven: See to it that you do not refuse Him that is speaking..."* God speaks to us from the Kingdom of Heaven. He speaks to us from His point of view. This is what hearing the voice of God is all about. It is about God transforming our minds. He wants us to be heavenly minded so that you will be earthly good. Don't ever allow anyone to convince you that you are too heavenly minded or spiritual to be any earthly good. This is a trick of the enemy to limit us to an earthly perspective.

Isaiah 66:1 says, *"Heaven is my throne and the Earth is My footstool."* This tells us that Heaven is in constant contact with the Earth. God in Heaven is always in touch with the Earth, and Jesus instructs us to ask it to invade Earth. He accomplishes this by His word. God transforms our mind by transforming our perspective through His revealed word— written and spoken.

The Mind of Christ

If we are to hear the voice of Heaven to release it into the Earth, and if God is giving us His perspective, how do we position our minds for this work? In "Preparing to Hear" I spoke of the *"get down position"*. The *"get down position"* is one of humility and submission. If we are to recognize and received divine communication from the mind of Christ we will have to develop a mind like His.

Paul says "let this mind be in you that was in Christ Jesus." (See Phil. 2:5) Notice the word *"let"*. This means we must make the choice to allow

Heaven's perspective into our mind. Some of the darkness in the minds of people is simply due to resistance and pride. Paul further goes on to say what kind of mind Christ had. He had a *"get down position"* mindset. It says, *"Who, being in the form of God, thought it not robbery to be equal with God: But made himself of no reputation, and took upon him the form of a servant, and was made in the likeness of men: And being found in fashion as a man, he humbled himself, and became obedient unto death, even the death of the cross" (Phil. 2:8).*

How does this relate to the Lord's Prayer? Jesus said **your** Kingdom come, **your** will be done. This is the mind of Christ at work and demonstrating to us His humility. He does not assume the will of God but He asked for the will of God. People often wonder how Jesus could always minster successful healings and miracles. He did so by saying this simple prayer. Once you invite Heaven's perspective to invade your earthly reality you will see the miracles happening too. When heaven manifests it self, the throne begins to manifests and He who sits on the throne becomes manifested. Then the voice of God, the audible voice of God is available to minister. You won't hear a still small voice in this type of manifestation, but a clear audible voice that will instruct you in daily provision-*give us this day our daily bread*; forgiveness-*forgive us our debts and we forgive our debtors*; direction-*lead us*; protection-*lead us not into temptation*; and deliverance-*deliver us from evil*. For these are the attributes of the Kingdom of Heaven. This is also the mind of God that is available to you. You have access to it and He wants you to see what He thinks toward you.

We also see how humility opens the heavens in Genesis 28:7-12. In this chapter Jacob has a dream of angles ascending and descending on a ladder that stretched between Heaven and Earth. Heaven was invading Earth, but what did Jacob do that preceded this event? It says he laid his head on a rock. He got into a "get down position." Once he was in a vulnerable position Heaven invaded Earth and it brought with it all of its resources. Your mind is open to receive Heaven's communication when you become dependent enough to willingly lay down your way of thinking, resting it on the rock— the stability which is Christ Jesus.

The Heavens Revelation of Christ

Jacob's episode with the angels ascending and descending on the ladder reminds me of another story in the gospels. Jesus asked the disciples who do men say that I am (what is man's perspective) and some said John the Baptist, Elijah, and/or one of the prophets. Then He asked them but who do "you" say that I am. And Peter says, *"You are the Christ, the Son of God"*, to which Jesus replies, *"Flesh and blood have not revealed this to you, but My Father in Heaven."* He goes on to say, *"...you are Peter and on this rock I will build My church and the gates of hell will not prevail against it"* (see Matt. 16:18). Jesus inquires of the disciples regarding what the Earth is saying about who He is, and only one person had the answer. And that answer came from Heaven. Peter had a revelation of who Jesus was and it was that revelation upon which the Lord would build His church. It is the revelation of Christ the Son of God that is the foundation for all further truth.

It was in this Heaven to Earth moment that Jesus says He would give us keys, not a key, but multiple keys. Keys perform the function of making doors accessible or inaccessible. These keys are the truths related to the Kingdom. He also said that the gates of hell will not prevail against the church. So we have keys to the kingdom and gates of hell. We are further instructed that with these keys, whatever we bind on earth will be bound in heaven, and whatever we loose on earth will be loosed in heaven.

Knowledge is a valuable commodity. Without it the people perish (see Hosea 4:6). Jesus gave us keys of knowledge and understanding in the knowledge of Him. To the disciples He also said *"To you it has been given to know the mysteries of the kingdom"* (Matt. 13:11). Please understand that you cannot progress beyond your knowledge. It is impossible to move forward productively if you are moving in blindness. In order for you to successfully make an impact you must be able to move in Heaven's revelation. You need keys to the gates that you hope to possess and keys to the gates that you intend to close. God recently gave me a vision of a person with a flashlight. He said, "See, people walk where they have light." Think about it. You point a flashlight at an area in front of you. You walk where there is light. This is also true spiritually. You cannot go beyond your level of revelation. This is why I stress to you the necessity to obtain a balance of truth from both a

237

practical and supernatural standpoint. What benefit is it to you if you have knowledge of how to experience supernatural increase if you do not also know what God's intentions are for how to manage that increase? Or what difference does it make if you have knowledge that allows you to manage your health, if you do not likewise have the revelation from God on how to access the power of supernatural deliverance when overwhelming health challenges arise? The revelation of Jesus as the Christ is multi-faceted and nothing in Hell can prevail or overcome this revelation in the life of the believer. However, this revelation is only the key to Heaven. There are **"keys"** to many areas of the heavens, such as finances, health, anointing, and so many more. There are also keys or revelations that **"close"** the gates of Hell in your life so that you can walk in victory. The funny thing about keys is that they can open and close the same door.

Earlier in "Ways God Speaks" I refer to a vision that I had in which God showed me how demons worked to destroy a Bible study. That was a key for victory. It was God showing me how to keep the enemy from advancing his earthly plan. The Heavenly plan was for us to keep praying, meeting, and encouraging each other. But more than that, it was a key of understanding for me. It taught me how the enemy worked and validated the scriptures in Ephesians 6:10, that says, *"That you may be able to stand against the WILES, SCHEMES, or PLANS, of the enemy."* God's light showed me that if I can get a view of the first step of the plan, then the second step would not be accomplished. My key could have closed the gates of Hell to that Bible study. Likewise God has keys to transform your mind into the mind of Christ.

Paul's Encounter with the Mind of God

There is a great example of how revelation transforms the mind in the story of Paul's conversion. It really does show us how an encounter with the mind of Christ can change our earthly perspective into that of heavens. Acts chapter 9 is where we can find such an example.

In this chapter we read of the Apostle Paul's conversion encounter with Jesus. During his encounters we see a few things happening that are fascinating. They are:

1) Paul (Saul at the time) has an encounter with Jesus in which he sees a light and hears God's voice. He has a vision.

2) When he opens his eyes from the vision he discovers that he is physically blind.

3) He is physically blind for three days, but he was spiritually awakened to pray to a God he formerly persecuted. He also had a second vision. We see that He was blind physically, but not spiritually.

4) Last, he receives his sight back. It only happens when scales have fallen from his eyes then he sees the physical world again.

There is a lot to see in this passage. When God started dealing with me about this passage I was excited by what I was seeing. I was excited because this passage holds keys to enable us to experience the freedom of transformation in our minds. We have dealt with the subject of the mind extensively in this book and chapter. We have also built a base understanding of the fact that our mind is a precious spiritual commodity for which God and Satan battle to control. For by controlling it, they control you. The difference is that Satan wants it so that he can exert control over you while God wants it so that He can empower you to control yourself. The Bible says, *"God did not give us a spirit of fear, but of love, power, and a sound mind."* The Greek word for sound mind means *self-control*. It suggests that the key to controlling oneself and your appetites is directly linked to your mind.

In our story of Paul Acts 9:2 describes for us how passionate Paul was in his pursuit to destroy the church. We can read about his zeal in the passages and how he breathed threats and murder against the church. He was definitely darkened in his mind. What makes this really interesting is the fact that Paul was not some random heathen that joined a passing crusade against the church. But to the contrary, he was a man of the temple. He was a devout Jewish scholar and he sincerely believed that what he was doing was in service to God. He was a very religious man. In fact he describes himself as being blameless regarding the law (see Phil. 3:6). You can be religious and yet have a darkened mind. God, however, was about to change Paul's perspective. And He did so with "light" and "truth". For it reads that a light shone all about him and Jesus spoke to Him.

It is also fascinating to consider the fact that Paul was the only person converted through this experience. We read that Paul was with his companions when this encounter occurred but there is no mention of their conversion. The Bible only tells us that they were perplexed hearing a voice and seeing no one. This tells me that the voice alone is not enough to convert the mind. It is only when God makes His voice LIGHT that you are converted. As I stated in the last chapter, revelation must lead to understanding to be productive. This is why some hear the call of salvation and others do not. It should be noted that this was a really important event in Paul's life. It was this encounter with the light and the voice that set the stage for the rest of what God did in Paul's life. His multitude of visions and revelations were the result of what happened next.

Paul's encounter with the light and the voice also had a profound side effect. For it showed us that the same light that gave Paul mental or spiritual sight also took away his physical sight. This is amazing because it parallels Peter's vision on the rooftop experience. God blinded Paul to the reality that held him in bondage. He had a distorted view of the church and this encounter blinded him to his original perspective. God did the same for Peter when He opened up his worldview. The fascinating thing is that both Paul and Peter are the only two disciples that God used to open doorways of Salvation to the gentiles. Likewise, in both cases He blinded them to the world around them. He blinded them to their original earthly perspective. He blinded Paul physically, and He blinded Peter by detaching him from reality. What was God doing to these two guys? He was pouring light and truth into them. He was giving them his perspective and He did so through His voice.

The voice of God changes our minds and opens it up to the truths of God's mind. I have said it a few times before in other places, but it bears repeating. You "have" the mind of Christ, but you need your mind transformed so that you can recognize His and distinguish your thoughts from His thoughts. It's really not that hard because His thoughts and ideas are not like your thoughts and ideas. As a matter of fact, I guarantee that you think much less of your self value than He does. Nor are His ways or perspectives like yours. If you get slapped, your way is to slap back. His way is to turn the other cheek. Just know that your thoughts are not like His.

The other interesting thing about Paul's experience is that while He was physically blind, he had spiritual vision. I said in the last chapter that we are prone to looking inward when our physical eyes close. This is what happened to Paul, being physically blind forced him into reflection. And while looking inward he was able to perceive what God was saying. God spoke to him when he was not distracted. There is an interesting parallel in the story of Elisha's servant's eye opening and the story of Paul's conversion. In the story of Elisha and his servant, which we have referred to often in this writing, we see that the army in the story is blinded and led by a lie into bondage. Remember when God granted Elisha's prayer that he led them into the captivity of the king of Israel. God blinded or darkened their minds and they were filled with the lie. But in Paul's case the same God blinded him and he was led into the truth. God closed Paul's eyes to earthly things and opened them to see into the Heavens.

Then after God opened Paul's eyes to God's plan in Heaven He then re-opened his eyes on Earth. But when He restored Paul's physical sight something strange happened. It says that while Ananias spoke to him something like scales fell from his eyes and his sight was restored. There is something important to see here. Whenever a reptile is ready to produce new skin, it sheds the old skin. This is what is happening in this story as well. Paul was shedding his old view of Jesus and putting on a new perspective. God's thoughts toward Paul were manifesting in his mind. The result of all of this was a transformed mind in Paul. His revelation, incubated, and finally it was activated in that we read of Paul preaching the same Jesus he previously persecuted. His revelation became an understanding!

The Process of Transforming the Mind

So far we have said a lot about the mind, heart, and imagination. We have said that the mind is a receptive place for the voice of God. We have also said that God wants us to have a mind that reflects His mind. We have said that the imagination is a tool of revelation for the hidden man in our hearts. It reflects who we really are at our core. Lastly, we said that both humans and God use the imagination as a mirror in us.

All of this has one goal in mind and that is the transformation of your mind from an earthly perspective into a mind with a heavenly perspective. But how do we use what we know to start the process of getting God's light?

Starting the Process with a Word

The first thing we need to understand to start the process of transforming our minds into the mind of Christ is that it all starts with a word from God. As with Paul's experience, it was his encounter with a word from Heaven that changed his perspective. It was the "rhema word" that Paul encountered. Even though it was a spoken word to Paul, I think it is very important to acknowledge the power of the recorded spoken word. Sometimes we place greater value on hearing a personal word from the throne over the scriptures. However we need to remember that the word of God is the word of God and it has the power to change, challenge, and transform the way we see.

Hebrews 4:12 says, *"The word of God is quick and powerful, sharper than any two edged sword, dividing asunder soul and spirit and is the discerner of the thoughts and intentions of the heart."* The word *"word"* in this passage is the Greek word *"RHEMA"*. It is a word that so far, I have not discussed, but it is a very important word. In other passages we will see the word *"word"* used and the Greek word for it is *"LOGOS"*. The Greek word *"LOGOS"* means "written word", whereas the Greek word "RHEMA" means "spoken word". I like to explain it this way. A logos word is like a full-scale 88 key piano. If you were to press all of the keys at one time you would hear a full range of sounds with no clear distinction. A *rhema* word is like a song melody. It is when God takes the written word and crafts a well-organized and distinct personal message. In the passage above we can see that the logos is the whole mind of God and that the rhema is an idea that He presents to us. From a practical standpoint the "logos" is the Bible. The rhema is a message that God uses to speak directly to your particular situation. This could be a verse lifted off the page or a word in your heart. If you are reading this book, this is a rhema for you.

The real power of this passage is that it tells us that God's word "rhema" and "logos" is full of power. It also tells us that its power is said to be actively working and performing a task in us. It also reveals to us that an important part of the mind's transformation process is that we learn to separate what is soul and what is spirit. The tool for the job is the word.

When we look at this passage we often assume that it means to divide between soul and spirit as if cutting a core away from the apple. However, to really understand this concept and the power of the word to change us, we must interpret it in light of the entire verse. The latter half of the verse tells us that the word of God pierces so far down that it discerns the thoughts and intentions. What this means is that God's voice goes deep into us where change happens. To understand it we must change the image we have held of a sword splitting things in half, and see it as sword going "deep" into us.

Real change happens when God challenges our motives. Remember, your spirit moves your soul. It creates the thoughts that lead to action. The word of God must go beyond your thoughts and change your very motivation and inspiration.

This is the starting point to allow Heaven to change our perspective. Our first line of defense is our Bible. It has more than enough information on God's perspectives on life. However the real magic happens when God breathes on a passage to make it personal for you. Reading 1 Peter 2:9 which says, *"You are a holy people are royal priesthood, a holy nations"* is really just text. But once God turns the voice of God into light, like He did for Paul—once He breathes on a passage the words become life.

This is what is meant by active. It is the moment when God brings a passage to life in a way that you have an "ah ha" moment. It is when God's thoughts towards you land in your heart and enlighten your understanding in a way that you can actively put that truth to use.

Daydreaming or Intense Meditation

Now I want to discuss a tool that God uses to open us up to the process of transforming our perspective. That tool is daydreaming! What is daydreaming? It is exactly as it sounds. It is dreaming during the day while in an awakened state. This is another thing that really has a bad connotation.

I am a natural daydreamer. This means that I was born with an innate ability to dream during the day. If I were to write a book on the subject I would title it "Dreaming with Your Mind Wide Open." I have come to absolutely love daydreaming, but this was not always the case.

When I was a child I was often rebuked for daydreaming. In fact, it became such a problem in school that it was believed to have interfered with my learning process—and to a degree it did. However, what was considered to be a negative in my learning process would later prove to be a positive in the kingdom of God. What most people never knew was that I was daydreaming about my future as an artist or whatever my heart was in pursuit of at that time. I was using my thoughts and imaginations to take me into the future I hoped to create for myself one day. I was daring to dream! It just happened to be at inappropriate times.

The result of my daydreaming meant that I had never been in a place of being uninspired. I have always been a dreamer; I always had an idea of what I wanted to do in my heart. Then I got saved and was taught to cast down imaginations. So I did. I cast down all imaginations. I took control of my thought life and it was a great help to me in many ways. However, because I did not have a complete and balanced understanding of the concepts presented in that passage of scripture, I was hurt in other ways.

Learning to take control of my thought life was a great help to me because it taught me how to be watchful. It also taught me to be attentive to what was happening in my mind. It further taught me not to allow any passing spirit to grab my attention and show me all kinds of evil things—this did happen. But it hurt me in other ways, because I did not know that I was only suppose to cast down those imaginations and thoughts that came against the ideas and principles of God. As a result I cut myself off from this ability and with its death also came the death of my inspiration and motivation.

Then a wonderful thing began to happen. God began to teach me about the power of daydreaming. He taught me that daydreaming is a very biblical thing to do and that it is a very important exercise in helping to shape your inner man. Guess who else knows this? Satan. After I explain it to you, you will be able to see how he is moving against you to cripple your ability to daydream.

Daydreaming is Biblical

How is daydreaming biblical? Daydreaming is really a form of intense meditation. For some of us such as myself, I am naturally sensitive to my thought life because I am introverted. I can very easily tune you out and turn inward for reflection. By reflection I mean that I can look inward at the hidden man and see what is happening—meditation is very natural to me. It is not something that I have to force to happen.

I have learned that daydreaming is really a listening tool of the spirit. This is why daydreamers and artists (visual and musical) in particular struggle with attention span. Daydreamers hear and see. Most artist see in their daydreams and most musical composers hear in theirs. If you spoke to them while they were in a moment of daydreaming you would find that they are hearing the songs or seeing the pictures, or movies in the invisible place. So daydreaming is to the invisible world is what listening with the ears is to the physical world. Learning this was a great relief and revelation. Now when I see people like Clive Barker, the creator of horror movies such as "Hellraiser", and see his artwork, I feel sorry for him. Why? He thinks that the creatures he sees are imaginary. However they are real and they are communicating with him to bring their mind into the earth. This is why so many artistic people suffer from depression. Being this sensitive to your thought life can lead to extreme worry and fear. This is why we need the word.

Now that I understand what daydreaming is I am very careful to vigilantly watch my thought life. I use this meditation gift as a way to put my mind in the word.

The Bible tells us to meditate over and over again. David says as I lay on my bed I will meditate… We are also commanded to meditate on whatever is good, lovely, pure, of good report, and on "anything" that is praise worthy or of value. This list is inclusive of your future.

One thing that I have had to learn is that God does not make mistakes. Who you are with all of your issues and perceived weaknesses is a reflection of a God that has a plan. What may be a negative to you can be a positive in the hand of God. The negativity surrounding daydreaming caused me to despise this ability because I was always told that it was worthless. I was told that it was a wasting of time. I heard it at school. I heard it at home. I heard it in the church. But I did not hear it from God.

God uses daydreaming in the most unusual way. As I stated earlier daydreaming simply means that you are spiritually sensitive. It does not take much for something in the spiritual realm to get your attention and show you all kinds of things. Most importantly, it means that you are sensitive to your own heart. Why is this a good thing? Remember I told you that your imagination reflects your heart. The Bible says out of the heart flows the issues of life (see Prov. 4:23). It also says that evil comes out of the heart (see Matt. 15:19). Most of you are very familiar with the evil in your heart. Most people, including myself, have had evil images of the things the heart desires to appear in our minds. The Bible also says this about the heart… that God would take out the stony heart and gives us a new heart (see Ezek. 36:26). This is really good news because it is means that God gives us His heart and as I said before, His heart reflects His imagination.

In the next chapter I tell you that one of the best ways to study God is to read the scriptures about Him and meditate. When I say meditate, I mean daydream. How? Allow your mind to just take off pondering the people and places and what they were doing. While you are pondering all these things you will begin to experience an opening up of truth. God will shed light upon your thoughts and give your mind revelation.

This has many benefits. Number one, you will begin to understand Jesus like you never have before. Two, you will find that it is easy to remember the scripture you are pondering because you are allowing yourself to interact with it. Three, you will begin to notice that your mind is seeing, hearing, and transforming. The experience with the daydream will assist in helping you to see from different vantage points. Lastly, it will assist you in building your faith. The Bible says that it is with the *"heart"* that one believes (see Rom. 10:10).

Seeing What You Believe

If it is with your heart that you believe, then it stands to reason that your imagination should be able to produce an image of your faith. Remember, your imagination reflects what is really in your heart. It reflects what you believe. How do I know that this is true? The same way that you understand this to be true!

Have you ever heard someone say I just can't imagine that? What are they really saying? They are saying I just can't see the possibility of that "in my mind" because I don't "believe in my heart" it is possible. The same is spoken in reverse. People also say, "I can see" that happening. Again this is an indication that your heart believes and projects a visual of what is possible.

So many times people struggle to really understand how to recognize faith. Some people confuse faith with chance. These people step into situations and hope that everything works out. Faith, however, is not hope! Faith is the substance that creates hope. To get our faith to really work for us we must first understand that it starts from deep within us, in the heart. If faith is present in the heart, it will produce an image of possibility in the mind. It is this possibility that fuels the transformation process. If God is to change your perspective you will need to allow Him to inspire the kind of faith that shows your mind His heart. You need faith to see Jesus returning for you. You need faith to see that you really are a special people. You need faith to see that you are forgiven and that you can come boldly before His throne of grace without a sense of guilt and shame. It is Faith that sees the change that you are after. If you can see it God's way, you will bring that inner vision into reality. The image that God shows you in your heart of the "new you" will begin to manifest Heaven's vision to the world around you.

Watering the Heart

This makes the imagination an absolutely vital tool in the process of transforming our minds. Likewise, daydreaming or intense meditation or contemplative thought, as it is also known, becomes even more valuable. It is so valuable because daydreaming waters your heart and assist in establishing our faith. Psalm 1:1-3 says this about using meditation to water and establish faith in our hearts, it reads, *"How blessed is the man who does not walk in the counsel of the wicked, nor stand in the path of sinners, nor sit in the seat of scoffers! But his delight is in the law of the LORD, And IN HIS LAW HE MEDITATES (DAYDREAMS) day and night. He WILL BE like a tree FIRMLY PLANTED by streams of water, Which yields its fruit in its season And its leaf does not wither; And in whatever he does, he prospers."*

The Apostle Paul likewise provides Timothy some insightful advice from which we can draw a conclusion. 2 Timothy 2:7 reads, *"Reflect on what I am saying, for the Lord will give you insight into all this."* Paul has just given some needed advice to the young pastor. In his counsel he provides Timothy some analogies to make a point. It is at this point that Paul realizes that the young man may not quite understand what he is saying. So he gives him instructions for how to get godly wisdom. And verse seven clearly makes a connection between meditation and revelation. When we allow ourselves to ponder and daydream it is in those moments that God breathes on us to enlighten the eyes of our heart.

The Wrong Image of You

These passages also speak of the power of daydreaming to shape our mind and establish deep and abiding faith. Some of you understand exactly what I am saying, because you are in a constant struggle to believe that a holy God can use you to accomplish His will. Your struggle is the result of your poor self-image. What is self-image? It is what you see about yourself in your own imagination based on what you believe about yourself in your own heart. It is your reflection of your faith or lack thereof.

When a person has not been enlightened by God with His heart's reflected image, that person will not see them selves from the heavenly vantage point. They will only see themselves from the earthly vantage point. It is usually derived from our comparing ourselves amongst ourselves. This is a limited view. And it causes a skewed self-image of either pride, as we consider ourselves better than others. Or it produces a poor self-image as we consider ourselves small in the sight of others.

Nebuchadnezzar and His Son Belshazzar had an over inflated self-image (read the book of Daniel). They both struggled to see themselves in the proper perspective of humans whom God allowed to be rulers. They saw themselves as gods and not men.

Gideon is an example of someone with poor self-image. God sent an angel who said, "Gideon, you mighty man of valor..." To which He (Gideon) responded, "I am least in my father's house." He struggled to be confident and rise to the occasion because of the image in his heart shown to his imagination. It was a warped self-image. He struggled to see what God's heart was showing him because of what his heart believed.

Saul also, struggled with poor self-image. The prophet Samuel gave Saul God's heart (His reflected image of Saul) by the voice of God, but like Gideon he saw himself as small in his own eyes. Then God gave him a new heart and the Bible says that he became another man. What kind of heart did God give him? He gave Saul the heart of a king. He gave Saul His heart so that he would have the right self-image. He gave Saul a heart that would believe!

Personal Examples of Daydreaming

So if God uses the daydreaming to transform our heart and self-image I want to give you some examples of how daydreaming has been used in my life to make permanent heart changes.

Pondering the Creation

As I have stated elsewhere is this book, I am an artist by trade and I have always been a visual learner. This means I learn and process information by what I see and experience. So one day as I was in conversation with God about creating I decided that I would make a sculpture of a human being. I wanted to get a better understanding of the subject. As I was creating this sculpture I got so lost in the process that I went into a perceptual vision. Remember perceptual visions occur when God takes something natural or physical and gives special meaning to it. This was the case with my sculpture. As I was sculpting I started pondering the process and God made me aware of a few things as I was working.

One thing I began to notice is the amount of time spent just deciding what it would look like. I also began to notice just how specific I was about the features and whether the eyes were to be big or small, whether or not it would be male or female, fat or tall. Why is this unique? It is unique because as an artist I have created many things, but this was the first time I was aware of the process.

This pondering led to some very fundamental understandings that deepened my appreciation for people. All us a sudden I realized that no one on the planet has control over the features that we sometimes despise. I also came to realize that there is not one detail of our design that God did not scrutinize. He knows every hair on your head, and you are exactly the way He wanted you. Last I came to understand that it must really hurt God's heart when we talk negatively about the appearance of the people He created. It is like walking up to Picasso and saying to him as he is painting, I don't like the way the paint goes to the left. It is insulting to alter His design.

This one moment of daydreaming produced fruit that remains. It transformed my perspective, my heart, and my mind. It was a seed or revelation that incubated and blossomed into an understanding.

Pondering the Creator

God used a similar situation to speak a life changing and mind transforming truth. Again as an artist I create all kinds of things. On this particular occasion I was creating characters for a children's book and I was doing a character bio. What most people do not realize is that anytime a character is created for a book, film, or play, the writer creates what is called a character bio. A character bio is exactly as it sounds. The writer creates a book for each character detailing age, sex, sexual preference, personality, social and economics status. They also develop the character's upbringing and the environment that shapes that character. This is what I was doing.

As I was creating the bio for my first character I decided that I wanted the character to come from a really harsh background. Likewise I was prepared to put him into some uncomfortable situations to help make my point. During the process I started pondering what was happening and I realized that this is what God does with us.

The Bible says that all things work together for the good. It does not, however, say that those things working for our good are actually good. I started realizing that God has planned each facet of our lives. You were born into the situation that God wanted you to be in. That was only part of the revelation. The other part for us to understand is that even those bad things that happened, (that God knew were going to happen), happened for a reason. That reason is the understanding that God gave me as I was creating a character bio.

I put my character into some really bad situations to develop the personality and character that I wanted. And I did so because I had planned for those who would read the book to grow from his encounters. I did it for those who would read or hear his story. Guess what? You are living epistles (see 2 Cor. 3:2) and God has allowed (not caused) some bad things to happen in the story of your life as well. He allowed them to happen because He intends for those who read or hear your story to be impacted.

This truth is reflected in the life of Joseph. Joseph had a dream of greatness that took him on a journey through slavery, servitude, and prison. However, in the end he realized that it was God's plan to get him into a place of destiny. That plan included some not so lovely things that we now read about for the purpose of growth.

People always say, "Kevin, how did you get that out of that situation?" You are more than likely thinking the same thing. The answer is simple… God takes advantage of daydreaming and meditation to teach us truths about Himself so that He can transform our mind into the mind of Christ. He wants to change your perspective and help you to see from the heavenly vantage point so that you can bring that perspective to the Earth.

Beyond Imagination

One of the things that you have to love about our God is the fact that He reveals His heart to us. Not only does He reveal His heart to us, but He reveals that in His Heart He sees us in ways that we don't see ourselves. Therefore don't daydream about your limitations. Meditate on His word. His word as I said earlier is alive and powerful. It shapes our way of thinking and protects us from thinking so small of ourselves.

I am never without a dream in my heart since I embraced the reality that God wants us to daydream. But even on my most creative day, I could never imagine in my own strength the vast possibilities that God has for my future. Notice that I said, in my own strength I could not imagine God's possibilities, but what about when God reveals His heart and mind to me?

Ephesians 3:20, says, *"To Him that is able to DO EXCEEDINGLY ABOVE or BEYOND what you are able to ask or IMAGINE according to His power that is at work in us."* What is the work that God is doing in us by His power? He is transforming us into His image by transforming our inner man. 2 Corinthians 3:18 says, *"But we all, with open face beholding as in a glass the glory of the Lord, are changed into the same image from glory to glory, even as by the Spirit of the Lord".* Likewise 2 Corinthians 4:16 says, *"For our inner man is renewed day by day".*

One of the most quoted scriptures in the Bible is 1 Corinthians 2:9-12 which says, *"...nor eye has seen nor ear has heard what God has prepared for those that love him..."* This is usually where the focus ends and most people are of the persuasion that we cannot know or do not know what God has prepared for us based on this verse. However, if you keep reading you will see that it says, **"***but God HAS REVEALED (past tense) THEM to us through His Spirit. For the Spirit searches all things, yes, the deep things of God. For what man knows the things of a man except the spirit of the man which is in him? Even so no one knows the things of God except the Spirit of God. Now we have received, not the spirit of the world, but the Spirit who* *is from God, THAT WE MIGHT KNOW THE THINGS that have been freely GIVEN to us by God."*

After reading this verse don't ever quote that scripture again to convince yourself that God has things that you do not have access to. You can know what is in the heart of God regarding your life. It has been freely given to us by God. It is a part of our inheritance and His heart will show you more than you can ask or imagine on your own.

Where are these things that God has freely given to us? Keep reading the verses. The answer is found in verse 16, it reads, *"For who has known the mind of the Lord that he may instruct Him?" But WE HAVE THE MIND of Christ."*

Understanding Strongholds

Finally, no discussion on the mind is complete without examining the subject of mental strongholds. I have often wondered about strongholds in the mind. What exactly is as stronghold? According to Google dictionary a stronghold is a place that has been fortified so as to protect something against attack. It is also a place where a particular cause or belief is strongly defended and upheld; where a group or party shares an idea or have come into agreement on an idea firmly planted.

As I said in the last chapter, we are capable of constructing systems in the mind. These systems are a network of ideas and beliefs that we gain through our experiences with our culture and environment. When we have built a strong enough system in which we think we have stability, that stable structure becomes a stronghold. A stronghold simply means that we have come into agreement with an idea or ideas and are so convinced by that idea that we have set up defenses around them. For instance, have you ever met someone with a substance abuse problem that just could not admit that they have a problem with addiction? Usually everyone around them can plainly see that a problem with addiction exists, but somehow this truth eludes the addict. They can't see the problem even though it has often times wrecked their lives and the lives of those around them. This is because they have come to believe an idea and have built in their minds layers of reasons to protect that idea. Those layers of reasons are the walls of the fortress that make up strongholds. It is not the idea, but the reasoning surrounding the idea. Sometimes there can be layers and layers of reasons binding people to destructive ideas.

Some of you have the same problem regarding hearing the voice of God. Even though you see that God speaks to people. Even though, you heard Him call you to salvation and even though the scriptures are full of stories pointing to a God that speaks in the Old Testament and New Testament. And even though I have provided more than enough scriptures to make you feel at ease about hearing voices, some of you will hold dearly to reasons you believe as to why God does not speak to people. These reasons are the stronghold protecting the idea or belief that you hold so dearly. Also, you will find that a spirit of fear is at the root or foundation on which this stronghold is built.

So how do you break through this wall and experience God freely? You need to change your belief. As we have been saying all throughout this chapter, you need to get a heavenly perspective. You need to search out the truth so that God can open your eyes to see. For instance I challenge you to search the scriptures for yourself, look to see if you can find a verse, story, or passage that ever said that God ever intended to stop speaking to mankind. If you do, put it to the scriptural test. Remember in "Signs of His Voice" one of the things we look for is consistency in the character of God as revealed in the scriptures. If you cannot find any scriptural reason to not hear the voice of God, then you need to ask yourself the most important question. Why do I believe that God stopped speaking to mankind?" You need to question yourself as to why you believe what you believe.

What you believe should have its roots in the scriptures and not in yours or someone else's opinion or logic. If it's just your opinion, then you will find that breaking your alliance with the spirit of fear and his beliefs and lies will tear down the walls—the walls that keep you from freely enjoying a fruitful relationship with God, where you are hearing His voice.

Clearing the Air

We've discussed so much about the mind, but what it all boils down to is the reality that your mind is like an antenna. It is used to tune into Heaven and Earth. Colossians 3:2 says, *"Set your mind on things above where Christ is seated, not on things of the Earth."* This is another way of saying tune into the right frequency.

Some time ago I went to bed in utter frustration with God. He had been teaching me something but I was not able to fully comprehend what He was teaching. I had the revelation and it was incubating and during the process I lost my patience. I really wanted to apply what I was learning and see the results. So I told Him I didn't want to deal with this issue anymore and fussed and pleaded for wisdom and went to sleep. When I awoke in the morning He cleared up my confusion with a vision that resulted in this understanding of the mind. In the vision there was a jukebox radio in front of me. It had a dial with two markings indicating that it had two channels. I immediately understood the vision. Then God started speaking to me about the ability to focus the attention of the mind. He said, "Kevin, put your attention on your foot. As I did I was aware of my foot." Then He said, "Put your attention on your fingertip, just one." As I did I became aware of that area of my finger. I did this with other parts of my body as well and noticed that I became aware of whatever I set my mind upon. This is because our mind can be intentionally focused upon objects physical or spiritual. This explains why we can be in a classroom with someone for a whole year or in some cases years, and never notice that person. It is because we have the ability to ignore or tune out things and people from our reality. The ability to direct ones attention is critical to hearing the voice of God and being aware of His presence. If you set your mind on Him (direct your attention to Him) your mind will behave like an antenna for your spirit and you will begin to perceive the reality of God. The same is true with anything in the spiritual realm. If you focus on fear the atmosphere around you will literally fill with fear and you will experience its effects.

This is why most people can only perceive God at church. This is because we expect Him to be there and it is a place where we naturally think about God. However, once we leave church our mind's attention is given to other things and the reality of God disappears. You should know that you can tune in at anytime and He will be right there in a way that you can sense and feel.

This understanding has been especially valuable for me. Why? It has been valuable because now the still small voice is audible. It is only still and small when I am out of focus, such as when I am at work engaged in projects or doing something such as driving. I obviously cannot have my mind on the road and in the heavens at the same time. I do, however, maintain enough awareness to hear the still small voice.

The still small voice is really a sign that your attention is divided. When we consider Elijah we can see that he was in a dark place when he heard that voice. Once He got to the entrance of the cave where there was light, he heard a clearly discernable voice. This symbolizes the focus of his attention. In the cave he was overcome with depression and His focus was on himself (tuned into himself). Once he got into the light at the entrance of the cave, his attention shifted to God. This is why the Lord passed by first. He wanted to get Elijah's attention off of himself and shift it to the entrance where the voice of God was speaking. Remember I said in the last chapter that before God speaks He will first get your attention. This is what He did in this passage as well.

So if your mind is like an antenna then you must understand that like any receiver it is subject to static. Static occurs when something blocks or distorts the signal from the transmitter. In *"Hindrances to Hearing"* we cover things that keep us from getting the signal, but what things in the mind actually distort the signal once it is received. By distort, I mean that there are things that cloud the mind and skew what we see.

Static can be caused by lies, an impure conscience, anxiety, sin, demonic interference, and hurt, pain, and unforgiveness. All of these can cause us to struggle in our communion with God. These are things that cloud the mind.

Lies

We've already discussed the static of lies and we understand that lies darken the mind and create strongholds. This phenomenon is really evident in Hollywood. Hollywood is filled with some of the most beautiful women and yet with all of their beauty they conceit to make changes to their appearance. They obviously see imperfections where we see perfection. One thing I have learned is that it never matters what people can see about you if you cannot see it yourself. Everyone's mind sees something and lies can distort your view of life.

Take Elijah for example. He sat in the darkness of a cave hoping for death and feeling lonely because he was filled with a lie. He had come to believe that all of God's prophets had been killed with the edge of the sword and he alone was left (see 1 Kings 19:14). This was not true. The first thing God does in the light of the cave is straighten out the lie. He told Elijah I have seven thousand who have not bowed their knees to Baal. In other words, brother I am not resting the entirety of my plan on the shoulders of one man! I have savings account. It is also interesting to see that Elijah's depression was clearly a form of self-induced delusion. It had already been communicated to him by Ahab's servant that some of the prophets were rounded up in groups of fifty and hidden in a cave. He knew that God had a reserve, but he chose to believe the lie. The result was a darkened understanding and a dark attitude that resulted in the still small voice.

Impure Conscience

Another thing that clouds the mind is an impure conscience. Paul mentions this faculty of the mind quite frequently in the scriptures. He and Peter warn us to keep it clear and to have a good conscience before God and men. When the conscience is affected by some inappropriate action we make, it floods the mind with thoughts that can result in feelings of guilt and shame. Guilt and shame are feelings that attempt to persuade us that we are not worthy of God's goodness. This often results in people running from God instead of to Him to find grace in time of need. We saw this in Isaiah when he cries woe unto me for I am a man of unclean lips (see Isa. 6:5). God wanted to speak with him but guilt and shame turned his attention to himself instead of tuning him into the God who was speaking to him. An impure conscience actually makes us hide from God. It can also make us feel so unworthy of what He has spoken to us. It can be just as paralyzing as fear. Feelings of being unworthy are one of the main reasons many never move into releasing the gifts of God into the lives of others. Feelings of unworthiness it say, "Why would God use me?"

Anxiety

This leads me to the next kind of static in our mind, anxiety. Another word for anxiety would be worry. Worry is a form of negative meditation. It is daydreaming about all the possible ways something can go wrong. If you look at the stories in the gospels of the disciples and the storms that they encountered, you will see anxiety at work. In each story there was a word from God and winds and waves that stirred fear in their hearts. There was a goal and something visible and something invisible at work. This is true with all anxiety. It is produced when our expectation from God is opposed by something we can see and something we cannot see. It is knowing that my God shall supply all my needs according to His riches in glory, while looking at a shutoff notice. Then fear whispers contrary thoughts in your mind and the storm moves from external to internal. It is when the spirit of fear contradicts the word of God.

This means that doubt is present and as we have said, doubt divides the signal and makes it hard to receive. As you can imagine it is hard to discern the voice of God when your mind is raging with all kinds of contrary thoughts. Please understand that worry doesn't quiet the voice of God, it just makes it hard to hear clearly. In fact when Jesus went to the disciples on the water they heard the voice in the midst of the storm. But I'm willing to bet it was not as clear on the water as it was when He Jesus got into the boat. In fact you can see that the word, "Jesus", was hard to discern in the storm. Therefore Peter says, Lord, "*if*" it is you. We also see this with Elijah. We see that it was worry that sent him into a cave with a suicidal mentality. However even in the darkness he could perceive the voice of God. It was still and small, but is shows us that God can get His voice to us even in the darkest hour of our lives.

Sin

Sin is a really dangerous static. I found out the hard way the result it can have on the mind's eye. The Bible says that *"The eye is the lamp of the body, if your eyes are healthy, your whole body will be full of light. But if your eyes are unhealthy your whole body will be full of darkness. If then the light is within you is darkness, how great is the darkness?"* (Matt. 6:22, 23). This passage is a reference to the rudder of the body, the mind. It is a reference to the mind seeing truth, but I believe it also applies to the sin that we play with in our minds.

Years ago, before I was married, I walked in a season of celibacy. That season would last 10 years. The first 5 years were fairly easy because God had extended to me grace to live that way. After the 5 year mark God began teaching me about marriage and I knew that this meant that I would soon be required to take a wife. The problem was that I really enjoyed my single life, sex was not a problem (thanks to grace) and the examples of marriages around me were not encouraging. I said to God, "Why would I mess up my life by adding the problems of marriage?" I then started to resist God's direction and I found a problem with every possible female I encountered. They were never good enough. Actually, they were great women, but I just did not want to be married.

After a few years of resistance God spoke to me and told me that His grace was no longer with me to stay single. Having an understanding of grace I knew that this meant that the life that was once easy to live would now be more challenging. Sure enough, my sex drive returned. I was then subject to the scriptures that say it is better to marry than to burn. I, however, continued to resist God's plan of marriage.

By this time I was in my seventh year of my celibacy and the intensity of the sex drive led to a season where I struggled with masturbation. It was not a long battle, because I was so convicted every time, but it was, however, long enough for me to cause damage to my mind's eye. The visions that once appeared in HD in my mind were now nonexistent. This is because I used my imagination, which was sanctified by God for His use, to picture one woman I lusted after. In fact we were both lusting after each other and she tried to entice me to fall with her many times. She wanted to be my wife but she was not living the type of Christian life that I wanted to be married to. She was so in love with me that she actually bought and tried love potion on me. The result was one of the most vivid dreams I have ever encountered. It was a sexual dream in which this woman and I fornicated. We both had this very real dream the same night! When I saw her the next day she just looked at me with wonder. Then she told me about her dream and I finished by describing to her all of the details such as the colors, the wallpaper and such.

This led to thoughts of her at night. I was spiritually compromised and because my mind's eye was so well developed, the lustful images of her in my mind also appeared in HD. So to protect me God closed my eyes and with it the dreams and the visions were gone! Yes this was a very hard lesson. I was blind for the first time in my walk with God. I repented and pleaded for my sight back, but God did not give it back until years later. This does not mean that He stopped speaking to me. I had repented and stopped this behavior so our relationship resumed as normal. I have always been able to hear God's voice, I just couldn't see His voice anymore.

So after years of maturity passed by, God began to open my eyes again. This time the visions were not in HD but they were standard definition. They were cloudy similar to what it looks like when you have a light layer of frost on a window in the morning. I could still see but the visions were not pure. They were cloudy.

Then in desperation I bought a book on seeing in the spirit. I bought it for two reasons. One reason I bought it was to compare experiences. The second reason was to see if anyone could help me repair my spiritual eyes. This book was a great help and I read it several times. It had some really practical advice on the subject. So I followed that advice and sure enough my vision was improving and I was recalling up to three dreams per night.

Then it happened again, but this time I didn't know what I had done wrong. That was until some time later. Before reading the book I had given up watching most things on TV. I just wanted to pursue God, but as time went on I slowly started being careless about what I watched. It was not until I woke up one morning with images of the Kardashian women in my mind that I realized that my mind was polluted. This is what led to this understanding of static.

I had learned from the book that I read that I needed to repent and sanctify myself every night before going to bed. And that is what I did for a while. Then I slipped into a casual attitude. Again I was blind. So God taught me something that I will share later in the chapter.

Demonic Influence

I wish I could tell you that my second bout with blindness was completely the result of my complacency, but that would not be all together true. The second bout with blindness was the work of demonic influence. In fact these creatures have directly confronted me several times in the learning process. They really hated that God was sharing all of this with me and they make me very aware of their displeasure. One day as I was lying on my bed I saw the most vividly red creature. It was only a partial view of his head and neck but it was so unbelievably vivid. When I saw it I knew that it was something evil so I said to the Lord, "What in the world is that?" Then I saw a picture of a large serpent swimming in water. I immediately understood it be Leviathan. I will not go into detail about what he is and what he does but just know that it was the beginning of a real battle!

After this encounter I started to really struggle with seeing clearly and sometimes with just seeing period. This is because demons do not want you to see. They want your mind to stay focused on the winds and waves not on Jesus. Please get this in your heart. Demons only have one real goal and that goal is to keep the believer distracted from seeing the reality of God's love for them and others. This is what every challenge they devise against you is set to accomplish. It makes you stop seeing things in the kingdom clearly. Make it your goal to keep your mind on Christ. If you can see Him, you will know what to do. Consider the man with the demons called legion in Mark 9. This man could not see Jesus clearly until the demons were removed. They were blocking his view of the savior.

Hurt and Pain

The last thing that can cloud our mind and distort the signal is unresolved hurt and pain. In reality it is the unforgiveness associated with the pain that distorts the signal.

I grew up in a home with a father that was a martial arts instructor. This being the case I have always been interested in martial arts and its practices. I was always impressed with the way they could ignore physical pain. This led to me instituting some of the pain resistant techniques into my life. This is how I was able to deal with some of the drama in one of my relationships from hell. When it was over I was able to walk away feeling nothing. Or at least that what I thought!

I wrote about it in detail in *"Ways God Speaks"*. I wrote about a dream in which I was saw myself doing violent things to this woman and how that revealed that I harbored unresolved pain in my heart. I learned that day that pain has a really important role in our lives. It is not there to make us feel uncomfortable, even though we know that it does. Pain is a signal to you that you have an injury that requires your attention. What I had done was train myself to override this signal so that I could keep moving forward in pursing what I wanted to do.

This practice is seen in every competitive arena and for sporting events it is a great discipline. We all admire people who can press through challenges to obtain a victory. You will find that this is necessary at different points in your walk with God as well. However, when it comes to hearing the voice of God, you have to stop and acknowledge the pain in your life.

Why you may ask? You have to acknowledge the pain because the reason your body alerts you to the reality of an injury is so you do not further injure yourself and others. Take stretching exercises for example. Many people during a stretch will get a sensation of pain when the muscle has been stretched to its maximum position. And even though the pain is indicating that the muscle cannot stretch any further, many will push it until it tears. Then they find themselves in the position of not only being less limber, but handicapped by the injury. Then their injury results in the disruption of the lives of those around them. This truth applies to spiritual pain as well. When we have unresolved hurt and pain in our heart, unforgiveness will cloud the mind. This happens because the area of our life where the spiritual pain resides becomes sensitive. So sensitive in fact that it may cause us to draw back or react defensively when someone innocently treads upon that painful area. It is similar to what we may experience with a cut on an arm that has not been properly addressed. The threat of exposing that area to touch controls how we interact with others. The same happens to us in our minds. When someone reminds us of a painful situation we look through the eyes of that pain and not with a clear view. Every man looks like a dog to a woman who has unresolved relationship pain. Every white man looks like a racist when there is unresolved racial pain. Every preacher looks like a crook to someone who has been robbed in church. Even God looks like an uncaring Father to someone with unresolved daddy issues. So pain can cloud your mind and can cause you to struggle to be obedient to God because your pain has contaminated His word to you.

Here is a personal example from my life. I grew up in an area that was predominately African American. We may have had 20-30 Caucasian students that I can remember in my graduating class of 600+ students. I also grew up with a mother that was very loving and accepting of all kinds of people. Even though I did not grow up with other races, her ways rubbed off on me. Also being in a predominately African American area meant that I did not have to deal with a lot of racism. This meant I was a little "green" in my experience.

Once I was old enough to work, my father secured me a job with the Federal Government and again my environment was predominately African American. However after 10 years or so the leadership changed and a Caucasian woman came in and hired an all-Caucasian staff for her supporting leadership. I thought nothing of it until the oppressive nature of racism started to rear its ugly head. God had given me favor with her so it did not directly affect me other than the fact that I was not allowed to advance into jobs that required that I showed intelligence. She managed everyone else with a very stereotypical perspective. Finally, she brought in a lady who really began to manage me with these prejudice ways. Then the first woman retired and a man was hired that recognized what was happening. He even came to my defense several times. He warned the other woman that she was setting herself and the agency up for an EEO case.

All of this really began to affect me. Then all of a sudden I found myself suspicious of every Caucasian person. I only saw them through the lens of these experiences. I realized it was not right and I asked God to take the feelings away but He never did. I was really struggling not to see all Caucasian people as hiding racial intentions. I was always wondering, even of Caucasian preachers, what they really thought about African Americans.

Then God taught me this and I could finally see how pain could cause you to see through its lens. This pain made it impossible to be comfortable in the presence of Caucasians. This was a real problem because I needed to be open to hear the voice of God for them as well. How I interacted with them needed to be such that they would be open and not closed to His love. Not only did it affect me being able to share but it also affected my ability to receive. I can remember watching old Oral Roberts videos with the intent of learning how he ministered deliverance and wondering whether he was bound himself by racism. As you can see this was really affecting me. Sometime later God showed me why the feelings remained. This is when I learned what I am going to share next.

How to Clear the Air

1 Peter 4:1 speaks of having a pure mind. A pure mind is a clean mind that is not clouded with things that hinders us from hearing, and seeing God's voice. While the idea of a pure mind may seem unobtainable, I remind you that the transformation of your mind is a process. It is not something that happens overnight. It is the product of intentional diligence in pursuing and obtaining that for which you were apprehended.

Therefore, you will find that there are some things that assist us with clearing the air. One thing that we already discussed was the power of deep meditation or daydreaming. Daydreaming as we have said is allowing God's word to wash you and root you in truth. Jesus said, *"Sanctify them by truth; your word is truth"* (John 17:17). Truth washes the mind but what else can we do? To explain it to you I need to tell you of a vision God gave me some years ago.

264

Sometime ago as I was sitting on the floor in prayer the Lord began to take me out in the spirit and show me a vision of windows. These windows were like an old filmstrip and in every one of the frames was an event in time. I did not at that time understand what I saw but would later discover that the vision was Hebrews 11:3, for *"By faith we understand that the worlds were framed by the word of God so that the things which are seen were not made of things which do appear"*. A word study of the passage revealed that the word "worlds" was not the word that we understand as the "cosmos" or planets. In the Greek it was the word "ion" for which we derive our word time. So the passage really reads, for by faith we understand that "time" was framed by the word of God.

This was a revelation on many fronts. It was a revelation on prophecy and the fact that God allows prophets to peer into these windows to see the events appointed and framed by time. For the Bible says such things as *"For the vision is for AN APPOINTED"* or framed time (Hab. 2:3). We also see that the word of God creates these time frames.

How does this relate to the mind? Your mind is constantly acting as a recorder capturing events in time. It is viewing these windows along the way of life. As a result you can go back in time to any point in the window of your life and relive a moment. This is what we call "memory". A memory is a peek back in time in your mind's file cabinet. Memories are very important and can be very real. Just ask anyone who has had to live through any type of trauma. They can tell you that they can go back in time and relive a memory with such intensity that it feels as if it was really happening to them again. The same happens in some pleasant experiences such as sexual and drug encounters. This is why we are tempted to return to a certain type of destructive behavior. It is because we are able to relive it in our minds.

As I said in the previous chapter about the imagination, there is more reality to what you experience in your mind than you and I could ever really be aware of. Also I am sure that everyone can agree that memories good and bad can feel, taste, smell, sound, and look real.

This leads us to two very important words in the Bible seen more than a few times in both the Old and New Testaments. They are "forgiveness" and "repentance". These two spiritual acts are more than just spiritual exercises that we do to help us maintain a healthy relationship with God. They are both ways to release the cleansing power of God in our minds.

Repentance

First up for discussion is repentance. Repentance is our response to sin that makes us right before God. Most people believe it is done for God's pleasure, but in reality it is designed for your cleansing. Have you ever noticed that neither Adam nor Eve ever bothered to apologize for their disobedience? Neither did the Cain when He killed his brother Abel. No one said God I'm sorry for what I have done. They just proceeded with trying to justify their actions. This is really the problem that God has with mankind; it is that mankind never wants to say to God I was wrong. Instead we find reasons to justify why we were right to do the things that we wanted to do. So Adam blamed Eve and Eve blamed the serpent. But it was Adam who obeyed the voice of his wife. It was Eve who considered the counsel of the serpent. Likewise it was you that did what you did in spite of God's clear commands not to do whatever you did.

The first stage of repentance is ownership of the sin. You must own or accept accountability for your disobedience. This is very important because God does not alleviate the feelings of guilt and shame until you do.

This is what Adam and Eve did in the Garden. They never allowed God the opportunity to forgive them. They never once apologized for their disobedience. Their guilt and shame not only affected their relationship with God but it affected their relationship with each other. You cannot begin to be comfortable in your own skin around other people until you can first be transparent with God. They didn't just cover up from God, they covered up from each other.

So repentance does not mean that you simply stop the disobedient behavior, but that you own your behavior and confess it to God. The Bible says, *"If we confess our sins He is faithful and just to forgive us and to cleanse us from unrighteousness"* (1 John 1:9). One of the keys to cleansing these guilty shameful memories in the window of time is confession. You have to go back in time and ask God to show you these areas where you struggle with guilt and shame and confess them to Him. You may find that going back to these moments in time are painful, but that's okay. As soon as you present them to God and apologize for the things you justified, He will erase and cleanse that memory so that the stain of sin is removed. It is important for you to know that sin *"stains"* (see Jer. 2:22), but the blood of Jesus washes (see Heb. 9:14). For the 1 John 1:7 says, *"... and the blood of Jesus Christ His Son cleanses us from all sin"*. Please learn to repent. Allow the finished work of Christ to cleanse your mind's conscience so that you can welcome His voice in your life.

Some people today are telling the saints that they don't understand their authority if they are living a lifestyle of repentance. This is not scripturally sound or true. Just read 1 John 1:7 again and you will see a clear need to repent of sin even after our conversion. Likewise we see a requirement of repentance for some healing scenarios. (see James 5:16) So confession and repentance should be a lifestyle. I personally find it to be an easy act because it is not only right, but respectful and loving to tell someone you love, I'm sorry I hurt you today. This should be especially easy for us as children of God because we already know that He will forgive us.

Forgiveness

The next mind cleaner is forgiveness. Forgiveness is a really hard subject to tackle because we are usually so emotionally tied to the offense. Some people like to say I will forgive but I won't forget. Is this really possible? To really understand forgiveness we have to examine some words. Isaiah 43:25 says, *"I, even I am He who blots out transgressions, for my own sake, and remembers your sin no more."* In other words God says I will forgive you and forget that there was an offense. The word "forget" in the original language means to lose from the mind. This was a rather disturbing definition for me, but it mirrors what God says He does in Isaiah. Also, we are commanded to forgive others like Christ forgave us (see Col. 3:13). It is a command to lose the offense from our mind in the same way that Christ lost our offense from His.

Before I learned this I sat before the Holy Spirit and asked Him to show me all those places of pain that I need to revisit and forgive. He immediately started taking me back to offenses. Some went all the way back to my childhood. It was an incredible experience because there were many instances that I thought were resolved but when the memory came up I could feel the pain of that time. Then I was able to relate how that pain was manifesting towards others tied to that offense.

For instance I often found myself wanting to prove my value to former classmates on Facebook. I could never figure out why I felt this need until the Holy Spirit brought back to mind a high school memory of a situation in which I was belittled before my classmates because my family had to live on a budget. That embarrassment stuck with me all those years. By this time I had been out of school 24 years, but I was still having these feelings. So I presented this to God and forgave that person who committed the offense.

Then I learned that as a genuine act of forgiveness I was going to have to lose it from my mind. This is where a new struggle began. I noticed that I was fine with forgiving the offense but I did not want to forget it altogether. I didn't really want to let it go. I was emotionally attached to that offense. This is when I learned that real forgiveness means giving up the right to the offense. See, the problem was that I felt a right to that image and I did not want to release it to God. It was mine. Forgiveness means that I grant a pardon from the offense and I give it to God to destroy.

Now I do understand that this is going to be especially hard for some people with certain traumas. Nonetheless if you want your mind to be free from that time frame then you have to give the offense to God. *(In cases of severe trauma I recommend that this is done with a friend, professional counselor, or an inner healing minister)* If not you will relive it over and over every time someone gets close to your area of pain. Satan will also use it against you in your prayer time to torment you. He will use such thoughts as such as, why would a loving God allow that to happen to you? He doesn't love you. He can't protect you. This guy is going to do the same thing to you. She is just as crazy as… It can go on and on. But if you purify your mind then you will be able to say that Satan has nothing in me. It is the pain, guilt, lies, and darkness within you that he uses against you.

Here is an example of how the devil can use your past to haunt your present. Due to the gift of word of wisdom on my life I am frequently sought out for counsel. On one particular occasion a young woman came to me for advice about a situation. She had previously told me about her traumatic past and it was pretty bad. She was pleasant but always had a very tough no nonsense demeanor. She was constantly in conflict with others, she couldn't get married, and she was just a very unpopular person. So on this day she was asking counsel about her conflict with her boss and I gave her counsel to submit to his authority. Then she burst into tears and said, "I just can't feel like a victim, I just can't." Suddenly, it occurred to me that all of the present conflict concerning her life was intimately tied to the events in the windows of her past. She had told me that she had forgiven her offenders but had pledged that she would never forget what they had done to her. By not forgiving and forgetting she was allowing Satan to afflict her with the painful memories in those windows. Even though she always had a very strong and tough demeanor, these memories were the chink in her amour. She could never allow herself to be vulnerable because she was scared of becoming a victim again.

Looking at this situation, ask yourself the question, is forgiveness beneficial to God or to man? It is beneficial to you. It is absolutely good for you so that you can be free to pursue the future that God has for you without dragging around painful and guilty memories from the past.

Remembering

This leads to the power of remembrance. The word remembrance in the Greek means to bring back to the mind and to record. The last part of this definition is really interesting. We all know that to remember things means to look back into a specific window in time. However, it also has another very important function. That function is that of recording or capturing images. God not only wants us to remember certain things but He also wants us to create new memories. How do we do this?

As I said your mind is always recording the windows of time so you must choose more carefully what you allow into the windows. Earlier I said I woke up with an image of the Kardashians in my mind. This is the memory that I created by what I allowed into my eyes. I learned that I had to ask God to purge that image from my mind and put into my mind images that when recalled would help me and not hurt me. This is very important for me because I have learned to dwell in the presence of God and the last thing I need popping up in my mind is beautiful women with big bottoms. So controlling the eye and ear gates is important to creating good memories

This also encourages us to be responsible in our behavior. For instance I am more aware of the types of images I put into the window of time for my children. I want their memories to be filled with images that give Glory to God. My kids have gotten use to the idea that daddy walks around the house talking into the air. They use to ask the question, "Daddy who are you talking to?" Now they know that I am talking to God and God is talking back to Daddy. This is the memory I am building in them so that when they are grown they will have this memory to draw upon. I want to remind them in the seasons of need that God is right there with them. And that He speaks to people. Ask yourself what kind of memories you are building for your children. How are you going to bind his law to your children so that they have a rich legacy of hearing the voice of God? Or are you going to build prisons of shame and guilt, lies, and pain for them?

All this boils down to the reality that your mind's memory must be edited like a movie. If you want freedom to walk in a transformed mind that is receptive to the voice of God. Then you have to allow God to edit the static out of you mind. Let him fine-tune you!

As I close out this chapter, I hope that you will take the time to put all of this information to use so that you can begin to open yourself up to the reality of your God. I hope that you know that your mind is so special. It is at the core of your spiritual life. What you do with it and how you treat it will determine your success in getting close to God and living the supernatural Christian life. Yes, I said supernatural Christian life. Some people really do not comprehend this reality. Some do not understand that Christianity is a supernatural life of encountering the supernatural God.

Section 5
Follow the Leader

Chapter Twelve
His Voice and His Character

The Voice on the Other End

I want you to picture this scenario. Imagine that you have just received a phone call from your husband of 20 years and he starts saying vulgar things to you over the phone. As he is speaking, you notice that the voice is similar but slightly different. But regardless of the voice, you're saying to yourself this could not be Dan, because you know that your husband does not talk that way. So you say, "This is not Dan! Who is this?" Suddenly laughter erupts on the other end of the phone. Then the caller finally reveals himself as one of your girlfriend's friends playing on the phone.

Many of you may not have ever really considered that there is a reality in this scenario. That reality is the truth that there is not much of a difference in hearing the voice of God than hearing the voice of a close friend over the phone. While you are on the phone with a person you are completely devoid of every major sense accept one. In this situation, you only have your ears for processing the information that you are receiving. You cannot touch, taste, smell, or see the person to verify their identity. Your only friends in this situation are your ears and what you know about that person's character.

You will find that this true with God also. You cannot see or touch Him, but you can hear Him. And you will decrease the chances of being deceived when you spend time with Him and invest in getting to understand Him..

The unfortunate part is that Satan is playing on the phones of many and they don't know it. They should know, but how can they, if they don't' understand the character of God? That is what this chapter is all about; "How to study the character of God". The Bible shows us exactly who He is and how He behaves. We can see that He is a person and we can examine what moves His heart.

The Bible also encourages us to "study" to show yourself approved before God, a worker that needs not to be ashamed" (see 2 Tim. 2:15). There is actually a teacher, whom I have come to respect, that teaches that we are not supposed to study the word but instead get revelation on the word. However, as he was teaching he knew all of the Greek and Hebrew words that were in the passages he was teaching. I thought it was a bit ironic. Don't let anyone confuse you regarding this matter. Revelation is increased when you show yourself approved. In other words, you will see that God will honor you with the deeper truths when you do the homework and study the culture of the people in the various books of the Bible, the original Greek and Hebrew words, and the various religious practices of the time. There are some things you just need to study to understand. Now, while I disagree with the point that he makes regarding studying, I do agree with the idea that God wants to reveal Himself. He is much too complex for you to think that in your own finite mind that you could comprehend His glorious nature through study alone. While there are things you must study, there are also some things that He must reveal.

So what I am going to encourage you to do in this chapter is to study the scriptures and study God allowing Him to reveal His nature to you. I am also going to show you how I study God and position myself for revelation.

I want to further add, that we are not studying the personality of God. We are studying His character. Personality is defined by the qualities of a person that define how they behave. For example a person may be funny, witty, passive, aggressive, etc. These are all personality traits. The scriptures do not show us much about God's personality. Even in the gospels we don't get a solid sense for Jesus' personality. We don't know if He was funny, or if He was emotional. What we see is His character. Character is defined not by what we do, but by who we are! And we can see that He was Holy. We can see that He was compassionate. We can see that He did not tolerate sin. We can see that He was merciful and so many other wonderful traits that if we take the time to learn, we will have greater confidence in knowing who is speaking to us. Then you will be able to say to the spirit of deception when he rears up…"That is not God. He does not act that way."

The Names of God

Have you ever had someone call you outside of your name or tell someone something about you that was not true? How did it feel? For most of us, what angered us so much is that someone used our name in connection with something that insulted our character. We may not consider the idea that our names say so much about our character, but they do. In fact, when you apply for a credit line they ask for your name and personal identification information just so they can see what other creditors have to say about your name. All of your character is summed up in whether or not you pay your debts. This is such a serious matter that you can't even get a good job if you have a bad name.

While we may not have ever given a lot thought to the relationship between names and character, we should realize that God is also subject to a background check. Every time someone thinks of God or is presented with some opportunity to serve Him, He is instantly put under a background investigation. In our minds, we unconsciously call God's character into question. For instance, every time you refuse to believe in His ability to solve your problems, you subconsciously say to yourself, I have done the research and I have concluded that this is not something that God can handle. God fails our background checks so often because we do not know the various names the patriarchs gave Him. These names are testimonies from great biblical heroes about how God demonstrated His faithfulness to them. They tell us His credit is good with them. Likewise, if we would take the time to learn what others have testified about Him, we will be in a better position for seeing God's hand at work in our lives.

Below are the various names God has been given by those to whom He has proven Himself faithful. Learning these is a good way to start building the safety net that will allow you to learn the voice of God. The Bible says that *"The name of the Lord is a strong tower. The righteous run in and are safe"* (Prov. 18:10).

> El-Shaddai – The Almighty God (Gen.17:1-2)
> Jehovah-Jireh – The Lord Our Provider (Gen. 22:14)
> Jehovah-Rapha – The Lord Our Healer (Exod. 15:22-26)
> Jehovah-Tsidqenu – The Lord Our Righteousness (Jer. 33:16)
> Jehovah-Nissi - The Lord is Our Banner (Exod. 17:15)
> Jehovah-Shalom – The Lord Our Peace (Judg. 6:24)
> Jehovah-Shammah - The Lord Is There (Ezek. 48:35)
> Jehovah-Sabaoth – The Lord of Hosts (Rom. 9:29)

El-Shaddai

This is something that God declared of Himself and later proved to Abraham. He says I am the Lord Almighty walk before me blameless. In this passage God tells us that He is Almighty. This simply means that He is full of "all might" or strength and power. This tells us that we can expect that God will speak to us in a way or with instructions that demonstrate this attribute of His name. Any voice that says such things as, "God is not able to do that" or "this is impossible" is not coming from God. This is not His character. If anything, you will find that He challenges us to do things based on the idea that He knows He is almighty.

Jehovah-Jireh

This is always an interesting one to consider. This means that God is a provider. Provider means pro (before) vide (vision). God is proactive. He is not at all surprised by the situations that come into our lives. Neither is He caught off guard about how to respond. He anticipates the need and then sets aside the resources to meet that need.

How does this relate to hearing the voice of God? This tells us that God does not speak to us in a panic. Sometimes when we feel pressure in a situation, we project to ourselves what we want God to say. Or sometimes we yield to the temptation Satan sends when he sees us in the wilderness. The voice that is pressuring you into decisions as if this is the only chance for an opportunity is not from God. He speaks to us from a place of knowing not from a place of ignorance. You see this type of pressure a lot when a salesman is involved.

We have all been victims of pressure. Sometimes we see a great deal and assume that it came from God, but the salesman is telling us it has to happen now. It's only for a limited time they say. This tricks a lot of us into unnecessary purchases. Just know that anything that is for you is for you. God knows what your needs are and He has made the provision before the need was present.

Just consider this example. The Bible says that Christ was slain "before" the foundations of the world (see 1 Pet. 1:20). He anticipated the fall of mankind and made provision for the need to be satisfied.

Jehovah-Rapha

This is another name that fascinates me. It fascinates me because there are people who say that God is not performing healings on a large scale. This is definitely not the voice of God speaking. The Bible shows us that this is a part of who He is; He **"IS"** a healer. It is His nature to heal.

If you hear a voice speaking to you and it is telling you that you should accept death because God is not healing anymore. Rebuke it in the name of Jesus, even if it comes to you per a human vessel. God does perform healings because He is **A HEALER**.

Jehovah-Tsidqenu

This particular name of God is absolutely beautiful. What this name tells us is that God covers our nakedness. Earlier in chapter 5, *Different Voices*, I told you that hearing the voice of God requires that you to be honest about who you are. This is the same concept. You need to realize that you are poorly dressed and that He wants to give you new clothes from His closet (see Zech. 3:3-5). He wants to you to exchange your shortcomings for His grace and forgiveness. We can see an example of this in the Garden of Eden. Once Adam and Eve realized that they were naked they sewed fig leaves together in an attempt to cover up their shame. Then God made for them adequate clothing. This is a depiction of who HE is. He covers us with His righteousness.

Therefore, we do not have to put up with voices that condemn, judge, and make us feel inadequate. I told someone once, who was being reminded of her failures by a loved one, "Don't let a dirty rag make you feel dirty". I told her, "you are dirty, and your righteousness is as a filthy rag. The difference is that you know you are dirty, and he doesn't." When we accept the fact that we are in rags, we can receive His riches. He is our righteousness.

Jehovah-Nissi

Have you ever been in a really low place and been surrounded by people who make you feel hopeless about the possibility of deliverance? In April of 2011 my mother died from uterine cancer. It was a challenging time in my life, but the voice of the Lord encouraged me all the way through. Even though she died, He never allowed me to think that He was not able to fix the situation or that He was small in the situation. He always reminded me that He is not the underdog in the war against cancer. This was the word He gave me to hold on to through this ordeal. And I told it to everyone who tried to innocently make me feel hopeless. I assumed He meant to heal her, but in the end His will prevailed.

The fact is that even though we may face insurmountable opposition, we are not to forget that our God is a God that raises a standard of victory. You may be wondering, how I can see victory in her death.

My mother never cried, moped, or became depressed about her situation. The cancer had spread to every part of her body, her heart, lungs, and brain, everywhere. And in the midst of it all she did not have one day of pain. This completely baffled the medical community. They often questioned her as to how it was possible, and the solider that she was, she always told them that it was her God that was working on her behalf. Everyone that came to visit her she preached Jesus to and encouraged them through their own problems. I remember on one occasion, right after she was told that she would die in a couple of months, that one of the young nurses was so impressed with how she was handling this devastating news. (Now what she did next was inappropriate but God was glorified all the same.) This young lady who was puzzled by how calm and pleasant mother was in face of the bad news, said to her, "Aren't you afraid?" To which my mother gently replied, "No." This nurse then began to ask her why, and my mother told her because she was in the hands of Her God. I don't know what happened to this young lady, but I promise you that she saw the banner of victory and a seed was planted in her heart. She witnessed the God of Peace and the God who is our Banner.

The Lord is He that will raise up a standard and a flag that announces our victory. My mother was like Sampson, she was having an effect on the lives of the living even in her death. And God showed His power in allowing her to die pain free. This encouraged the hearts of all who witnessed His keeping power. Like I said, she never had one day of pain. It was so baffling to the doctors that one of them thought she was delusional and gave her morphine anyway. He soon came to accept that by some miracle she was not in pain. God was showing us victory from another perspective.

He was confirming for us His word that He is not inferior in the war against cancer. He made it clear, that though cancer had tormented others, it would not torment His daughter.

It was not the outcome we wanted, but He said to me, "I am not inferior in the war against cancer," and He demonstrated that He was able to bring her to Himself in a way that others could not figure out.

The final victory was to take place in her hospital room. She had died, and my father, brothers, and I went to the hospital to view the body. When I walked into the room and saw her body, I felt the warmest sense of peace and as I looked at her all I could do was smile. I know this sounds strange but that's how I felt, like smiling. Even though I would miss her God assured me by manifesting His presence in her hospital room, that He is not the God of the dead, but the living. There is victory even in death for the believer. For the scriptures say, *"Oh death where is your victory"* (1 Cor. 11:12).

279

This is the point I am trying to make, when God speaks to us, He does so from the standpoint of victory. He does not speak to us in hopelessness as if He were somehow the underdog.

Jehovah-Shalom

Sometimes we can be tempted to fear when we encounter stressful situations. This is when we need to know that God is our peace. God does not inspire nor speak to us from a place of fear. When you encounter situations and you hear voices that are telling you things that are filling your heart with fear, you can be assured that it did come from God. The Bible say's *"God did not give us a spirit of fear, but of love, power, and a sound mind"* (2 Tim. 1:7). Likewise, Romans says, *"For we have not received the spirit of fear again to bondage"*.

You will also notice that God shows us everything about Himself but fear. We see Him grieved, angry, and joyful, but there is not one passage that presents God as one that experiences fear. Fear is not in His nature and His voice will not come from a place of fear.

Going back to the death of my mother, I can remember being at her funeral and still having a smile on my face. I greeted each person as they came through with a hug and a smile. I was at peace with God's decision. Then, they closed the casket and the reality began to set in. I was never going to see her again in this life. As the service went on different preachers got up to say a word of encouragement and they were kind words but they were solemn. Then my grandmother's Pastor got up to speak and the word she spoke changed the whole atmosphere of the service and restored my peace immediately. She said, *"Why are we sorrowful. We don't sorrow as those who have no hope"* (1 Thess. 4:13). Those words struck me to my core and carried me through with incredible peace.

I said it before, we do not have a God who does not cause us to be victorious. Even is death the believer wins. For to be absent from the body is to be present with the Lord (see 2 Cor. 5:8). God's voice produces peace even when we should feel otherwise.

Jehovah-Shammah

Jehovah Shammah means the Lord is there. Please keep in mind as we go through these names and that these names tell us *who God is*"! This is another one where we need to renew our minds. We like to say things like the "Lord is coming" and "where is God?" This tells me that we do not understand this character trait of God. You do not need His presence to show up to speak to you. You have access to Him because He *"is there"* already. He is always there, that's why I am teaching you how to come into that reality. If you can get into that reality, you will begin to both feel and hear God clearly and more often. Do yourself a favor and take these types of phrases out of your vocabulary and thinking. God is there and waiting to fellowship with you.

Jehovah-Sabaoth

One of the things that this name tells us about God is that He is the Lord of all creation. It testifies to His greatness and the honor that He deserves.

I remember early on in my developing relationship with God, that I got so comfortable with Him that I started to call Him JC. He put up with it for a while then He reminded me that I am but a vapor that appears on the Earth for a second and that He is the God of all creation. He reminded me that He is not one of my homies. You should keep this in mind as well. Even though Abraham was considered the friend of God, he was still very careful during his negotiations with God for Sodom and Gomorrah.

This name also means that He's got the whole world in His hand. And because He does we do not need to worry.

The real mystery of this name is unpacked in the idea of the vastness of God. In the Bible God says *"Heaven is His throne and Earth is His footstool"* (Isa. 66:1). As I meditated on what this means, I was filled with reverent fear, and utter amazement. Consider the implications of God's size. We know that the universe is unimaginably vast. Our galaxy alone is but one of billions. Our sun is 93 millions miles away from earth. If we were to travel there by plane it would take us 21 years. Now think about how big God must be that all of time and space exist inside of Him! Think about how big He must be that He has no beginning and no end.

If we were to really put it into perspective, just image going to the beach and holding one grain of sand in your hand. That would be the Earth in His hand. So how much bigger is He than you and your puny problems? For me the thought of it all was so overwhelming! I told God when He revealed it to me, that it was more truth than my little human mind could handle! Just think about it.

After you catch your breath, consider the reality that such a powerful and vast being wants to talk to you. Do you think that He is worried about anything? When He speaks to you He will speak to you from the position of one who uses the Earth as a footstool. He will be sure of Himself. He will not be timid. If you hear a voice speaking to you in uncertainty, it will not be God. I said it in an earlier chapter that God speaks with authority not suggestively or passively. He tells us what to do as the Lord of all creation and He is so big that He has no reason to be fearful of anything. Not even Satan.

These are only some of Gods names that He was given by those to whom He revealed Himself. There are others such as Elohim, the branch of righteousness, the Word of God, the Good Shepherd, and King of Kings and many more. The Bible also shows us other characteristics of His person such as compassion and mercy, goodness, kindness, and justice. We also have the fruit of the Holy Spirit that communicates the character of God. I encourage you to study the rest of the names so that you can begin to recognize the voice on the other end of the phone.

Studying God

How can we use our personal Bible study time as a way to get to know the character of God? We put God under investigation. As I said before, you already subconsciously do it, why not do so with purpose. Take your doubts and questions to the Bible and God will clarify for you what is holding you back.

282

The word "investigate" means to track the foot prints of. When all of us were in grade school, we were at some point required to do a book report. Often it was a biography on an historical figure and then we reported to the class what we discovered about the person through our reading. We can use the same principles to study God. The only difference is that we are not studying the dead. My method of studying God somewhat resembles an interview.

When I study I take small sections or passages of scriptures at a time. I also read through the stories about God in the Old and New Testaments several times looking to see how God dealt with the situations. I consider those involved, what they did, what they didn't do, how God felt about it, and how He responded. I even study the customs and social atmosphere of the time.

If you are going to seriously consider studying the word then you will need to buy some resources. You will need a good Bible dictionary. The Bible dictionary is a great resource for researching the custom, culture, and history of the various groups of people in the Bible. It is also a great resource because it usually has maps of the territory of that day. This is invaluable for helping you to imagine the distance they walked and how each landmark related to one another.

The next thing you will need to purchase is a concordance and/or lexicon. These are invaluable when it comes to studying the word. The language of the original biblical text was far more expansive than our English vocabulary. For instance, we use one word to describe love, and the original language uses five words to indicate different types and levels of love. As you can see, this is how people find themselves promoting weird doctrines or in battles with what is called "apparent conflicts" in ideas.

A topical Bible is also a really great resource for the serious student. Topical Bibles present all the scriptures in groups based on subject matter. For example all the scriptures that relate to grace from the Old Testament to the New Testament are grouped together in a way that makes cross-referencing ideas easy.

The Spirit of Revelation

One other thing that we need to consider is the idea that there really are some things that you will only see in the scriptures if God opens them up to you. This is what the Bible refers to in Ephesians 1:18 as the spirit of wisdom and revelation in the knowledge of Him.

Something that I think you are able to see all through my writing is that there are some things I clearly received via revelation. This whole subject and all of the scriptures are not a product of my study time. Rather, they are the culmination of my study time. When we show ourselves approved through study God rewards us with more insight into His person. Studying is our way of showing God that we are attempting to draw near to Him. Revelation is His way of drawing close to us. When we show Him that we hunger and thirst for righteousness He fills us with His light.

The fact that you are reading this book tells me that you are willing to study. To receive revelation from God all you need to do is take the passages you have been studying and meditate on them. You will find that as you meditate, meaning to think about from every possible angle, God will begin to open up truths and parallels in the scriptures. You will begin to see things in the word you never saw before.

Revealing Parallels

For example, God showed me a parallel in Acts and 2 Kings. When Jesus was taken up from the disciples, the Bible says that they saw Him as He was taken up. A few days later the Holy Spirit fell on them and they were endued with power. In 1 Kings, Elijah tells his young disciple Elisha whom had been faithfully following him, that if he sees him when he is taken away, he will receive a double portion. As they are speaking a chariot separates them and as Elisha is looking at his teacher being taken away, he receives his teacher's mantle and is empowered with double his teacher's anointing. Can you see the parallel yet?

I could go really deep into the whole teaching and what all He showed me about the Church living and receiving the double portion anointing, but that

284

is a subject for another book. This is not something that you would normally see through your personal study. This is something that God has to show you or someone else has to point out to you.

Revealing the God Who Sees Our Potential

Another example would be found in Genesis 1:1. It reads that the Earth was void and without form. That verse alone was a springboard of insight. God showed me His character is so few words. He showed me by this passage that what He sees is our potential.

Notice that He did not call Earth nothing. Have you ever heard that phrase "God stepped out into nothing"? God showed me in this small passage that he does not call the Earth "nothing" even though we see that it was nothing. *"God calls those things that are not as though they were"* (Rom. 4:7). He calls it Earth before He ever formed a thing. This is good news, because this means that no matter what condition we may be in, we know that He is not calling us by where we are, but by what He has purposed. He sees and speaks to your potential.

Revealing God in Warfare

One of may favorite and all time helpful revelations from God deals with the topic of warfare and the kingdom of God.

Ephesians 6:10-18 outlines for us the reality that we are in a war. It also declares to us who and what we are fighting. It further provides us with knowledge of our weapons and the armor provided for doing battle.

One day as I was preparing to teach my workplace Bible study, the Holy Spirit started talking to me about this passage. This is what He revealed to me. The following was not obtained during my study time it was given to me at work as I was doing my daily tasks.

When you look into the passage you will notice that there is no protection for the backside of the body. God showed me, that this is because we are a kingdom that is advancing forward towards a goal. We are aggressively

285

taking the promises in front of us; we are pressing toward the goal of the high call of God.

This idea is also reflected in our weaponry. You will notice that the enemy has "darts" or arrows in his arsenal. These are long-range weapons. They are designed to kill, slow down, and intimidate a "forward" moving threat from a safe distance. We however, have "swords". A sword is a close range combat weapon. What was God showing me? We have a shield of faith to use to protect us as we move forward into the things of God. It protects us from darts of fear, intimidation, and discouragement so that we can continue to move forward. Once we are close enough to obtaining the promise then the "rhema" word or voice of God speaks to help us press into the promise. The sword is an indication that at some point in the battle it becomes personal and intense. I'm sure most of you have heard it said that the battle is most intense right before you get your breakthrough. Well this is the scriptural reference for that idea. It is at this moment when meditation and quoting of the word is critical to you obtaining your promise.

We can see the parallel for this as well as Israel moves forward to take the promise land. They never looked or went backwards. Those of the previous generation who continued to look back to the "good ole days" in Egypt were killed in the wilderness. We can also see this idea when God instructs Gideon to only take those into battle who lapped up water with their hands. Those who put their faces in the water were disqualified because they represent those who lose focus in battle.

This again is an example of something that God reveals. No amount of study can connect the scriptures in such a way. And I could go on and on with the insights God has given me about Himself. I hope that these examples show you the value of allowing the voice of God to minster to you. I like to think of him as the baker. If we add the study ingredients of egg, sugar, dough, and salt, He will blend it all together and we will begin to rise with the revelation of His person.

Looking for Consistency

Last, I want to put one final rule in place. When you study God you are looking for consistency. Do not attribute a particular trait to His character because of something you found in one passage of scripture. In fact you will find safety in knowing that God uses the scriptures to expose us to a principle then He illustrates that principle for us in a story. The truth should be consistent with what we actually see happening in the biblical stories. Also, the Bible says, *"Let every word be established in the mouth of two or three witnesses"* (Duet. 19:15). This means, that whatever God has revealed about Himself once, He has revealed somewhere else in the scriptures.

This is really important in some areas of life in particular. One of which is marriage. I was one of those persons waiting for a voice from heaven to point out my wife from across the room. As you can see from my story in a previous chapter about a woman I went after because of a dream, that I was looking for God to direct me by supernatural means to a natural end. Then God helped me to look for His character in the situation. He allowed me to see that there are "NO" biblical instances of Him directing people as to whom they are to marry by supernatural means, except when He instructed Hosea to marry a prostitute. The only other closest example of this is seen in the story of Isaac and Rebecca. And in that story God led Abraham's servant to the Rebecca and not Isaac.

Why am I using this issue? I am using this issue because it is a perfect example of what it means to study the ways of God and His character. I have known and seen many people who got married because of a dream, vision, voice, or prophecy and watched the horror latter unfold when the marriage fell apart. I have also seen those who have waited beyond their fruitful years because they were waiting on such a supernatural experience.

We must always search for *how God does things* in the *"scriptures"* to protect us from these types of errors. We should see the principle at work in a story. When we study the ways of God we will see that He allows people to choose a spouse, for it reads, *"When A MAN FINDS a wife, he has found a good thing."* Not only do we see that He allows us to choose, but He provides us with more than a few instructions on "how to choose"! He tells us we must be equally yoked, to stay away from angry people, to avoid harlots, and many other such things to help us make informed healthy decisions.

Another great example of looking for the ways of God can be seen in some of today's popular teachings on deliverance. One of the teachings say that in order to cast demons out of the lives of people that the person must not have unconfessed sins. It teaches that demons have rights to us over the issue of sin. They also teach that you cannot cast a demon out of a person that wants the demon to stay.

However, when you look at the scriptures, you will find no such examples. Again the principle should be consistent with the illustrated account presented in the scriptures. I do believe however, that you can invite them in for the scriptures say *"Do not give place to the Devil."* I also believe that you can repent and cast them out with just as much ease as they were invited in. We have many examples of Jesus casting out demons and never once did we see Him ask a demon if He had rights to torment the person's life. In fact on one occasion He cast out a demon from a woman's daughter and the girl wasn't even present. He simply said to the woman it is done and when she arrived home the demon was gone out of the child. (see Mark 7:24-30) Neither did we see such in any of disciples' ministries. What we do see as we track God's footprints through the scriptures is an occasion where the disciples could not cast out a demon. And Jesus makes it absolutely clear that if we are having a problem casting out a demon it is not a issue with the person. It is an issue with "our faith" or it may be a lack of "prayer" and "fasting". Lastly, He tells us that there is a "kind" of demon that is hard to cast out when these elements are not in place in our lives (see Matt. 17:21, Mark 9:29).

You will also see that the issue of whether or not the person wants the demon to stay is not an issue. Paul cast out a spirit of divination from of a slave girl against her will and the demon's will (see Acts 16:18). We also see that she never had a chance or option to repent. Peter's shadow alone sent many demons to flight (see Acts 5:12-16). We also see that even the garments from Paul's body were enough to get the job done (see Acts 19:11-12). I have more to say on this topic but I will save if for another book.

Theses are examples of studying God. This is how we track His footprint in the word. You are looking and investigating the *how* and the *what*. You want to know **WHAT WOULD JESUS DO** or **WHAT DID JESUS DO**? This type of study protects us from bad theology passed down from generation to generation.

Please do not misunderstand my point regarding marriage. I am not saying that you are not to consider God in searching for a spouse. For we are told to acknowledge Him in all of our ways... Only God knows if this person is a good choice for your future. However, don't sit around waiting for the heavens to crack open, it will probably never happen. God's word reveals that he has created a natural process and that He involves Himself in that process—the process of people meeting, finding common interests, and falling in love. This is His way as seen in the scriptures.

Hopefully you have been enriched by the idea of seeking God, for if you seek you will find. God knows all about you and He would like to tell you a little more about Himself. If you learn to investigate Him you will find more than you bargained for awaiting you. You will discover more about who He is and how he moves. You will also find protection from deceiving spirits that may whisper in your ears or preach from your pulpit. Either way you will find great peace in knowing Him who died for you.

Chapter Thirteen
The Voice and the Unction

Follow the Leader

One of my favorite verses in all of scripture is Philippians 2:13. It reads, *"For it is God who works in you to will and to do in order to fulfill his good purpose."* Wow, so much is said with so few words.

My wife can validate the fact that I am going to preach and teach this passage to anyone that comes to me for advice on what action to take in any given situation. It is a passage that gives us great insight into the leading of God's Spirit. It pretty much tells us that if we really want to know what the will of God is in any given situation that all we need to do is look inward.

There was a time of a few years when God rarely spoke to me. In that time of not hearing His voice He taught me this verse. This verse became everything to me in that season. I have waited on job opportunities using this principle. When I say waited, I mean I waited in place as long as three years until God led me to another opportunity. And those opportunities were major opportunities when they finally arrived. I can remember my wife getting frustrated with the idea that I would not seek out another job. She could not understand why I was waiting, but I promise you she understands why now. Waiting on God's leading has put me into my career field as a highly paid graphic designer even though I am uneducated. As I go into more detail on this principle I will share more of this testimony.

So far most of this book has been about hearing the voice of God, but this chapter is specifically dedicated to the leading of the Spirit of God. For the scriptures declare *"As many as are led by the Spirit of God are the sons of God"* (Rom. 8:14). I would love to tell you that God is going to speak to you about what to do in every situation, but the truth is sometimes He leads us through the valley and the shadow of death, (see Psalm 23:4). Also, Jesus said He would lead us and guide us into all truth (see John 16:13). In fact if you can learn this principle you will be saved from the heartache so many suffer when they hear a voice other than God's.

Asleep in the Passenger Seat

As I was writing this chapter I was reminded of a vision that the Lord gave me. In the vision, Jesus and I were in a car and He was driving. I was in the passenger seat asleep. God said to me, "Let me drive." This vision is very precious to me and I often recall it to my memory to remind myself that He's in control and He knows where He is going. Sometimes when we follow God we want Him to tell us where we're headed and what will happen next. But often we are called to be like Abraham and just follow. He said to Abram *"Get out of your country to a place I will show you"* (Gen. 12:1). Wow. Is that all? Yep, that was all the instruction he received. What's more amazing is the fact that Abraham obeyed God with such little instruction.

This passage sets up a scenario and reveals a principle. That principle is that God speaks to us and He leads us. Even Jesus said, *"My sheep hear my voice and THEY FOLLOW Me"* (John 10:27). Moses also becomes a great example of this principle. For God spoke to Israel by Moses, but He Himself led them in a pillar of cloud by day and a pillar of fire by night. He spoke to them and He led them.

So it is not only important to hear the voice of God, but it is equally important to know and understand how to follow His Spirit.

How can we follow Abraham's example? What principle would help us to be more like Abraham? Hebrews 4:10 says, *"For he that is entered into His rest, he also hath ceased from his own works, as God did from his."* What does this mean?

The first principle of following God's lead is learning how to rest. Earlier in *"Elements of Hearing"* we learned about stillness. Real stillness is achieved when we learn to how to rest. If you are wondering what the difference is between the two, stillness is defined by an action, while resting is an attitude of trust. Resting occurs when we learn to be comfortable enough to let God be in the driver's seat of our life. Psalm 46:10 says, *"Be still and know that I am God."* This passage validates the idea of rest, for it says be still "first, and "know" second. You cannot know the experience with God until you first learn to rest.

Jesus further invites us to rest when He says in Matthew 11:28-30 *"Come to Me, all who are weary and heavy-laden, and I will give you rest. Take My yoke upon you and learn from Me, for I am gentle and humble in heart, and YOU WILL FIND REST FOR YOUR SOULS. For My yoke is easy and My burden is light."*

How do we rest? We rest by taking His yoke. Jesus is once again using a similitude to communicate to the people an idea in a visual language using concepts they understand. The yoke in biblical times was used to tie up animals to prevent wandering. Today we would recognize it as the reigns used to control horses or a leash used to walk dogs. This verse today would have been written as, let Me take the reigns or leash... It is a depiction of God's ability to lead us, but we must choose to follow Him. It does not read, I will give you My yoke, but instead it reads, *"take My yoke"*. So how do we rest? We learn to accept the idea that God is humble and gentle. We accept the idea that He wants what is best for us and that all of His decisions for our lives are made with the best intentions. If you can settle that idea in your heart then you will cease from your works and enter into His rest.

Togetherness: Team Work

Another important concept is the concept that God is working "with us" not "for us". Many of us experience so little in our Christian experience because we are waiters. Even though you are resting, you are not waiting. The scriptures say that the Holy Spirit is our helper (see John 15:26). He assists us in doing what God has for us to do. That tells us that you have role to play in seeing the things of God come to pass in your life.

There is a popular saying that says, if you take one step, God will take two. Surprise, not true! God does not work "for us" He works "with us". There is only one place in scripture to which this can be applied as truth. James 4:8, where it states *"If you draw near to God, He will draw near to you."* Pressing into an intimate place with God; initialing worship to God is the only thing that God gives us control over. It is the only area in which we can make the first move and expect God to follow. Other than that, this is an unscriptural statement and we are to allow God to lead us.

What about moving in faith? Shouldn't I move first and expect God to do His will? Shouldn't I seek if I hope to find. Knock if I want a door to open? What does the Bible say about how faith operates?

The Bible says, *"Faith comes by HEARING and HEARING by the word of God"* (Rom. 10:17). Faith is not demonstrated by stepping out hoping God will meet your expectations. For example, let's consider the idea of knocking. Which door will you knock on? Will you knock on all of them? Will you knock on one of them? What happens when more than one door opens? To which will you apply your concept of faith? Can you see the problem with this kind of approach to following God? It can lead to confusion and confusion has nothing to do with God, *"For God is not the author of confusion"* (1 Cor. 14:33). He knows where He is going and you need to acknowledge that you don't.

When we use our faith to follow God it should be the result of having heard the voice of God and responding to it. Once we have heard the voice of God we are to apply our faith to demonstrate trust and obedience to Him. It is a team effort—God has a part to do and so do you. The Bible is clear that we are subordinate partners with God in accomplishing His will. For as many as are *"led"*...My sheep *"follow"*... for "He will *"guide you"* into all truth. I cannot stress this enough. You cannot follow God from in front of Him.

So if we are to find God's best then we must learn to rest and we must learn to cooperate with our guide and follow His lead.

Desire: He Wills in Us

*"And I will put my spirit within you, and **cause you** to walk in my statutes,*

and ye shall keep my judgments, and do them" (Ezek 36:27).

This is where we get into the part of our main verse in Philippians 2, *"He wills in us"*. The passage above from Ezekiel is very revealing. It tells us that God is going to put a new spirit *"IN US"* and *"CAUSE US"* to do his will. What is He saying? I thought God was a gentleman. Is He saying that He is going to force us into doing His will? No, the key word in this verse is spirit. As we have defined earlier in previous chapters, the word spirit means breath or wind. It is the basis from which we get the word inspire and inspiration. Motivation is also a word that we can use to represent spirit. So what God is saying in the verse above is that He is going to "inspire" or "motivate" us to do His will.

How does this relate to the passage in Philippians that reads, "He wills in us…?" In the New Testament God gives us the Helper who inspires us to do His will. How? He does so by giving us the desire to do what He wants us to do.

Often we complicate the process by over thinking the plan of God. Finding God's will becomes easier to discern when we learn to follow the desires that He places in our hearts. Ezekiel 36 reads, *"And I will give them one heart, and put **a new spirit within them**. "And I will take the heart of stone out of their flesh and give them a heart of flesh, **that they may walk in My statutes and keep My ordinances and do them**. Then they will be My people, and I shall be their God."*

Often I hear stories about people who say that God called them to a particular kind ministry. But they seem very leery and almost disgusted by the idea that they claim came from God. They clearly know that they don't want to be a part of the ministry that they are getting involved with. I use this verse in my counsel to those in this type of dilemma to help them understand that God gives us the desire to do what He wants us to do. If you hate the idea of doing something that God has told you to do, then there is a very big chance that you are not following God. Remember His yoke is easy His burden is light.

How does this apply to everyday life scenarios? If you learn how to rest in the Lord and not move ahead of Him, then you find that He always has a desire placed in your heart for your next move. He will literally motivate or inspire you to do what He is asking you to do.

Here's one example from my life. A few years ago I was in a job that was going nowhere. By this time I had a family of 3 kids and a wife. My wife was a wonderful stay-at-home mom and I really needed a new job. I also desired a job with career latter. Up until that point I always had jobs because I did not have a skillset, but I really wanted a career.

Prior to entering my season of need I started to have a renewed desire do art and I knew that God was leading me into an art-based career, specifically in the area of graphic design. The problem was that I did not have a college degree. All of my art experience was in the area of illustration. So over the next three years I sacrificed going out to lunch. I literally went out to lunch maybe 3 times in 3 years total. Everyday during my lunchtime I studied graphic design principles and graphic design programs. Three years I stayed this course in spite of the fact that I needed more money. I was convinced that this was God's direction and it was somewhat antagonizing to my wife. This was partly due to the fact that all I had was a desire to move in that direction. I didn't even know how I would get into the field of graphic arts without a degree, but I had a desire to go in this direction.

Two and a half years into my studies God began to create opportunities for me to create graphic products in my office. That led to several successful products that positioned me for the real opportunity. By the time I was into the third year when one of my co-workers crossed paths with a senior designer in our art department who was working alone. He was the supervisor and all of his employees had retired. This co-worker upon learning about the situation communicated to him that I had been creating graphic products upon request around the office that were very visually appealing. Long story short, I was allowed to work part time in the graphic department 2 days a week. That two days was all I needed to show what I could do and it was not long after that I was made a full-time graphic designer.

To what do I attribute this incredible move of God? It was all because I was able to rest and follow the desire God had placed in my heart.

After reading this chapter some of you are going to experience a great sense of freedom and relief. A lot of times we get involved in things because we want to be seen or we see a need and we assume that God wants us to do something about it. Then once we get involved and start working in that area we find that we are operating in dread the whole time and nothing about the experience is enjoyable. We're just grinding our way through hoping to reach the end soon. Or we just consider it our way of suffering for Christ. Not only do we not enjoy it but, we find it difficult to remain faithful. That is because we are not *"FAITH FILLED*. You must be faith filled to be full of faith, and as I said earlier, faith comes by hearing God's direction.

Learn the Value of "NO"

I have over the years learned to say no to opportunities that are not from God. Sometimes I just flat out say I don't have a desire to participate in this event. Which always prompts a response like, you really don't need all of that for this, or it's just going to be…. I then gently explain it to them this way. If I get involved in this event even though I don't have a desire to do so, I am going to struggle with being consistent and productive. And If I struggle with being consistent and productive then your event will in some way be affected adversely. We have all worked on projects with people who did not want to be involved. What generally happens is everyone else who wants to be a part of the event finds them selves picking up the slack. I want to be a blessing and not a hindrance. This usually helps them to accept my answer of "no".

For those of you to whom God calls to lead events or to work as event planners, you should really read the book of Nehemiah and Ezra. You will see the value of this principle there. Nehemiah had a desire placed in his heart to rebuild the walls of Jerusalem and the Bible does not say he rallied the troops, put out flyers, or that he tried to persuade people into accepting his dream. He just followed God and the Bible says that God stirred the hearts of those who would help him. In other words God willed in them to do for His good pleasure. This resulted in them being able to stay the course until they were finished despite very dangerous opposition.

This brings me to another important point. There is value in following His lead. Other than having a desire to do His will you will find that the desire, motivation, inspiration, or passion that God gives you for an assignment is long suffering. What do I mean? When you try to do something in your own strength you will eventually get weary and fail to produce any real fruit. But when God inspires you to do something He gives you a sustaining grace to see the product through until it is completed. Ask Jeremiah. He tried to walk away from ministry, but soon discovered that the call of God and the leading of the Spirit was not something he could ignore. It was God at work in him "willing" to do ministry through a sustaining inspiration.

Ability: He Works in US

This brings us to the latter part of Philippians 2, which reads, *"...and WORKS IN US to do..."* We also see this idea presented in the verses from Ezekiel 36 in which it states *"I WILL CAUSE them to WALK in My ways."* These verses are clear indications that God wants us to accomplish His will, but He's not expecting us to do it in our own strength, *"For it is not by power nor might but by My Spirit says the Lord"* (Zech. 4:6).

I call this the principle of grace. It is when God gives us the ability and or opportunity to accomplish an assigned task. Whenever I teach on grace I use Philippians 2 as my foundation. It so eloquently and vividly points out that there are two components to grace—*"He wills"* or inspires, which we have already covered, and *"He does"*.

Going back to the story of Nehemiah we see this principle at work. As we examine the story we can see that God gave Nehemiah and his volunteers the desire to rebuild the wall and the ability and opportunity to do the work.

The comfort of following God's direction can be found in the fact that where He drives us He provides for us. What is He providing? He provides us with the ability and the opportunity to fulfill His will. When we attempt to make the will of God happen we find ourselves with little Ishmael's. Ishmael represents the product of Abrahams and Sarah labor. They had the desire for something and assumed the responsibility of bringing God's desire to pass, which has had long reaching effects historically.

When God leads you into a path you do not have to worry about the, who, what, when, where, and why. He takes care of all the details. For instance, if God has called you to preach, He is calling you to yield to Him as He preaches through you. He will provide the word, and the opportunities to do what He called you to do. He called Moses to preach and He had a speech impediment. Even though God could not inspire the kind of faith in Moses needed to use Him as a Prophet, He still provided Aaron as a mouthpiece to Moses. Read also, the story of Gideon in Judges 6. God does the same for him. He inspires him with an idea and then He provides him with the ability and resources to get the job done.

Referring back to my story of how God led me into the graphic design field, I can see where this principle was at work. God gave me a desire to move into a career in the arts, and then He provided me with the ability and resources. Once I started moving with God in this new direction a former graphic designer called me to the graphics department before he retired and personally told me what subjects I needed to study to get started. He also gave me more than a few books from his collection. As I read and studied I eventually came to a place where I needed more than books. I needed to be in a classroom environment. That led to God opening up avenues for me to pay cash to go school. After a year of school the finances dried up, but that was ok. I had taken all the classes I needed to set a firm foundation in place. It was not too long after that the opportunity arose. So God gave me a desire and then provided the resources and the opportunity for follow His direction.

I Have Will, But No Work

Sometimes we find ourselves in the place where we have desire, but no ability, or ability but no desire. What does this mean and how should we respond in such a situation? First I must inform you that this is perfectly normal in the process of following the Spirit of God.

When we find ourselves in the place of desire, but no ability or opportunity to manifest that desire, then we are in a place of preparation. God explained it to me this way. Imagine that you are scheduled to play a part in a Broadway production. What would be the process? Would you show up the day of the performance, jump on the stage and expect to be successful? Probably not! First you would practice your lines at home. Then you would come to many rehearsals, some in character and some out of character. Then when the day arrives and the curtain is drawn you are more confident in doing what you are assigned to do because of all of the preparation that went into the process before the performance.

God handles His kingdom in the same way. He gives us a desire to go in a certain direction, then He expects us to prepare for the day He draws the curtain. So many people never get their curtains drawn because they do not properly prepare for the opportunity to do what He calls them to do. Then there are those at the other end of the spectrum who just jump right out in front of the curtain end up hurt and or embarrassed.

Remember I said earlier, God works with us, not for us and we are not waiting, we are working. Well, this is the work part. When we are waiting for God to fulfill His desire He placed on the inside of us we are to work. We should be like the actor who practices his lines, studies his craft, and shows up to rehearsal.

When I got the direction from God to get back to doing art, I immediately bought many books and started to study my craft. As mentioned previously, I even took some college courses. Lastly, I practiced in my private times and did volunteer graphic work to build up my skills. Why? Because I knew one day that God would draw the curtain and I wanted to be ready to perform for His glory.

Moses and Gideon are still good examples of this principle. Moses had a desire from God to help his native people. So he jumped on stage in front of the curtain, which resulted in him committing sin. He killed an Egyptian and ended up on the backside of the desert, herding sheep for 40 years (see Acts 7:25). Gideon also, had a desire from God to help his people find relief from their oppressors. And so the scriptures say that he was threshing wheat in the wine press (see Judg. 6:11). I'm not entirely sure what he was doing, but it sounds like he was a making a mess. He was mixing things together that did not belong together.

300

Hopefully, theses two examples will help you to understand the importance of following the formula. Desire + Ability/Opportunity = Grace (God's manifested purpose).

I Have Work, But No Will

Well that covers what happens when you have "will" but not ability or opportunity, but what about when you have the ability and opportunity but no desire?

I cannot think of a biblical example to explain this one. I can only reference my personal experience as it relates to having the ability to do something but lacking the drive.

Most of you do not realize that I have had this information for nearly twenty years. I started writing this book in 1996. What happened you may be ask? God made me wait? How did He do this? He took the desire away. At first, I thought ok, you want me to wait a while, and there must be more you want to show me. Well there was more, but not twenty years worth.

It sounds strange doesn't it? I had the information and I had the ability to communicate this information. I had nearly everything I needed to write this book. In fact I was single with no kids. I had all the time in the world to write this book, but I no longer had the grace to do it.

So what did I do? Well at first I waited and waited and waited. Then I got tired of waiting and I decided I would proceed to write without the desire. After a while I started to think that I had missed God. It seemed like a fair assessment since so much time had passed. So I sat down to write and as I did my thoughts got jumbled and the task just seemed overwhelming and tedious. So after a few unsuccessful attempts I decided to let that idea go. It was clear to me that He was not going in that direction at that time.

Next I started a blog so that I could at least provide the principles to those who might be hungry for this subject. And again my thoughts were jumbled, two pages took forever to write, and I struggled to even remember to visit the page to make updates. Eventually, I forgot about the blog altogether.

Then one day it all came back. "YEARS" later! Now I have the desire and the ability to write this book. The first 208 pages were written in 30 days! I was steadily cranking out pages like crazy and there was an endless stream of revelatory thought. I could actually feel God assisting and directing me with every subject. It was an incredible experience.

In fact, the principles I outline in the book are the same principles I used to write this book. I wrote when He gave me the desire and the ability. When I got off track and sensed confusion, I went back and erased the area creating conflict, and then I re-tuned into God and kept writing.

Elijah's Example

Lastly, we can see that desire and ability and opportunity principles at work in the life of the prophet Elijah in 1 Kings 17:1-7. In this passage we find the story of Elijah at the Brook Cherith. In the story God leads Elijah to a brook in a time of great famine and there provides food via the ravens. Finally, after some time passes the ravens cease feeding him and the river dries up. When the provision has dried up Elijah knows, that it is time to move on to the next location. What we see in the story are these principles at work. God led Elijah to a place where there was ability and opportunity. And when he had no more ability and opportunity he knew that it was time to move.

We can also see this idea at work in the next few passages (see 1 Kings 17:8-15). Elijah upon leaving the brook was instructed to go to a widow's home, who God had commanded to feed him. Upon arriving he finds that the widow has a jar of oil and a piece of bread. That was all the food she had. This makes this a really interesting story, because God told Elijah that He was going to supply food by the hands of this widow, but she doesn't have food to give him. Then Elijah demonstrates what happens when God is leading us. He moved into the supernatural because he knew that the leading of God brings provision. This is a great example of the fact that where God lead's us, He provides for us, even when the provision is not readily apparent.

In summary I would like to say, remember the formula. You need both God's desire and God's ability to fulfill His good pleasure. If you find that you have desire and no ability, then you are in a season of preparation. You should start looking for God to open doors that will coincide with preparing you for the direction that He is taking you.

Likewise, if you find yourself in the position, that you have ability and opportunity, but no desire, then you may be in a season of waiting and preparation also. God is more than likely getting the audience seated in the auditorium of your life. You should continue in preparation. Or it may be that you simply missed God and you should let that idea go and retune for His direction. Remember just because you can do something does not mean that you should.

Allow God to lead you and you will always be like Elijah, you will always know where the water is when no one else does.

Section 6
Putting it
All Together

Chapter Fourteen

Practicing the Presence

The Secret Place

For years Psalm 91 was one of my favorite passages of scripture to read. At one point in my life I read it almost every day. I can't say the same is true today, but what remains the same is the truth that God gave me from its wisdom. It presents a truth so real that if you allow yourself to really grab a hold of it, it will heighten your awareness of the reality of the ever-present God.

It says, *"He who dwells in the secret place of the Most High shall abide under the shadow of the Almighty. I will say of the Lord He is my refuge and my fortress My God in Him will I trust."* The key words in this passage are dwell, place, and shadow. All three of these words are unique because they point to the idea of a place in God.

It says, he who "dwells." This tells us that there is a way to live in the conscious awareness of God. Then it says in the "secret place." This tells us that there is a location. Finally, it reads, "shall abide in the shadow." Now this is the really important word, because it tells us that we can dwell in a secret place where we are so close to God that we are in "his shadow" or in "His presence".

A shadow is an interesting phenomenon. It occurs when light is being blocked by the presence of an object. It sometimes seems otherworldly. What makes it so fascinating is the fact that it validates the presence of a reality. The shadow itself is a representative of a real object and it always leads us to the reality of that object if we follow it to its source.

This is the wisdom of this passage. For it tells us that while we may not be able to see the source object, which is God, we can see its affects. Shadows are visible, yet intangible, just like God. What this passage is inferring, is the idea that when we learn to make God a dwelling place we will become acutely aware of His reality. I would like you to also take notice to the fact that it does not say, "he that visits" it, says, "he that dwells".

Some of us are in the habit of visiting with God and what God desires is that we come into a place of dwelling with Him. If we purpose to make God our dwelling, then the rest of the Psalm applies to our lives. Before He can be your fortress, He must be your dwelling.

How do we make God a dwelling place? We learn to do as Proverbs 3:6 commands, *"In ALL your ways ACKNOWLEDGE HIM, and He will direct your paths.* This passage clearly lays out a way for God to speak to us and lead us. It says that our ability to receive divine direction is directly linked to our willingness to acknowledge Him. Acknowledge simply means that we recognize and or accept the reality of God's presence with us. By giving God the opportunity to direct our paths, we will find that we are sharpening our senses and heightening our awareness of His presence.

In this chapter I want to give you practical exercises that you can use in "real-time" situations to practice the presence of God. Notice that I said "real-time" situations. I say "real time" because, there are so many people seeking experiences from God—Many of whom are being encouraged by books that feed into their desires for such. I am not going to give you exercises that promote encounters, because real intimacy with God fosters encounters. What I mean is this, you don't need to seek a supernatural encounter with God. He is supernatural and all encounters with Him are supernatural. Even those you may regard lightly such as a scripture planted in your heart.

Chase the King, Not the Castle

I also think it is worth noting again that a lot of people are chasing supernatural experiences with the idea that if we ask God for a fish, He will not give us a stone (see Luke 11:11). But I would like to strongly caution you that while we may know that God will not give us a stone, if we push into areas without His permission and/or help we will find that Satan has no problem giving us the rock we so eagerly desire. I've shared this a couple of times in this book, that I have witnessed firsthand what happens when people get so caught up in the supernatural that they press into it without God and find themselves indwelled with a familiar spirit. Please do not get caught up in the hype. Allow God to give you the experience that He desires for you to have.

One last word on this subject, there is a group to whom Jesus will say depart from me I never knew you. And they will respond with but we prophesied in your name, we cast out demons in your name, and worked "many" miracles in your name (see Matt. 7:22). These are all people who believed that they could validate their faith by supernatural encounters. This is why God gave me this assignment. There are a lot of books on hearing God's voice and seeing visions and having encounters, but they lacked adequate measures of discernment. And as I said before, I am not against the supernatural. I have had and continue to have many supernatural encounters as well; I have seen angels and demons, I've had and visions and dreams, heard the audible voice of God and demons. I operate in the gifts; I see the cloud of the Holy Spirit on a regular basis, almost daily. On top of all of this I have seen and walked in both the natural and spiritual realms simultaneously all day. I know all about supernatural encounters and experiences, but in all I have been blessed to experience, I allow God to lead me as He desires. I do not seek visions, dreams, and encounters. I acknowledge God in my decisions and He alone decides how He will manifest His direction. He encourages us to pursue spiritual gifts not supernatural experiences (see 1 Cor. 14:1).

In fact God has spoken to me to point out to you that Paul spoke against boasting about such encounters, for it reads *"It is doubtless not profitable for me to boast. I will come to visions and revelations of the Lord"* (2 Cor. 12:1). In fact, to keep him humble God allowed a demon to afflict him to keep his ego in check. *"And lest I should be exalted above measure **by the abundance of the revelations**, a thorn in the flesh **was given to me, a messenger of Satan to buffet me**, lest I be exalted above measure."* (2 Cor. 12:7-10). Therefore, you should consider the reality that a lot of revelation may come at a cost. So your experiences with supernatural may put you into a position where God may see the need to keep your ego in check.

I can tell you from experience, that a lot of revelation means increased and very real warfare. I could tell you countless stories just from what has happened since I started writing this book. Am I trying to scare you? Of course not. But as I have said in *"The Voices of Deception"* the spiritual realm is not a playground. It all seems fun until you have to really be there for the intended purpose of being there.

So again I say, be open to the supernatural but chase God and seek the kingdom and all of its righteousness. If you do, God will take care of the rest.

My Concept of Waiting

You will also find that God has given me a different understanding of waiting on Him. So I will not give you exercises that require you to sit around for hours literally waiting for Him to show up. Why? As I said in a previous chapter, He is Jehovah-Shammah, the God who is there; "always there". You don't need to wait for Him to show up, He is already present. The old concept of waiting was not designed for Him, but it was for you to learn discipline and to kill your flesh. And I acknowledge **"it as a good practice"**. But if you can incorporate this new idea of waiting, you will see that getting into the presence of God is simply you choosing to be aware of His reality.

The other reason that I encourage incorporating this new waiting method, is the fact that God does not work for us, He works With Us. You should know that just because you sit on the floor for 5 hours doesn't mean that God is going to speak to you. He is not our bellhop, He will speak when He is ready, and your job is to be ready when He does. While you may not like or agree with this idea, the reality is that sometimes the things we want to hear are things that we are not ready to hear. God told me it would be twenty years before I really started doing what He wanted me to do. Then He went on to other topics and no matter how much I pressed him about ministry, He only spoke to me about my current assignments. Looking back, I can see why He chose to deal with me that way. I was in no way ready for what I wanted to do. My spiritual life at the time was great, but my professional life and personal life sucked. In His wisdom, He directed and spoke to me about those areas first. Now twenty years later He's back to discussing ministry.

So please, please do these exercises expecting God to encounter you in the way He chooses. You may experience seeing a vision, you may not. You may even get an angelic visitation, I don't know. But in the end God will meet you at some point in the day and you will not miss Him if you keep your mind stayed on Him.

Also, I am not going to give you exercises that help you to see and hear by imagining Jesus sitting on the couch with you. This is impractical in my opinion. I believe that there are real life situations occurring in your life right now that God is more than willing to speak to you about. As such, these exercises are designed with everyday matters in mind.

Practical Exercises

Exercise: The Leading Teams

This is an exercise God gave me to do with a session I was teaching that greatly helped the participants to identify with the concept of following God's leading. This exercise will give you a sense for the feeling of being led. This exercise requires two people and a rope.

First decide who is going to be led and who is going to do the leading. Next, tie the rope around the person who is to be led and blindfold them. Make sure the knot of the rope is by the belly button and that the rope is tied pretty snug against the body. Then the person doing the leading will gently, and I mean gently tug on the rope in a direction. When the person being led feels the tug they are to follow in the direction of the tug. Repeat the process several times guiding them to various areas.

If you do this right, you will have a point of reference for how following God's spirit feels. Another thing to keep in mind is that this is meant to simulate the feeling of inspiration.

Exercise: At Work

Yes, God cares about how you do your job. In this exercise I encourage you to ask God how to solve a problem at work. That problem can be a how to handle a problem with an employee. Or it may be a work related problem that you have not been able to solve. Still your thoughts and wait for the answer. It may come as a sudden knowing, a mental vision, or even a voice. If it doesn't come at work you may be in for a dream.

The goal of this exercise is for you to realize that Jesus is willing to be your life partner. You will find that you are a better employee with His assistance. This understanding was great for me, God made me work harder than my own boss. This led to a few job offers from other supervisors that noticed my hard work. If they only knew my boss was the Holy Spirit and that it was His standard that got their attention.

You may be questioning what Jesus and the building of the kingdom has to do with your job. Jesus is interested in your witness and how you represent His name in the workplace. When I allowed God to be my boss in the workplace others benefited others as well. There was a guy in the office that was turned off by the legalism of the church, until he met me. He thought I was a cool Christian and he could tell that I really enjoyed being a Christian. I was always full of joy even in times of chaos. One day he said to the entire office, "if I'm going to be a Christian I want to be like Kevin. He lives right and still enjoys life". This blessed me to no end and it was all because of my witness at work, so yes Jesus is interested in meeting you at work.

Exercise: The Knowing

This exercise is something that you can do anytime, anywhere. This involves learning how to experience the inner witness of the Holy Spirit. Think of a situation in which there is a decision to make. Don't choose anything dire, but something simple like should your child go to a particular place. Ask God the question and look for the light, inner swelling, and a desire. Now run a series of answers through the same process. You will notice that the Holy Spirit responds to the truth. When there is no truth you will feel nothing or you will feel a sense of emptiness. In extreme cases you may feel a sensation of withdrawal on the inside of you.

312

I use this method all the time. I use it to discern books and teachings (especially online teachings) as well as with people. Sometimes when listening to a new preacher I look for a kindred witness that connects me to what he or she is saying. One day while searching the internet my search led to a video of a popular prophet. As I listened to him I noticed that I had absolutely no inner response from the Holy Spirit. So I ignored the idea He was selling. My next search led me to an evangelist preaching the same message but with slightly different ideas. Even though the subject matter was the same the Holy Spirit responded so favorably to this evangelist that I listened to his message intently. God also blessed my family and myself, inspiring in us a deeper relationship with Him that has remained. As for the prophet, I tried several times to listen to him teach. Every single time God responded with a feeling of withdrawal. This is what the witness does. It sorts out what is and is not of God. It works because the Holy Spirit has your best interest in mind and He will respond favorably to those things and people that are kingdom things and people. This is how I knew not to buy a home during the housing market scandal. I asked God what to do and I felt the emptiness. I look for this even in checking my dreams and visions and voices. If the voice vision or dream does not register in my inner man then I ignore it. On more than a few occasions I was able to avoid deception by the enemy. If you really learn to trust the inner witness, you will be able to say the same.

Exercise: Pray for Someone

This exercise is designed to increase your hearing during prayer. Remember prayer does not mean getting up early in the morning or praying before bed, but that you remain in a place of continued engagement with God. So even on the drive home from work you can pray and ask God if there is someone He would like for you to pray for, then wait looking for a response. You may hear or see something and then you may feel a stirring or rising in your inner man. Listen for the first words of the prayer. Once you hear them just open your mouth and start flowing with God to the best of your ability. This may happen in your native language or in a gift of tongues.

Exercise: Worship

Be filled with the Spirit singing to yourself… The next exercise encourages you to allow the Holy Spirit to lead you into worship. This is really simple. Just ask God to fill your heart with worship. Either immediately or sometime there after you will hear a song stirring in your heart. Just sing it and when it changes, change with it. It will almost be like listening to a radio. For instance I hear songs all day as if I'm listening to an inner radio.

Sometimes God will lead us into an encounter by starting with worship. I told my story in a previous chapter of how I followed the worship in my heart and as I focused or gave more attention to it, how it became audible and then God spoke to me in an internal audible voice. And this occurred while I was at work, not sitting and waiting. I am going to drive this point home as many times as I can. You can worship and interact with God all day not just in your prayer closet at home. Remember He is with you "always" and He will never leave you.

Also remember to engage God in worship with "all "of your invisible attributes. Allow yourself to feel the meaning of the words of the song. Get your heart, mind, and imagination involved.

Exercise: Marriage

One important aspect of marriage was lost in the garden and marriages have suffered dearly as a result. We should note that God never intended for it to be man and woman. His original intent was that it would be Himself, man, and woman. So this exercise is designed to assist you in your marriage.

First ask God if there is something nice that you can do for your spouse. Or you can ask Him about how their day went and then ask Him how to best respond.

This could look something like this. You ask God how your wife's day went and He may tell you it was a hard day. He may then direct you to buy her a simple card of encouragement. When you get home and find that she had a terrible day and then give her an encouraging card, you may find an overwhelmingly loving response.

314

Exercise: Arguments

This is another one designed to improve relationships but it can only be practiced in the midst of a disagreement.

If you are in an argument with your husband for instance, ask God to show you "yourself" in the situation. I always go to God first before I bring my issue to my wife. Why? I want to ensure that I don't cause further damage to the situation.

For instance, one day my I decided I was going to confront my wife about not putting her shoes in the closet. However, before I did I decided to talk to God about the situation. As we were talking He gently brought to mind that I was doing the same thing. Maybe not as often, but I still did that same thing. He reminded me to get the log out of my eye before attempting to remove the stick from hers. This saved me an unnecessary argument. In fact, I have avoided many such arguments by talking to God first. You will be surprised by how often you are wrong. And when you're not, God has a way of working it out without you making a mess.

Another instance of this occurred right before I wrote this book. I was coming into the end of the twenty-year period and God was stirring my heart to action. So I started doing more in terms of giving up a lot of things that were not sin, but were distracting. It just so happened that it was some of the things that my wife and I enjoyed watching together. This seemingly sudden change caused some uneasiness and a spirit entered the house to try to distract me. I could see him in my face attempting to distract me from my writing of this book. And when he was unsuccessful, he decided to sit next to my wife. At that point I knew this was going to be trouble. For the next few days this thing did everything to try to cause an argument between us. Nonetheless, God had shown me the source and so I listened to Him as to how to respond. Therefore, every potential argument was diffused by the wisdom He spoke to me. He told me how to respond and what to say and my wife and I grew even closer through the experience. Later, I exposed the thing and it left. As I mentioned earlier my wife was not accustomed to seeing this side of my gifting, and I was not sure how to explain it to her so this thing was allowed to operate longer than I would have liked.

What I want you to take from this story is the reality, that God can be the best counselor in your marriage if you would only allow Him to speak to you about how to navigate the good and bad times. In fact, my wife and I have had only good times, and that is because we listen for His voice in how to deal with each other.

Hopefully you can see the benefits in allowing God to be a part of your everyday life. As I stated before, my interest is that you will see and hear God. This book is designed to help you develop a natural walk with God where communion with Him is second nature. By natural I mean that I want you to see God in your everyday life experiences such as your job, marriage, and relationships, etc. Most people only seem to want God moving in their ministries, but He told me that He wants to be a part of your everyday experiences. It is His desire to do life with you as a life partner and guide. He says that there is so much more that He would do if you allow Him the opportunity to be in your space. I want you close, closer than close. I want you to know Me from experience and not just from what you have heard or read. I will make My word alive in you and through you, if you only give me the opportunity to be close. Take this invitation to draw near to Me, for if you do, I promise that I will draw near unto you. I love you with an unimaginable love. Says the Lord.

Chapter Fifteen
Journaling the Vision

Write the Vision

One of the most practical ways to inspire your own growth in hearing the voice of God is to learn the art of journaling. Believe it or not journaling is a biblical principle. We can clearly see this idea reflected in Habakkuk 2:2, which says, *"Write the vision and make it plain on tablets that he that reads it may run by it."* In this passage God Himself instructs the prophet to write down what he sees. But it is most evident in the concept of the canonized scriptures. For what is the Bible but a collection of writings? It is a collection of letters from Paul, Peter, Isaiah, Jeremiah, Moses, etc. In fact, these are just the canonized scriptures, but in biblical times many believers recorded their relationships with God. What we have in the Bible is only a portion of a few people's encounters. Please don't misunderstand what I am saying. I believe in the Bible as an infallible work of God, and that He coordinated the decisions regarding which of the many writings were to be canonized. Likewise I also understand that there are many books written by the early church believers. They are not authoritative and neither do I care to read them, but the point is that journaling should be a normal Christian custom.

Writing has also been the major resource whereby mankind has been able to learn of many cultures from previous times. It serves the most basic necessity of creating a record of the culture, people, time, and discoveries of that time period. It will also serve you in the same way as well. Having a written record of your encounters with God will serve you in ways that are beyond your expectations. In fact as I am writing this book I am in a series of dreams. Yes, a series. They are happening every night and each one builds on the previous night. It is God expressing a message to me in my sleep and it is a flowing sequence of dreams all based on a similar message. Also, they are happening in twos. What I mean is I am remembering two dreams each night with themes that flow into the next one. It has been absolutely incredible.

What if I was not recording these dreams? What if I just dismissed them as pizza dream babble? I would be missing pieces of a very important conversation with the Creator, especially since they are about how to proceed with this book and other areas of my life. So get in the habit of journaling. The term journaling does not only refer to recording your dreams and visions. I am referring to all encounters with the Lord. I journal my dreams and visions, my scripture revelations, my scripture ponders, my perceptual vision, and even those unpleasant encounters *(I believe that all things are working for my good even though they seem bad and that all experiences are learning opportunities)*.

Not only should we write down the things God speaks to us in audible voices, dreams and visions, and impressions, for record keeping sake, but because there are many other benefits to us personally. Below are just a few of those ways in which journaling benefits our lives.

1. We remind ourselves (1 Tim 4:12-16)
One of the benefits of journaling is that it serves as a record of our encounters with God. In your scripture reference above, Timothy is told to take those things that God has said to him and meditate of them. He encourages him to use them to stir up the gifts that God has deposited in him. You will find that journaling will be one of the biggest sources of encouragement in seasons of lack, stress, pain, and pressure. It will give you something to mentally chew on as a way to water your faith.

2. It encourages our faith (Rev. 12:11)
The Bible says and we overcome by the word of our "testimony". One reason David was able to face Goliath is because he had access to prior experiences with God. He was able to overcome facing the giant in front of him because He was able to look back into the records of God in his life. He was also able to see where God had worked miracles in his life by helping him to overcome a lion and a bear (see 1 Sam. 17:36).

3. **It is a record of your growth**

One of the things I most appreciate about journaling is being able to look back on the things that God said and seeing the growth. There were some things in my journals that clearly reflect my growth. I was able to see some of the things that I struggled to incorporate into my life at the time and how now those things are no problem at all.

4. **It's easier to check it against the scriptures (1 John 4:1)**

One of the most important things to learn to do is test the spirits. 1 John 4:1, tells us clearly not to believe every spirit but to test them. 1 Corinthians 14:29, further builds on this idea in its instructions to the prophets, for it reads, *"Let the prophets speak two or three and let the others JUDGE."* You will find this much easier to do if you get in the habit or journaling.

5. **It is a sign of your expectation from God (Hab. 2:2)**

Habakkuk says, *"I will look and see what He will answer."* I have personally increased my awareness of my dreams by putting pen and paper next to my bed. You would be surprised how responsive God is to such a seemingly small act. Journaling is one sure way to show expectation. John in Revelation recorded the visions as they were happening. He did not have to run around looking for pen a paper. This tells me that he was ready and expecting that God would speak to him at any moment.

Make it Plain

One thing that you will soon come to discover about the voice of God is that God frequently speaks in parables, and dark sayings (see Num. 12:1-8). Sometimes He speaks plainly but most of the time He will speak in a way that requires you to interpret. This will definitely be true with visions and dreams. They rarely depict reality. Why does God speak this way? I believe it is because a picture is worth a thousand words. Also, a picture or pictorial statement is much easier to remember than long dialogs.

The fact that He speaks this way means that we must be prepared to receive and interpret His communications. Jesus is seen often speaking in parables and then unpacking the truths hidden inside each facet of the story. He was making it plain for the disciples so that it had practical application for their lives in the kingdom.

This is also what He is requiring of you. He expects you to make it plain so that it has a practical application for those who may read it, hear it, or share it.

How do you interpret the communication? The first thing you need to understand is that God communicates with us on a personal level. What I mean is that while there are some consistent manifestations such as color, most of the images and visuals that He will use when communicating with you are things that *"you understand"*. Sometimes well-meaning authors will create books in which they will include a multitude of symbols and their meanings. While I respect their efforts to create an easier way for people to interpret their visionary encounters, it should be noted that there are not two dreams that are alike in the Bible. Each was distinct and tailored to the recipient. Even Jesus used parables that were understood by that generation. God is "personal" and so is His communication with you. He actually considers how you learn and process information.

Now, I am not saying do not read these books, because there are clearly some things that will be consistent and they are good for reference. However they are good for reference only. For instance you will see God using the stars to communicate to Abraham that he would have more descendants than he could count. You also see the same type of thing happen with Joseph in his dream of twelve stars bowing down to him as the son. What you see is God speaking to that generation by what they understood, astronomy. But you would not expect God to do the same today. This is a technological generation. He may give you dreams that reflect such. You should expect that your encounter with him will be personal to you. In other words you may understand it, just you. If you want others to understand it then you will need to make them plain for everyone else.

For instance, I am a natural visual learner. When I was in school they told me I had a learning disability and put me in special classes. However, when I became a man, one thing that I learned about myself was that I acquire knowledge by what I experienced and visualize. When I am in conversations and people are describing people, places, things, and concepts I actually see images of those things in my mind as it is processing the information. Once I discovered this I taught myself all kinds of things by drawing or creating an image of what I did not understand. So when God speaks to me in pictures, He is speaking right up my alley. And the images and movements He chooses are things that I understand naturally.

Some people examine every color seen and every clothing detail such as the type of shoes worn. They generally search for the deepest of meaning. However, regarding myself, God rarely embeds that deep of a meaning into our encounters. He speaks to me in a way that I naturally understand. You will find that the same is true from you. So get the dream books for reference, but do not use them exclusively to interpret your encounters. Your encounters are tailored just for you.

A really good example of the idea of "personal communication" was mentioned earlier in this book. I wrote about a time when God spoke to me about He-man. He spoke to me about something I was familiar with personally and generationally. He also taught me a great lesson about His word and His Spirit. But He may not have chosen to communicate the same subject to you the same way because you may not even know who He-man is! So you should expect that his communication with you is personal.

Just imagine how you would feel if I just walked up to you and started telling you about God speaking to me about He-man. You would need me to make it plain and applicable for you to be able to extract any value from it. The same will be true with you. You will receive unique and personal communication from God and you will need to make it plain if others are to be enriched by the encounter.

I also want you to notice that after you have made it plain, that the rest of the verse in Habakkuk 2:2 says, to make it plain "on tablets". In other words after you have made the revelation applicable for others, write it down-journal it.

It's Not Just for You

Finally, journaling the encounter and making it plain has a broader application, *"...that he may run who reads it."* This points us to the reality that God often thinks in big pictures. He's got more than you in mind when He speaks. So many people right now are seeking encounters in which they are the only people enriched. 1 Corinthians 12:12 makes it perfectly clear that God's goal is that each joint supplies it part and causes growth to the body. Your encounter with God is not only for you! It's for all to whom it has been appointed within your sphere of influence.

I recently read a book that was filled with some pretty incredible encounters with God. At first glance it would really make you suspicious. I was suspicious until God validated the book by a tangible anointing and the inner witness. It was also a scriptural book and I could relate to many of the experiences. As I read it I also got clarity for some of my own experiences in the Lord. But what I really appreciated about the book was the incredible risk the author took in revealing his experiences. He really put his head on a chopping block for all the skeptics to mock him. But the reality is this, he's got the revelation that what God is doing is bigger than him. His book blessed me so much that I am planning to send him a free copy of this one to let him know how appreciative I am for him sharing his journal with the whole world.

Again I would like to point out the Bible as a perfect example of how the encounters and experiences with God are intended to be recorded for others to "read" and "run". The word "run" in the passage simply means that a work has been recorded that will be inspiring to those who read it. Are you ready to inspire someone?

322

Final Thoughts

Communicating solid biblical truth regarding the ability to discern the voice of God is one of my passions and my prayers. Habakkuk 1:3 says, *"Why do you cause me to see..."* God did the same to me. He showed me something, and then He told me something. It was that something that I saw that has sparked this passion. I saw people from all levels of Christian ministry from the pulpit to the pew asking that question. Is this God? Or is this me? Or is this the devil? I saw people making bad financial decisions. I saw people making bad life decisions and I heard the pain in the voices of those who wished that they could know for certain that it is God that is speaking to them.

This is what I saw first, and then God told me something. He forged a sword through His word, and put it into my hands as a weapon and a tool for helping the body of Christ grow in intimacy with Him. It is a word and a seed. It is a word that I take great pleasure is planting. I am so excited about what God wants to do in the life of His people. And I cannot wait to see Him give increase to us in this much-needed area of Christian living.

It is has been my prayer and passion that you have been enriched by the principles presented in this book. I prayed so earnestly everyday as I was writing, God please help me to make this practical and inspiring. I want each person that reads this book to go on to developing a relationship with God that is beyond what they could ever imagine or think. When I started writing on this subject, one of the things I noticed is that while there were a lot of good books on how to hear God's voice, they all lacked what I thought would ease the readers doubts about who they are hearing. **This book is meant to be a companion to those books.** The Bible says that we know in part we prophesy in part (see 1 Cor. 13:9). I have come to respect the fact that everyone has been given a part to share and this is mine. My hope is that I was able to provide you with a solid biblical basis for discerning what you hear and that it will produce the kind of certainty that will allow you to comfortably grow in your relationship with God.

Thank you for endeavoring to go higher and may our God satisfy your heart in seeking Him.

I also hope that I made it clear that hearing God's voice is not an issue for the believer in Jesus Christ. We all hear His voice and my desire and what I attempted to do was to help you distinguish His voice from all the others. Again we all hear voices. That is how God designed the human. The question to answer is which voice belongs to God. Remember it's not about whether God gives you a rock or a fish. It's about you knowing the difference between the two!

Setting Goals

I started this book with a very important question, "Does God still speak?" One of the things I pointed out in that chapter is the necessity of understanding that the Bible was written for our example. The Bible is nothing more than a love story about God and mankind and it is full of stories showcasing men and women who walked with God.

This is why I encourage you to read the Bible differently. Read it looking for ways to be closer to the Creator. I have learned that it is wise to study those who have been where I want to be. Some of you want ministries and gifts and miracles and material things. And that's ok! However, if you look in the scriptures you will see that these things are all outpourings or overflows of the relationship of men who sought God.

Moses says to God, in Exodus 33:13 *"Show me Your ways that I may know You."* This must be our ultimate goal. If we are to really have any significant impact this must be the cry of our heart. So the last thing that I want to encourage you to do as you start this quest is to use the great men of God as your examples of what you can have with God. I personally have six examples that I admire and study. I want the kind of relationship with God that these men had. They are Enoch who walked with God until God took him, Abraham the friend of God, Moses God's friend that He spoke to face-to-face, Elijah whom God protected and gave power to, Paul whom was willing to suffer to satisfy God's heart, and David whom God loved because he was a seeker of His heart.

These great men inspire me to know Him. Not seek His power or His gifts, but to simply know Him and understand His ways. You may or may not have these same goals. My point is that you find those who have what you want with God and find out why they were so special to God. God testifies of all His great people. Enoch walked with God. Abraham was God's friend, Elijah was great, David was a man after God's own heart, and Moses was more humble than any man of Earth. These are not just facts about these men, but these are the words that God Himself testifies to about these men. What will He say about you! Make it your goal to find something that God can testify to about you to those who come after you.

One Last Thing

I would hate to assume that everyone reading this is a Christian. If you are not a believer in Jesus Christ and struggle to understand the concepts of this book, you should know that this is completely normal. The Bible says that unless you are born again you cannot see or understand the things of God.

John 3:3

Jesus replied, "Very truly I tell you, no one can see the kingdom of God unless they are born again."

It also says that in order to have the born again experience that one who comes to God must first believe that He is and that He is a rewarder of those who diligently seek Him.

Heb. 11:6

And without faith it is impossible to please God, because anyone who comes to him must believe that he exists and that he rewards those who earnestly seek him.

Your first step toward a brand new life is your acknowledgement of the reality and existence of God. He promises that if you do He will reward you for seeking Him out.

Your next step is to confess with your mouth and believe in your heart that Jesus Christ died on the cross for your sins so that you could enter into a glorious relationship with a welcoming God, who has been waiting for you.

Romans 10:9

If you confess with your mouth that Jesus is Lord and believe in your heart that God raised him from the dead, you will be saved.

Then you need to repent, which simply means to go the other way. Let go of the lifestyle of wickedness and turn towards righteousness. I hear you saying but how?

Acts 3:19

Repent, then, and turn to God, so that your sins may be wiped out, that times of refreshing may come from the Lord,

This is the great part. You do not have to do this on your own. When you accept Jesus as your Lord and Savior He will give you the Helper the Holy Spirit and He will do the job of inspiring in you the very nature of righteousness.

John 15:26

When the Helper comes, whom I will send to you from the Father, that is the Spirit of truth who proceeds from the Father, He will testify about Me, and you will testify also, because you have been with Me from the beginning.

For God imputes or transfers to us His righteousness when we give Him our confessions of nakedness. His Spirit will fill you and empower you to live this life we call Christianity. God made him who had no sin to be sin for us, so that in him we might become the righteousness of God.

2 Corinthians 5:21

God made him who had no sin to be sin for us, so that in him we might become the righteousness of God.

Yes it is that simple. Just say Lord I know I have been wrong and I repent (I am sorry) for the life that I lived. Say Lord, I give you my weakness and my sins and I accept your forgiveness and your righteousness. Confess with your mouth, Lord I believe that Jesus Christ your only begotten Son died on the cross for my sins and was resurrected for me. Then ask Him to fill you with His Spirit and go on with your life living empowered to do right.

If you do not have a church home, then you will need to find one quickly. The Bible tells us that we should be a part of family of like- minded people who can strengthen us and encourage us and help us to grow in the things of God.

Colossians 3:16

Let the word of Christ richly dwell within you, with all wisdom teaching and admonishing one another with psalms and hymns and spiritual songs, singing with thankfulness in your hearts to God.

If you have done all of this, then I would like to say welcome to the family. Now if you read this information again I promise you it will make much more sense. The kingdom of God is not a kingdom that allows one to window shop. You have to come inside to understand it for the Bible says, *"TASTE AND SEE that the Lord is Good"* (Psalm 34:8). You don't get to see until you first taste!

Extras:
Prayers that I Pray

Prayer of Intimacy
Exodus 33:13

Father I pray please, if I have found grace in thy sight, show me now Your way, that I may know thee, that I may find grace in thy sight.

Prayer of Wisdom and Revelation
Ephesians 1:17-20

Father God of our Lord Jesus Christ, the Father of glory, please give me the spirit of wisdom and revelation in the knowledge of Jesus: May it result in the eyes of my understanding being enlightened; that I may know what is the hope of his calling, and what the riches of the glory of his inheritance in the saints, and what is the exceeding greatness of Your power toward us who believe, according to the working of your mighty power, Which You wrought in Christ, when You raised Him from the dead, and set Him at His own right hand in the heavenly places,

Prayer for Spiritual Vision
2 Kings 6:17-20New King James Version (NKJV)

Father I pray the prayer of Elisha, and ask you to open my eyes that I may see, that I may see your kingdom, and see the truth in all situations. Enlighten me to see beyond the facts but to see the truth in any situation.

Prayer for God's Manifested Will
Matthew 6:9-13, The Lord's Prayer

Father I invite the kingdom of heaven to come and manifest in my life. I ask that your will be done. Please help me to manifest in the earth you plans in the heavens.

Prayer for Opening of Spiritual Ears
Isaiah 50:4

Father open my ears to hear that I might have a word in season for him that is weary.

328

About the Author

Kevin Winters is a prophetic minster that has been walking with God for 23 years. His passion is that you 1) know that God is intimate 2) know how to walk in His purpose for your life 3) know how to walk in Holy Ghost power, and 4) know how to do spiritual warfare and be victorious. God has gifted him to teach and preach under a prophetic utterance that demonstrates insight and revelation. He is an author, a poet, and a visionary. His ministry is marked by the wisdom and insight that God has given him. God has made him a deep thinker and to most that hear him he is considered a balanced source of revelation.

Currently, Kevin shares God's word through his online ministry. He can be heard weekly on YouTube and Facebook sharing what God is saying and doing in the world in this hour. He also shares his heart is written form via blogging.

By trade he is a Visual Communication Specialist with the Federal Government. In this capacity he serves as a lead graphic designer and illustrator. His hobbies include making music, creating art, martial arts, and enjoying his family.

He resides with Tanya, his wife of 13 years, in Maryland. They have four beautiful children, Autumn, Caleb, Aaron, and Noelle. They are also long time members of the prestigious First Baptist Church of Glenarden where they serve under the leadership of Pastor John K. Jenkins, Sr.

To hear or read Kevin's teachings visit one of the sites below.

http://doinglifeonfire.org/

www.facebook.com/doinglifeonfire

doinglifeonfire.youtube

Reach out to Kevin
doinglifeonfire@yahoo.com

Recommended Reading

The following books are recommended as companion books to this one. As I said the Bible is clear that we see *in part*... and know *in part*. As a supporter of good information I recommend that you also read these books by these authors regarding the subject of the voice of God. These are books that layout the many ways we may experience God speaking to us. This book is meant to cover discernment; these books cover the voice of God in detail and provide useful exercises to help you grow in the experience of learning to hear His voice.

I also recommend that you pick up a copy of my other book, *You Can Hear the Voice of God Clearly: How to go from the still small voice to the clear voice of God.*

As a disclaimer, I want to re-emphasize that I judge works of God and not just individuals. It is inevitable that someone will take issue with various authors listed for teaching that they disagree with. That being the case, I advise that you judge each author's work separately to see how it measures up to God's truth. That does not mean that I agree with all of their teachings, but again, as for these particular works, I believe them to be God's truth.

Seeing The Voice of God:
What God is Telling You Through Dreams and Visions
By Laura Harris Smith

Hearing God's Voice Made Simple
Seeing in the Spirit Made Simple
By Praying Medic

How to See in the Spirit
By Michael Van Vlymen

4 Keys to Hearing God's Voice
By Mark and Patti Vikler

The Seer
By James Goll

7 Secrets to Power Praying: How to Access God's Wisdom and Miracles Everyday
By Jane Glenchur

To hear or read Kevin's teachings visit one of the sites below.

DLOF
Doing Life On Fire

DoinglifeonfFire.org

www.facebook.com/doinglifeonfire

KevinWinters.youtube

Reach out to Kevin

doinglifeonfire@yahoo.com

For more teaching on this subject visit Kevin's YouTube channel and click on the playlist titled "How to Hear the Voice of God".

25385855R00194

Printed in Great Britain
by Amazon